A DAYBOOK
OF PRAYER

Meditations, Scriptures, and Prayers
to Draw Near to the Heart of God

INTEGRITY
HOUSE™

Nashville, Tennesse

A DAYBOOK OF PRAYER

Copyright © 2006 by Integrity Publishers

Published by Integrity House, a Division of Integrity Media, Inc.
660 Bakers Bridge, Suite 200, Franklin, Tennessee 37067

ISBN 10: 1-59145-476-X
ISBN 13: 978-159145-476-2
Printed in the United States of America

A DAYBOOK
OF PRAYER

*Meditations, Scriptures, and Prayers
to Draw Near to the Heart of God*

INTRODUCTION
YOUR DAILY LIFELINE

What would happen in your life if you committed time every single day of the year to learning something powerful and profound about prayer? And then spent time with God in prayer each day?

Prayer is your lifeline to the One who created you; who redeems you; who has plans and a purpose for your life; who desires a daily relationship based on trust and communication. God is ready to meet with you each and every day of the year, to hear what is on your heart and mind, to provide you with the reassurance, guidance, and wisdom you need to live the life He intends for you.

A *Daybook of Prayer* is a great resource that provides you with an inspirational Bible verse, a significant teaching on prayer from classic and contemporary Christian thinkers, and a poignant prayer starter for you to put into words your own petitions and praise before the Father.

What would happen if you devoted part of every day of the year to prayer? Your life—and your world—would never be the same.

DON'T HOLD BACK

Cast all your anxiety on him because he cares for you.

1 PETER 5:7

Tell God all that is in your heart, as one unloads one's heart, its pleasures and its pains, to a dear friend. Tell Him your troubles, that He may comfort you; tell Him your joys, that He may sober them; tell Him your longings, that He may purify them; tell Him your dislikes, that He may help you to conquer them; talk to Him of your temptations, that He may shield you from them; show Him the wounds of your heart, that He may heal them; lay bare your indifference to good, your depraved tastes for evil, your instability. Tell Him how self-love makes you unjust to others, how vanity tempts you to be insincere, how pride disguises you to yourself and others....

People who have no secrets from each other never want for subject of conversation.... They talk out of the abundance of the heart, without consideration they say just what they think. Blessed are they who attain to such familiar, unreserved intercourse with God.

—FRANÇOIS FÉNELON

Heavenly Father, I want to share everything with You, both good and bad. Help me to open myself to Your loving Spirit. Amen.

GOD IS LISTENING

The LORD has heard my plea;
the LORD will answer my prayer.

PSALM 6:9 NLT

You can talk to God because God listens. Your voice matters in heaven. He takes you very seriously. When you enter his presence, he turns to you to hear your voice. No need to fear that you will be ignored. Even if you stammer or stumble, even if what you have to say impresses no one, it impresses God, and he listens. He listens to the painful plea of the elderly in the rest home. He listens to the gruff confession of a death-row inmate. When the alcoholic begs for mercy, when the spouse seeks guidance, when the businessman steps off the street into the chapel, God listens.

Intently. Carefully.

Lord God, thank You that You so attentively hear my prayers. Help me rest in Your love today, Lord. Amen.

—MAX LUCADO, from *The Great House of God*

ON OUR DARKEST DAYS

If I ascend into heaven, You are there;
If I make my bed in hell, behold, You are there.

PSALM 139:8 NKJV

> *O Lord, You see me as I am, You see my darkest moments, and You faithfully stay beside me. Help me turn even my darkest moments over to You. Amen.*

It's easy to be honest before God with our hallelujahs; it is somewhat more difficult to be honest in our hurts; it is nearly impossible to be honest before God in the dark emotions of our hate. So we commonly suppress our negative emotions.... But when we pray the psalms, these classic prayers of God's people, we find that will not do. We must pray who we actually are, not who we think we are, not who we think we should be.

In prayer, all is not sweetness and light. The way of prayer is not to cover our unlovely emotions so that they will appear respectable, but expose them so that they can be enlisted in the work of the kingdom.

—EUGENE H. PETERSON, from *Answering God*

WAIT UPON THE LORD

But those who wait on the LORD will find new strength.
They will fly high on wings like eagles. They will run
and not grow weary. They will walk and not faint.

ISAIAH 40:31 NLT

I wonder how many wonderful gifts are left wrapped in heaven because they were never unwrapped on earth? They just remain there, unasked for. James wrote plainly, "You do not have because you do not ask" (James 4:2 [NKJV]). In other words, if we would ask more, we would have more.

But what about the times when we do ask? Sometimes the answer is "yes," sometimes it's "no," and many times it's "wait."... Do you know what that's doing to your Christian life? It's building muscles of faith.

God says, "I know what I'm doing. You can trust Me." And let me assure you. He is a good God, and you can trust Him whether He answers "yes," "no," or "wait."

—CHARLES SWINDOLL, from *Perfect Trust*

 Lord, I know that You know what's best for me, and I know that You will never abandon me. Please help me see Your hand in my life today, and please use my circumstances to make me more like You. Amen.

GOD'S SURE PROMISES

All these faithful ones died without receiving what
God had promised them, but they saw it all from a
distance and welcomed the promises of God.

HEBREWS 11:13 NLT

God knows exactly when to withhold or to grant us any
visible sign of encouragement. How wonderful it is when we
will trust Him in either case! Yet it is better when all visible
evidence that He is remembering us is withheld. He wants us
to realize that His Word—His promise of remembering us—
is more real and dependable than any evidence our senses
may reveal....

Delayed answers to prayers are not refusals. Many prayers are
received and recorded, yet underneath are the words, "My
time has not yet come." God has a fixed time and an ordained
purpose, and He who controls the limits of our lives also
determines the time of our deliverance.

—L. B. COWMAN, from *Streams in the Desert*

 Lord, I know that You have good plans for Your people,
even when I can't see You at work. Today, Lord, I pray
for Your perspective and the ability to endure the time
between with grace and perseverance. Amen.

CONTINUAL PRAYER

Continue in prayer, and watch in
the same with thanksgiving.

COLOSSIANS 4:2 KJV

What is prayer? Not the utterance of words. They are but the vehicle of prayer. Prayer is the attitude of a person's spirit, and the elements of prayer may be diffused throughout our daily lives....

Our continual submission to God's will is...essential for all prayer. Many people believe that

> *Heavenly Father, I want to be willing and obedient to do the things You ask me to do. As I remain in continual prayer, I know You will help me to follow You. Amen.*

praying is urging our wishes on God, and answered prayer is God giving us what we desire. The deepest expression of true prayer is not, "Do this, because I desire it, O Lord." Rather, it is, "I do this because you desire it, O Lord."

So there should run all through our daily lives the music of continual prayer beneath our various occupations, like some prolonged, deep, bass note that bears up and dignifies the lighter melody rising, falling, and changing above it. Then our lives can be woven into a harmonious unity based upon a continual communion, a continual desire after God, and a continual submission to Him.

–ALEXANDER MACLAREN

JANUARY 7

EVERY MOMENT

Pay attention to my prayer,
for it comes from an honest heart.

PSALM 17:1 NLT

Prayer is for every moment of our lives, not just for times of suffering or joy. Prayer is really a place; a place where you meet God in genuine conversation.

Have you ever said, "Well, all we can do now is pray"? Instead of beginning with prayer, we sometimes resort to it after all other resources have been used. When we come to the end of ourselves, we come to the beginning of God. We don't need to be embarrassed that we are needy. God doesn't demand that we pray in King James English, or even with eloquence. Every feeble, stumbling prayer uttered by a believer is heard by God. A cry, a sigh, a "Help!" are all prayers, according to the Psalms.

–BILLY GRAHAM, from *Day by Day with Billy Graham*

 Father, I want to pray all day, directing every thought
and sigh toward You. Help me see reminders of
Your presence throughout the day, Lord. Amen.

A PRAYERFUL HEART

Blessed are the pure in heart,
For they shall see God.

MATTHEW 5:9 NKJV

The Scriptures say, "Pray without ceasing" (1 Thessalonians 5:17 KJV). This should be the motto of every true follower of Jesus. No matter how dark and hopeless a situation might seem, never stop praying. It's not only to resolve our problems that we should pray, but to share in the strength of God's friendship. For us, prayer should be not merely an act, but an attitude of life.

> *Lord, I pray that You would create in me a pure heart. Please refresh my gratitude to You and teach me to trust You wholeheartedly. Amen.*

Do we pray for God's will, or demand our own way? Prayer needs to be an integral part of our lives, so that when a crisis comes we have the strength and faith to pray for God's will. Someone said that strength in prayer is better than length in prayer. However, Martin Luther said, "I have so much to do today that I shall spend the first three hours in prayer."

—BILLY GRAHAM, from *Day by Day with Billy Graham*

THE DUTY OF PRAYER

"Will he always call upon God?"

JOB 27:10 KJV

The neglect of the duty of prayer seems to be inconsistent with supreme love to God, and is against the will of God so plainly revealed. Living in such a neglect is inconsistent with leading a holy life....

A holy life is a life of faith. The life that true Christians live in the world, they live by the faith of the Son of God. But who can believe that that man lives by faith who lives without prayer, which is the natural expression of faith? Prayer is as natural an expression of faith as breathing is of life; and to say that a man lives a life of faith and lives a prayerless life is every whit as inconsistent and incredible as to say that a man lives without breathing. A prayerless life is so far from being a holy life that it is a profane life. He who lives so lives like a heathen who does not call on God's name. He who lives a prayerless life lives without God in the world.

—JONATHAN EDWARDS

Heavenly Father, I do not want to be someone who leads a "prayerless life" in this world. Help me to be always seeking You, living a life of faith and holiness. I want to take joy in spending time in Your presence, in worshiping You, and in living a life that is completely devoted to You. Amen.

PRAYING IN FAITH

I will lie down and sleep in peace,
for you alone, O LORD,
make me dwell in safety

PSALM 4:8

Whatever we ask of God...

Whatever we voice in thanksgiving to God...

Whatever we declare to be the attributes of God...

We must offer with faith.

We must truly believe that when we ask of God, He answers.

We must truly believe that He is worthy of all our thanksgiving and praise.

> *Lord God, today I just lay everything in Your hands. God, I'm anxious, but I believe in Your power and goodness, and I believe in your praiseworthiness. Thank You for Your love. Amen.*

We must truly believe that He is totally capable of handling all things according to the fullness of His plan and purpose for our life.

—CHARLES STANLEY

HEALING PRAYER

Now Simon's mother-in-law was lying sick with a fever;
and immediately they spoke to Jesus about her.

MARK 1:30 NASB

Into Simon's house illness had entered; fever in a deadly form had prostrated his mother-in-law; and as soon as Jesus came, they told Him of the sad affliction, and He hurried to the patient's bed. Do you have any illness in the house this morning? You will find Jesus the best physician by far; go to Him at once and tell Him all about the matter. Immediately lay the case before Him. It concerns one of His people, and therefore He will not regard it as trivial. Notice that immediately the Savior restored the ill woman; none can heal as He does. We dare not assume that the Lord will remove all illness from those we love, but we dare not forget that believing prayer for the sick is far more likely to be followed by restoration than anything else in the world; and where this does not happen, we must meekly bow to His will by whom life and death are determined. The tender heart of Jesus waits to hear our griefs; let us pour them into His patient ear.

–CHARLES H. SPURGEON

 Lord Jesus, thank You for Your compassionate heart. I know You hear all of my prayers. Thank You for the healing of body and spirit that comes when I pray. Amen.

THE GLORIOUS TASK OF INTERCEDING

And whatever you ask in My name, that I will do,
that the Father may be glorified in the Son.

JOHN 14:13 NKJV

Intercession is very important. A little girl prayed for her friend till she also found the Lord Jesus as her Savior. Together they began to pray for a third girl. Then the three of them for a fourth and the four of them for a fifth—the chain reaction in the hearts of little children by intercession.

Father, thank You for Your love for me and the world. Holy Spirit, please guide my prayers and lead my thoughts to those who need Your love. Amen.

Will you not ask the Lord to use you for this chain reaction—that this may begin in your heart and then continue? Pray for one, then together for a third, then the three of you for a fourth.

In 1 Timothy 2:1-2 [KJV] Paul says: "I exhort therefore, that, first of all, supplications, prayers, intercessions, and giving of thanks, be made for all men; for kings, and for all that are in authority; that we may lead a quiet and peaceable life in all godliness and honesty."

I have experienced that nothing makes us as free as interceding for others.

What a heavy task! But how glorious!

–CORRIE TEN BOOM, from *Not I, but Christ*

A PRAYERFUL COMMUNITY

May the Lord make your love increase and overflow for
each other and for everyone else, just as ours does for you.

1 THESSALONIANS 3:12

*Lord, I know that
relationships are so
important to You. God,
please lead me close to You
and teach me to love, so
that I can show Your love to
those around me. Amen.*

Prayer is the strength of our individual and community existence. It is through prayer that we find the heart of our love relationship with Jesus as individuals, and it is through the love relationship of Jesus working in individual lives that communities prosper in peace and unity. It is in the solitude of prayer that we find our true Companion, and thus learn to be better companions of others. It is in the inner silence of prayer that we hear the living word of God, and thus learn to speak words that flow from the love of God to one another.

—JOHN MICHAEL TALBOT, from *Regathering Power*

GOD IN OUR MIDST

Cast your burden on the Lord,
And He shall sustain you.

PSALM 55:22 NKJV

What prayer as asking presupposes is simply a personal—that is, an experientially interactive—relationship between us and God, just as with a request of child to parent or friend to friend. It assumes that our natural concerns will be naturally expressed, and that God will hear our prayers for ourselves as well as for others....

Accordingly, I believe the most adequate description of prayer is simply, "Talking to God about what we are doing together."... Prayer is a matter of explicitly sharing with God my concerns about what he too is concerned about in my life.

—DALLAS WILLARD, from *The Divine Conspiracy: Rediscovering Our Hidden Life in God*

 Lord, help me remember today that my life is about You. Help me remember that You're right here in the midst of everything that's pressing for my attention. Help me remember that You want to live life with me. Amen.

JANUARY 15

AN UPRIGHT HEART

I desire therefore that the men pray everywhere,
lifting up holy hands, without wrath and doubting.

1 TIMOTHY 2:8 NKJV

Praying must come out of a clean heart and be presented and urged with the "lifting up of holy hands" (1 Timothy 2:8). It must be strengthened by a life aiming, unceasingly, to obey God, to attain conformity to the divine law, and to come into submission to the divine will.

Let it not be forgotten, that, while life is a condition of prayer, prayer is also the condition of righteous living. Prayer promotes righteous living and is the one great aid to uprightness of heart and life. The fruit of real praying is right living. Praying sets him who prays to the great business of working out his salvation with fear and trembling. It puts him to watching his temper, conversation, and conduct.... It gives him a high incentive to pursue his pilgrimage consistently by shunning every evil way to walk in the good.

–E. M. BOUNDS

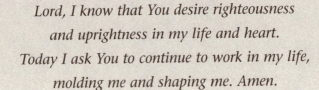

*Lord, I know that You desire righteousness
and uprightness in my life and heart.
Today I ask You to continue to work in my life,
molding me and shaping me. Amen.*

REACHING OUT IN FAITH

Listen to my cry for mercy
as I cry to you for help,
as I lift my hands toward your holy sanctuary.

PSALM 28:2 NLT

There are things we can do to increase our faith, such as read the Word of God. Faith comes simply by hearing it (Romans 10:17). When you take the promises and truths in His Word and declare them out loud, you'll sense your faith increasing.

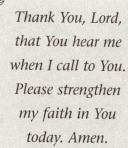

Thank You, Lord, that You hear me when I call to You. Please strengthen my faith in You today. Amen.

Praying increases our faith as well because it's how we reach out and touch God. At one point a woman reached out to the Lord believing that if she just "touched the hem of His garment" she could be healed. Jesus told her that her faith had made her well, and she was healed at that very time (Matthew 9:20-22). Every time we reach out and touch Him in prayer, our lives are healed in some way and our faith is increased.

–STORMIE OMARTIAN, from *The Power of a Praying Woman*

KNOW MY HEART

And I am sure that God, who began the good work
within you, will continue his work until it is finally
finished on that day when Christ Jesus comes back again.

PHILIPPIANS 1:6 NLT

Pray earnestly—you might even kneel or take a moment to write out these words as a covenant to God—Psalm 139:23-24: "Search me, O God, and know my heart; try me, and know my anxieties; and see if there is any wicked way in me, and lead me in the way everlasting" (NKJV).

But beware! If you make that your earnest prayer before the Lord, be ready! God wants to shine the spotlight of His Spirit into your life to show you elements of attitude and behavior that need to be confessed and repented. It may be discouraging at first, but the result will be a richer life with a greater understanding of His astounding grace.

–DAVID JEREMIAH, from *Captured by Grace*

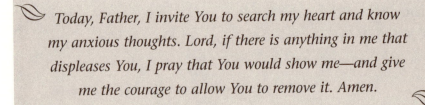

Today, Father, I invite You to search my heart and know my anxious thoughts. Lord, if there is anything in me that displeases You, I pray that You would show me—and give me the courage to allow You to remove it. Amen.

BARRIERS TO JOY

In all my prayers for all of you, I always pray with joy,
because of your partnership in the gospel from the
first day until now, being confident of this, that he
who began a good work in you will carry it on
to completion until the day of Christ Jesus.

PHILIPPIANS 1:4–6

Ask yourself two questions:

Is there any unconfessed sin in my life?

Confession is telling God you did the thing He saw you do. He doesn't need to hear it as much as you need to say it. Whether it's too small to mention or too big to be forgiven isn't yours to decide. Your task is to be honest....

Are there any unsurrendered worries in my heart?

"Give all your worries to him, because he cares about you" (1 Peter 5:7 [NCV]).

The German word for *worry* means "to strangle." The Greek word means "to divide the mind." Both are accurate. Worry is a noose on the neck and a distraction of the mind, neither of which is befitting for joy.

–MAX LUCADO, from
When God Whispers Your Name

Dear Heavenly Father, I pray that You would show me the things that keep me from enjoying my life in You. Please help me build confession into my prayer life, and may my prayers foster in me a rich, joyful dependence on You. Amen.

CONFESSION IS GOOD FOR THE SOUL

Draw near to God and He will draw near to you.

JAMES 4:8 NKJV

Confession does for the soul what preparing the land does for the field. Before the farmer sows the seed he works the acreage, removing the rocks and pulling the stumps. He knows that seed grows better if the land is prepared. Confession is the act of inviting God to walk the acreage of our hearts. "There is a rock of greed over here. Father, I can't budge it. And that tree of guilt near the fence? Its roots are long and deep. And may I show you some dry soil, too crusty for seed?" God's seed grows better if the soil of the heart is cleared.

And so the Father and the Son walk the field together; digging and pulling, preparing the heart for fruit. Confession invites the Father to work the soil of the soil.

−MAX LUCADO, from *In the Grip of Grace*

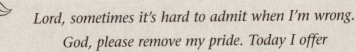

Lord, sometimes it's hard to admit when I'm wrong.
God, please remove my pride. Today I offer
my whole life to You. Amen.

A CLEAN HEART

Create in me a pure heart, O God,
and renew a right spirit within me.

PSALM 51:10

I want you to look upon this idea of cleansing your heart not as a judgment that your heart is dirty, but as God's call for you to get completely right before Him so He can bring all the blessings He has for you into your life. See it as God preparing you for the important work He has ahead for you to do....

In order to see positive changes happen in your life, you have to be open to the cleansing and stretching work of the Holy Spirit. You have to allow Him to expose your heart so you won't be deceived about yourself and your life. You have to invite Him to create a clean heart within you.

—STORMIE OMARTIAN, from *The Power of a Praying Woman*

Lord, as painful as it is to present my sinfulness to You for cleansing, I know that it's ultimately for my good and Your glory. God, I know that it is because of Your love that You desire purity in my life. Today, Lord, I pray that You would cleanse my heart. Amen.

DIVINE MOMENTS

The LORD is close to all who call on him,
yes, to all who call on him sincerely.

PSALM 145:18 NLT

Imagine considering every moment as a potential time of communion with God. By the time your life is over, you will have spent six months at stoplights, eight months opening junk mail, a year and a half looking for lost stuff (double that number in my case), and a whopping five years standing in various lines.

Why don't you give these moments to God? By giving God your whispering thoughts, the common becomes uncommon. Simple phrases such as "Thank You, Father," "Be sovereign this hour, O Lord," "You are my resting place, Jesus" can turn a commute into a pilgrimage. You needn't leave your office or kneel in your kitchen. Just pray where you are. Let the kitchen become a cathedral or the classroom a chapel. Give God your whispering thoughts.

—MAX LUCADO, from *Just Like Jesus*

God, I know that You are with me always.
I give you my moments today, Lord God.
Please direct my thoughts toward You and allow me
to see You today in the middle of the mundane. Amen.

PRAYER CHANGES ME

I want men everywhere to lift up holy hands in prayer,
without anger or disputing.

1 TIMOTHY 2:8

The late Dr. Donald Barnhouse, greatly admired American pastor and author, once came to the pulpit and made a statement that stunned his congregation: "Prayer changes nothing!" You could have heard a pin drop in that packed Sunday worship service in Philadelphia. His comment, of course, was designed to make Christians realize that

Heavenly Father, I know that of all the changes that prayer can bring, the greatest change takes place within my heart. Help me to be receptive to Your leading as I pray. Amen.

God is sovereignly in charge of everything. Our times are literally in His hands. No puny human being by uttering a few words in prayer takes charge of events and changes them. God does the shaping, the changing; it is He who is in control. Barnhouse was correct, except in one minor detail. Prayer changes me. When you and I pray, we change, and that is one of the major reasons prayer is such a therapy that counteracts anxiety.

–CHARLES SWINDOLL

THE ANSWER FOR EVERY NEED

*But by His doing you are in Christ Jesus, who became
to us wisdom from God, and righteousness
and sanctification, and redemption.*

1 CORINTHIANS 1:30 NASB

God is not a retailer dispensing grace to us in doses. God is not measuring out some patience to the impatient, some love to the unloving, some meekness to the proud in quantities that we take and work on as a kind of capital. God has given only one gift to meet all our need—His Son, Christ Jesus. As I look to Him to live out His life in me, He will be humble and patient and loving and everything else I need—in my stead....

"Lord, I cannot do it, therefore, I will no longer try to do it." This is the point where most of us fail. Pray instead, "Lord, I cannot do it, therefore, I will take my hands off. , from now on, I trust You for that." I depend on Him to act, and then, I enter fully and joyfully into the action He initiates. It is not passivity. It is a most active life trusting the Lord like that.

–WATCHMAN NEE

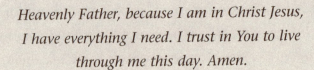

*Heavenly Father, because I am in Christ Jesus,
I have everything I need. I trust in You to live
through me this day. Amen.*

YOUR FATHER WAITS FOR YOU

[Jesus said,] "When you pray, go into your own room,
shut your door and pray to your Father privately.
Your Father who sees all private things will reward you."

MATTHEW 6:6 PHILLIPS

Christians often complain that private prayer is not what it should be. They feel weak and sinful. Their heart is cold and dark. It is as if they have so little to pray, and in that little, no faith or joy. They are discouraged and kept from prayer by the thought that they cannot come to the Father as they ought or as they wish.

Child of God, listen to your teacher, Jesus! He tells you that when you go to private prayer, your first thought must be this: "The Father is in secret, and the Father waits for me there."

...Get yourself into the presence of the loving Father. "As a father has compassion on his children, so the LORD has compassion on those who fear him" (Psalm 103:13 [ASV])....

Just place yourself before God and look up into God's face. Think of God's wonderful, tender, compassionate love. Just tell God how sinful and cold and dark all is. It is the Father's loving heart that will give light and warmth to yours.

–ANDREW MURRAY

Heavenly Father, thank You for all the gifts You continually give me on a daily basis. Thank You for being a loving Father who longs to meet all of my needs. You are worthy of my praise. Amen.

MORE THAN A PHYSICAL TOUCH

[Jesus said,] "The thief does not come except to steal, and
to kill, and to destroy. I have come that they may have
life, and that they may have it more abundantly"

JOHN 10:10 NKJV

While in prayer, not particularly thinking about myself, a Voice seemed to say, "Are you yourself ready for this work to which I have called you?" I replied, "No, Lord, I am done for. I have reached the end of my resources." The Voice replied, "If you will turn that over to me and not worry about it, I will take care of it." I quickly answered, "Lord, I close the bargain right here." A great peace settled into my heart and pervaded me. I knew it was done! Life—abundant Life—had taken possession of me. I was so lifted up that I scarcely touched the road as I quietly walked home that night. For days after, I went through days working all day and far into the night, for there was not the slightest trace of tiredness of any kind. I seemed possessed by Life and Peace and Rest—by Christ Himself.

Nine of the most strenuous years of my life have gone by since then, and the old trouble has never returned, and I have never had such health. But it was more than a physical touch. I seemed to have tapped new Life for body, mind, and spirit. Life was on a permanently higher level. And I had done nothing but take it!

—E. STANLEY JONES

Lord, as I spend this time in prayer with You, You renew me, body, mind, and spirit. Thank You for the abundant life You have given to me. Amen.

DELAYED, BUT NOT REFUSED

I am exhausted from crying for help; my throat is
parched and dry. My eyes are swollen with
weeping, waiting for my God to help me.

PSALM 69:3 NLT

Why does God delay to answer a prayer? First, perhaps God loves to hear the voice of prayer. "The prayer of the upright pleases him" (Proverbs 15:8). You let the street musician play a long time before you throw down money for him, because you love to hear his music.

Second, God may delay an answer in order to humble us. God has spoken to us abundantly in the Bible to forsake our sins, but we would not listen to God. Therefore, God lets us keep speaking to Him in prayer, and seems not to hear us.

Third, God may delay to answer because God sees we are still unprepared for the blessing we ask. Our spiritual impurity is not yet boiled away. We would have God swift to deliver, and we are slow to repent.

Finally, God may delay to answer in order that the blessing we pray for may be more highly valued and sweeter when it comes. The longer a merchant's ships stay in foreign countries, the more the merchant rejoices when they come home weighed down with spices and jewels.

–THOMAS WATSON

Lord, even when You do not answer right away, I know You hear me when I pray. Teach me patience as I wait on You. Amen.

PREPARING TO PRAY

Then Jacob woke up and said, "Surely the LORD
is in this place, and I wasn't even aware of it."

GENESIS 28:16 NLT

God's Presence is universal. There is no place in the world—not one—that is devoid of God's Most Holy Presence.... This is a truth that all followers of Jesus readily admit, but all are not equally alive to its importance.... Because we are not seeing God with our physical eyes, we are too apt to forget God and act as though God is way far away.

While knowing perfectly well that God is everywhere, if we do not think about it, it is the same as if we did not know it. Therefore, before beginning to pray, it is always necessary to rouse your entire being to a constant, unswerving remembering and thinking about the Presence of God. In Old Testament days, when Jacob beheld the ladder that went up to Heaven, he cried out, "Surely the LORD is in this place, and I wasn't even aware of it." By saying this, he meant that he had not thought about it, because, surely, he could not fail to know that God was everywhere and in all things. Therefore, when you are preparing to pray, you must say with your whole heart, "God is indeed here."

–FRANCIS DE SALES

 Heavenly Father, as I prepare to enter Your presence,
help me to say, with reverence and awe, "You are
indeed here." I worship You in this place.

YOUR PRAYER HELPER

The Spirit helps us in our weakness. We do not know
what we ought to pray for, but the Spirit himself intercedes
for us with groans that words cannot express.

ROMANS 8:26

"The Spirit himself intercedes for us." "To intercede for" means
to act the part of a court advocate in behalf of someone....

All true prayer is due to the influence of the Holy Spirit. The
Holy Spirit not only guides you in the selection of the things for
which to pray, but also gives you the appropriate desires. Please
do not suppose that the Spirit itself prays or utters the inarticulate groans the apostle is speaking about here. The Spirit is said
to do what the Spirit causes you to do. More is meant here than
that certain desires and feelings are awakened in your heart by
a mere external influence. The Holy Spirit dwells inside the
Christian believer as a principle
of life. There is, however, a
meeting together, a joint operation of the Divine and human,
especially in those emotions,
desires, and aspirations which
we are unable to clothe in
words. Although these desires
are not and cannot be articu-
lated with words, the eye of God
who searches the heart can read
and understand them.

—CHARLES HODGE

*Lord, I thank You for
sending me Your Spirit to
intercede with me as I pray.
I yield myself to Him,
allowing Him to pray
through me, especially when
I don't know how to pray.
Thank You for this great
"prayer helper." Amen.*

PRAY SHAMELESSLY

[Jesus said,] "I say unto you, Though he will not
rise and give him, because he is his friend,
yet because of his importunity he will rise
and give him as many as he needeth."

LUKE 11:8 KJV

The man must feed his friend, for hospitality is a sacred duty.
So he goes to another friend for *three loaves,* i.e., three small
loaves which would suffice for one man. But this second
householder has shut his door and gone to bed with his children.... He raises no difficulty about giving the bread, but the
bother of getting up is quite another matter....

But the man is persistent. He will not go away, nor will he let
his friend go back to sleep. And where friendship cannot
prevail, *his importunity* (lit. 'shamelessness') wins the day. The
lesson is clear. We must not play at prayer, but must show
persistence if we do not receive the answer immediately. It is
not that God is unwilling and must be pressed into answering.... But if we do not want what we are asking for enough
to be persistent, we do not want it very much. It is not such
tepid prayer that is answered.

–LEON MORRIS, from *The Gospel According to John*

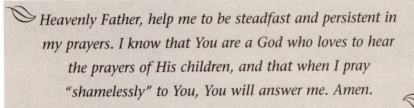

*Heavenly Father, help me to be steadfast and persistent in
my prayers. I know that You are a God who loves to hear
the prayers of His children, and that when I pray
"shamelessly" to You, You will answer me. Amen.*

A MIGHTY WEAPON

[Jesus said,] "But the tax collector stood at a distance.
He would not even look up to heaven, but beat his
breast and said, 'God, have mercy on me, a sinner.'"

LUKE 11:8

Prayer is a mighty weapon if it is done in the right mindset. Prayer is so strong that continual pleas have overcome shamelessness, injustice, and savage cruelty.... It has also overcome laziness and things that friendship could not bring about. For, "although he will not give him because he is his friend, yet because of his appeals he will rise and give to him." In addition, continual requests made an unworthy woman worthy....

Let us pray diligently. Prayer is a mighty weapon if used with earnestness and sincerity, without drawing attention to ourselves. It has turned back wars and benefited an entire undeserving nation.... So then, if we pray with humility, beating our chests like the tax gatherer and saying what he did, "Be merciful to me a sinner," we will obtain everything we ask for.... We need much repentance, beloved, much prayer, much endurance, and much perseverance to gain the good things that have been promised to us.

–JOHN CHRYSOSTOM

Lord, I want my prayers to be mighty and effective.
Teach me how to make my prayers a mighty
weapon for Your Kingdom. Amen.

COMMUNION WITH GOD

> But I have stilled and quieted my soul;
> like a weaned child with its mother,
> like a weaned child is my soul within me.
>
> PSALM 131:2

Prayer is first of all, communion with God. Our blessed Lord Himself, in the days of His flesh, is seen again and again leaving the company of His disciples and going out into some desert place on a mountainside, or into a garden, that His spirit might be refreshed as He bowed in prayer alone with the Father. , from such seasons of fellowship He returned to do His mightiest works and to bear witness to the truth. And in this He is our great Exemplar....

We are told to continue in prayer. This does not mean that we are to be constantly teasing God in order that we may obtain what we might think would add most to our happiness or be best for us, but we are to abide in a sense of His presence and of our dependence upon His bounty. We are to learn to talk to Him and to quietly wait before Him, too, in order that we may hear His voice as He speaks to us.

—H. A. IRONSIDE

 Heavenly Father, I love to spend time in Your presence, abiding in You. Teach me to hear Your voice as You speak to me. Amen.

CHILDLIKE PRAYER

The LORD is like a father to his children,
tender and compassionate to those who fear him.

PSALM 103:13 NLT

Nothing is more central to the spiritual life than prayer, for prayer ushers us into perpetual communion with the heart of God. And there are many things to learn about this life of constant conversation with the Holy One.

Abba Father, I am Your child. I bring to You all of my needs and place them before You, knowing that You care for me.

But we must beware of making things too complicated. Like children coming to their parents, so we come to God. There is awe to be sure, but there is also intimacy. We bring our heart cries to a loving Father. Like the mother hen who gathers her chicks under her wings, so our God cares for us, protects us, comforts us (Matthew 23:37).

So no matter how much we study the labyrinthine realities of prayer, let us forever come as children to a loving Abba who delights to give and to forgive.

–RICHARD J. FOSTER, from *Prayer: Finding the Heart's True Home*

FEBRUARY 2

PRAYERLESSNESS

Yet no one calls on your name or pleads with
you for mercy. Therefore, you have turned away
from us and turned us over to our sins.

ISAIAH 64:7 NLT

The worst sin is prayerlessness. Overt sin, or crime, or the glaring inconsistencies which often surprise us in Christian people are the effect of this, or its punishment. We are left by God for lack of seeking Him. The history of the saints shows often that their lapses were the fruit and nemesis of slackness or neglect in prayer.... Trusting the God of Christ, and transacting with Him, we come into tune with men.... Prayer is an act, indeed *the* act, of fellowship. We cannot truly pray even for ourselves without passing beyond ourselves and our individual experience.... Not to want to pray, then, is the sin behind sin. And it ends in not being able to pray.... We do not take our spiritual food, and so we falter, dwindle, and die. "In the sweat of your brow ye shall eat your bread." That has been said to be true both of physical and spiritual labor.

–P. T. FORSYTH, from *Prayer and Worship*

Heavenly Father, praying can be difficult at times, but I long for fellowship with You. Help me to persevere in my prayer life, so that I may grow closer to You. Amen.

PAY ATTENTION

[Jesus said,] "And so I tell you, keep on asking, and you will be given what you ask for. Keep on looking, and you will find. Keep on knocking, and the door will be opened."

LUKE 11:9 NLT

"Blessed are the drowsy ones for they shall soon drop off to sleep!" wrote Nietzsche, and his satirical warning holds for those who do not pray. For prayer is awakeness, attention, intense inward openness. In a certain way sin could be described, and described with a good deal of penetration, by noting that it is anything that destroys this attention. Pride, self-will, self-absorption, doublemindedness, dishonesty, sexual excess, overeating, overdrinking, overactivity of any sort, all destroy attention and all cut the nerve of effective prayer. Just as sleep is upset by any serious mental disturbance, so attention is dispersed when unfaced sin gets the ascendancy. If prayer is attention, then it is naturally attention to the highest thing that I know, to my "ultimate concern," and this human prayer means a moving out of a life of inattention, out of the dispersion, out of "the Gethsemane sleep" into the life of openness and attention to the highest that I know. God can only disclose the Divine whispers to those who are attending.

–DOUGLAS V. STEERE, from *Prayer and Worship*

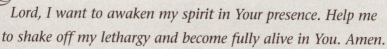

Lord, I want to awaken my spirit in Your presence. Help me to shake off my lethargy and become fully alive in You. Amen.

GIVE GOD YOUR WHOLE LIFE

[Jesus said,] "For everyone who asks receives; he who seeks finds; and to him who knocks, the door will be opened."

LUKE 11:10

Heavenly Father, I give my life, in its entirety, over to Your loving care. I want to do Your will in every area of my life. Amen.

Now if we conclude that we must be pious in our prayers, we must also conclude that we must be pious in all the other aspects of our lives. For there is no reason why we should make God the rule and the measure of our prayers, why we should look wholly unto Him and pray according to His will, and yet not make Him the rule and measure of all the other actions of our life. For any ways of life, any employment of our talents whether of our bodies, our time, or money that are not strictly according to the will of God, that are not done to His glory are simply absurdities, and our prayers fail because they are not according to the will of God.... It is our strict duty to live by reason, to devote all of the action of our lives to God.... If our prayers do not lead us to this, they are of no value no matter how wise or heavenly.

—WILLIAM LAW

PRAYING THE PSALMS

How long, O LORD? Will you forget me forever?
How long will you hide your face from me?

PSALM 13:1

The Bible contains many recorded models of prayer—150 psalms, the Lord's Prayer, and the prayers of saints from Abraham to Paul....

As for the Psalms, I am always intrigued to find how Christians relate to them, for it took me years after my conversion to feel at home in them. Why? Partly, I think, because the view of life as a battle which the Psalms embody took longer to root itself in my heart than in my head; partly because the middle-class misconception that tidiness, self-conscious balance, and restraint are essentials of godliness—a misconception which makes most of the Psalms seem uncouth—possessed both my head and my heart for longer. More and more, however, the psalmists' calls for help, their complaints, confessions of sin, depressions, celebrations of God, cries of love for him, challenges and commitments to him, and hopes placed exclusively in him, have become the emotional world of my prayers and I think this is how it should be.

—J. I. PACKER, from *Knowing God*

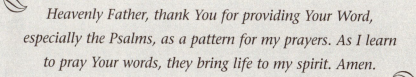

Heavenly Father, thank You for providing Your Word, especially the Psalms, as a pattern for my prayers. As I learn to pray Your words, they bring life to my spirit. Amen.

PRAY WITHOUT CEASING

Pray continually.

1 THESSALONIANS 5:17

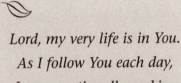

Lord, my very life is in You.
As I follow You each day,
I pray continually, seeking
to be in Your presence,
moment by moment. Amen.

Our thinking about prayer, whether right or wrong, is based on our own mental conception of it. The correct concept is to think of prayer as the breath in our lungs and the blood from our hearts. Our blood flows and our breathing continues "without ceasing"; we are not even conscious of it, but it never stops. And we are not always conscious of Jesus keeping us in perfect oneness with God, but if we are obeying Him, He always is. Prayer is not an exercise, it is the life of the saint. Beware of anything that stops the offering up of prayer. "Pray without ceasing…"—maintain the childlike habit of offering up prayer in your heart to God all the time.

−OSWALD CHAMBERS

PASSIONATE PRAYERS

My soul thirsts for you;
my whole body longs for you
in this parched and weary land
where there is no water.

PSALM 63:1 NLT

Ardent desire is the basis of unceasing prayer. It is not a shallow, fickle tendency, but a strong yearning, an unquenchable desire which permeates, glows, burns, and fixes the heart. It is the flame of a present and active principle ascending up to God. It is ardor propelled by desire that burns its way to the throne of mercy and gets its request. It is the determination of desire that gives battle victory in a great struggle of prayer. It is the burden of a weighty desire that sobers, makes restless, and reduces to quietness the soul just emerged from its mighty wrestlings. It is the inclusive character of desire which arms prayer with a thousand requests. It clothes it with an indestructible courage and an all-conquering power.

—E. M. BOUNDS

 Lord God, today I pray that You would rekindle a new love for You in my heart. Remind me of the goodness of knowing You. May I seek You with renewed passion today. Amen.

A LIFE OF PRAYER

Pray without ceasing, give thanks in all circumstances;
for this is the will of God in Christ Jesus for you.

1 THESSALONIANS 5:17–18 NRSV

Lord, I long to be in Your presence every moment of every day. Through my prayers, I seek to be with You, to know Your peace, all day long. Amen.

Let us not be content to pray morning and evening, but let us live in prayer all day long. Let this prayer, this life of love, which means death to self, spread out from our seasons of prayer, as from a centre, over all that we have to do. All should become prayer, that is, a loving consciousness of God's presence, whether it be social intercourse or business. Such a course as this will ensure you a profound peace.

–FRANÇOIS FÉNELON

PERSISTENCE IN PRAYER

[Jesus said,] "Ask and it will be given to you; seek and
you will find; knock and the door will be opened to you.
For everyone who asks receives; he who seeks finds;
and to him who knocks, the door will be opened."

MATTHEW 7:7–8

This is the lesson of the parable in Luke 18:1-8 about the widow. She was so persistent and importunate in her refusal to let go of the judge that he was overpowered and had to help her in spite of himself. How much more, Christ argues there (Luke 18:7), will God give us if He sees that we do not stop praying but go right on knocking so that He has to hear it? This is all the more so because He has promised to do so and shows that such persistence is pleasing to Him. Since your need goes right on knocking, therefore, you go right on knocking, too, and do not relent.... By urging you not only to ask but also to knock, God intends to test you to see whether you can hold on tight, and to teach you that your prayer is not displeasing to Him or unheard, simply because His answer is delayed and you are permitted to go on seeking and knocking.

–MARTIN LUTHER

*Heavenly Father, I knock on Your door, and I keep on
knocking until I hear from You. Help me to be patient,
yet persistent, as I wait for Your answer. Amen.*

PRAY LIKE THIS

[Jesus said,] "Pray then like this: 'Our Father
in heaven, hallowed be your name.'"

MATTHEW 6:9 ESV

No man will pray aright, unless his lips and heart shall be directed by the Heavenly Master. For that purpose he has laid down this rule, by which we must frame our prayers....

This form of prayer consists, as I have said, of six petitions. The first three, it ought to be known, relate to the glory of God, without any regard to ourselves; and the remaining three relate to those things which are necessary for our salvation. As the law of God is divided into two tables, of which the former contains the duties of piety, and the latter the duties of charity, so in prayer Christ enjoins us to consider and seek the glory of God, and, at the same time, permits us to consult our own interests. Let us therefore know, that we shall be in a state of mind for praying in a right manner, if we not only are in earnest about ourselves and our own advantage, but assign the first place to the glory of God.

–JOHN CALVIN

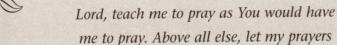

*Lord, teach me to pray as You would have
me to pray. Above all else, let my prayers
bring glory to Your name. Amen.*

THE NECESSITY OF PRAYER

Is anyone among you suffering? Then he must pray. Is anyone cheerful? He is to sing praises. Is anyone among you sick? Then he must call for the elders of the church and they are to pray over him, anointing him with oil in the name of the Lord; and the prayer offered in faith will restore the one who is sick, and the Lord will raise him up, and if he has committed sins, they will be forgiven him.

JAMES 5:13–15 NASB

Words fail to explain how necessary prayer is.... Surely, with good reason the Heavenly Father affirms that the only stronghold of safety is in calling upon his name [cf. Joel 2:32]. By so doing we invoke the presence both of his providence, through which he watches over and guards our affairs, and of his power, through which he sustains us, weak as we are and well-nigh overcome, and of his goodness, through which he receives us, miserably burdened with sins, unto grace; and, in short, it is by prayer that we call him to reveal himself as wholly present to us. Hence comes an extraordinary peace and repose to our consciences. For having disclosed to the Lord the necessity that was pressing upon us, we even rest fully in the thought that none of our ills is hid from him who, we are convinced, has both the will and the power to take the best care of us.

–JOHN CALVIN

Lord, I turn over all of my needs to You. You are my El Shaddai, the great Need-meeter. I trust in You to care for me. Amen.

KINGDOM PRAYERS

[Jesus said,] "Our Father in heaven,
hallowed be your name,
your kingdom come,
your will be done
on earth as it is in heaven."

MATTHEW 6:9-10

In honor of His own Son whose death made possible the full invasion of divine power into the impossibilities of earth, God will do nothing apart from the prayers of the people His Son redeemed. The power is His; the privilege is ours.

We who are in Christ have no reason to fear or surrender to hell's program. We have been redeemed to be prayerful agents of God's blessing, authority, and power on earth; to pray for the earthly manifestation of His heavenly righteousness and will.

That will happen when we seek God's kingdom first.

–EUGENE H. PETERSON, from *Like Dew Your Youth*

 *Today, Lord, I want to seek Your kingdom first—
today, Lord, let Your will be done on earth as it is
in heaven. I pray for opportunities to participate
in Your redeeming work, O Lord. Amen.*

IN SPIRIT AND IN TRUTH

[Jesus said,] "God is Spirit, and those who worship
Him must worship in spirit and truth."

JOHN 4:24 NKJV

You do not feel in the spirit of prayer; you have no spiritual uplift; you are simply indifferent. Give that unhappy mood no heed. You know very well what you ought to do. You ought to present yourself before God; you ought to say your prayers. Do that, and the devout attitude, the bended knees, the folded hands, the quiet and the silence, the lips busied with holy words, will induce the consciousness of the divine presence, and help you to pray in spirit and in truth.

Lord, there are times, to be honest, when I don't feel like praying. During such times, help me to persist in doing what I know is right. Help me to always pray in spirit and in truth. Amen.

—GEORGE HODGES

THE SERVICE OF PRAYER

"Moreover, as for me, far be it from me that I should sin against the Lord by ceasing to pray for you, and I will instruct you in the good and the right way."

1 SAMUEL 12:23 ESV

Heavenly Father, allow my prayers to lift someone's burden today. Show me who needs Your loving touch and allow me to intercede for them. Help me make a difference in someone else's life. Amen.

Perhaps we do not think enough [about] what an effective service prayer is, especially intercessory prayer. We do not believe as we should how it might help those we so fain would serve, penetrating the hearts we cannot open, shielding those we cannot guard, teaching where we cannot speak, comforting where our words have no power to soothe; following the steps of our beloved through the toils and perplexities of the day, lifting off their burdens with an unseen hand at night. No ministry is so like that of an angel as this—silent, invisible, known but to God.

—ELIZABETH RUNDLE CHARLES

PRAYING FOR EACH OTHER

[Jesus said,] "Greater love has no one than this,
that he lay down his life for his friends."

JOHN 15:13

Prayer is the greatest gift we can give to anyone. Of course, if someone needs food, clothes, and a place to live, those needs must be met. But in giving that way, we can't neglect to pray for them as well. Material things are temporary, but our prayers for another person can affect them for a lifetime.

We can never move into all God has for us until we first move into intercessory prayer. This is one part of our calling that we have in common, because we are all called to intercede for others. God wants us to love others enough to lay down our lives for them in prayer.

−STORMIE OMARTIAN, from *The Power of a Praying Woman*

*Lord, remind me today that my faith can move
mountains in the lives of those close to me.
Thank You so much, Lord, that You hear our prayers
for each other. And I pray that You would give me
a sacrificial love for Your people. Amen.*

GIVE GOD YOUR TROUBLES

Therefore let all who are faithful offer prayer to you; at a
time of distress, the rush of mighty waters shall not reach
them. You are a hiding place for me; you preserve me from
trouble; you surround me with glad cries of deliverance.

PSALM 32:6–7 NRSV

What are the things we should lay before the Almighty God
in prayer? Answer: First, our personal troubles. In Psalm 32,
David cried out, "You are my hiding place; you will protect
me from trouble and surround me with songs of deliverance"
(v. 7). Likewise, in Psalm 142, "I cry aloud to the Lord… I pour
out my complaint before him; before him I tell my trouble."
When we pray we should keep in mind all of the shortcom-
ings and excesses we feel, and pour them out freely to God,
our faithful Father, who is ready to help. If you do not know
or recognize your needs, or think you have none, then you
are in the worst possible place. The greatest trouble we can
ever know is thinking that we have no trouble for we have
become hard-hearted and insensible to what is inside of us.

–MARTIN LUTHER

*Heavenly Father, I lay all of my troubles
before You, all of my needs. Thank You for
hearing my cry and rescuing me. Amen.*

WHY?

Turn and answer me, O LORD my God!
Restore light to my eyes, or I will die.

PSALM 13:3 NLT

Some people would tell you not to ask God questions like, "Why?" I am not one of those people. I believe that asking God "Why?" indicates that we have the faith to know that He, and only He, has the answer. I believe "Why?" is a question that ultimately shows faith. However, once we ask the question, we must be willing to rest in His timing for the answer. For some situations the answer may come fairly quickly, for others, very slowly, and for some, not until we see Him face to face. If we trust in the sovereignty of God, we wrestle our way to peace in the knowledge that if an answer is for our highest good, the God who loves us will not withhold it.

Lord God, when I face the hard seasons of life, I know that You are with me. I know that You have a plan. Please hold onto me, Father, and give me greater faith to face my trials. Amen.

–LANA BATEMAN, from *The Heart of Prayer*

THE GOD OF OUR LORD JESUS CHRIST

For this reason, because I have heard of your faith in the Lord Jesus and your love toward all the saints, I do not cease to give thanks for you, remembering you in my prayers, that the God of our Lord Jesus Christ, the Father of glory, may give you a spirit of wisdom and of revelation in the knowledge of him.

EPHESIANS 1:15–17 ESV

So when Paul reminds himself that he is praying to "the God of our Lord Jesus Christ" he reminds himself that he is praying to the God of our salvation, he is praying to the God who has originated and brought to pass all the things we have been considering from verse 3 to verse 14 in our chapter. He is praying to the God who has, before the foundation of the world, chosen and elected us and planned His glorious purpose in Christ for our final complete salvation. What a difference it makes to prayer when you begin in that manner! You no longer go to God uncertainly, or with doubts and queries as to whether He is going to receive you; you remember and realize that you are praying because He has done something to you, and drawn you to Himself in and through "our Lord Jesus Christ."

–DAVID MARTYN LLOYD-JONES

Heavenly Father, You are the "God of my Lord Jesus Christ," my Creator and Savior. There is no other God but You. I can be certain that You hear and answer my prayer. Amen.

HOW TO PRAY
WITHOUT CEASING

Now He was telling them a parable to show that at
all times they ought to pray and not to lose heart.

LUKE 18:1 NASB

How, then, shall we lay hold of that Life and Power and live
the life of prayer without ceasing? By quiet, persistent practice
in turning all of our being, day and night, in prayer and
inward worship and surrender, toward him who calls in the
deeps of our souls.

Mental habits of inward orientation must be established. An
inner, secret turning to God can be made fairly steady after
weeks and months and years of practice and lapses and fail-
ures and returns....

Begin now, as you read these words, as you sit in your chair,
to offer your whole selves, utterly and in joyful abandon, in
quiet, glad surrender to him who is within.... Walk and talk
and work and laugh with your friends. But behind the scenes,
keep up the life of simple prayer and inward worship. Let
inward prayer be your last act before you fall asleep and the
first act when you awake.

–THOMAS KELLY

Lord, I want to pray at all times and not grow weary.
Thank You for strengthening me. Amen.

PASSIONATE PRAYERS

He said: "In a certain town there was a judge who neither
feared God nor cared about men. And there was a widow
in that town who kept coming to him with the plea,
'Grant me justice against my adversary.'"

LUKE 18:2–3

Passionate people hang in there when the going gets tough. They persist, they persevere, they never lose heart, and they never quit. Proverbs 24:16 says, "For a righteous man may fall seven times and rise again" (NKJV). Jesus told the parable of the persistent widow "that men always ought to pray and not lose heart" (Luke 18:1 NKJV). Combine these two scriptural principles, and you have the idea of a person who keeps praying and keeps persisting until success is certain—an unbeatable formula.

The apostle Paul urged that we be "not lagging in diligence, fervent in spirit, serving the Lord" (Romans 12:11 NKJV). And he said to the Corinthian Christians, "But we have this treasure in earthen vessels, that the excellence of the power may be of God and not of us . . . . Therefore we do not lose heart. Even though our outward man is perishing, yet the inward man is being renewed day by day" (2 Corinthians 4:7, 16 NKJV).

–DAVID JEREMIAH

Lord, I want to be passionate in my prayers, persistent until I receive an answer. Help me to lift my fervent prayers to You and to never lose heart. Amen.

HE WILL ANSWER

[Jesus said,] "The judge ignored her for a while, but
eventually she wore him out. 'I fear neither God nor man,'
he said to himself, 'but this woman is driving me crazy.
I'm going to see that she gets justice, because she is
wearing me out with her constant requests!'"

LUKE 18:4-5 NLT

It looks as if he did not hear you: never mind; he does; it must
be that he does; go on as the woman did; you too will be
heard. She is heard at last, and in virtue of her much going;
God hears at once, and will avenge speedily. The unrighteous
judge cared nothing for the woman; those who cry to God are
his own chosen—plain in the fact that they cry to him. He
has made and appointed them to cry: they do cry: will he not
hear them? They exist that they may pray; he has chosen
them that they may choose him; he has called them that they
may call him—that there may be such communion, such
interchange as belongs to their being and the being of their
Father. The gulf of indifference lay between the poor woman
and the unjust judge; God and those who seek his help, are
closer than two hands clasped hard in love: he will avenge
them speedily.

–GEORGE MACDONALD

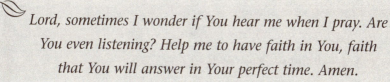

*Lord, sometimes I wonder if You hear me when I pray. Are
You even listening? Help me to have faith in You, faith
that You will answer in Your perfect time. Amen.*

WAITING

[Jesus said,] "And will not God bring about justice
for his chosen ones, who cry out to him day
and night? Will he keep putting them off?"

LUKE 18:7

Waiting is part of ordinary time. We discover God in our waiting: waiting in checkout lines, waiting for the telephone to ring, waiting for graduation, waiting for a promotion, waiting to retire, waiting to die. The waiting itself becomes prayer as we give our waiting to God. In waiting we begin to get in touch with the rhythms of life—stillness and action, listening and decision. They are the rhythms of God. It is in the everyday and the commonplace that we learn patience, acceptance, and contentment....

In a world in which *Winning Through Intimidation* is the order of the day, I am attracted to people who are free from the tyranny of assertiveness. I am drawn to those who are able to simply meet people where they are, with no need to control or manage or make them do anything. I enjoy being around them because they draw the best out in me without any manipulation whatsoever.

–RICHARD J. FOSTER, from *Prayer: Finding the Heart's True Home*

Lord, I know that waiting is a part of life, and that You would have me learn patience in my prayers. As I give my waiting times to You, teach me to be content in every circumstance. Amen.

THE GOODNESS OF GOD

[Jesus said,] "And shall God not avenge His own elect who cry out day and night to Him, though He bears long with them? I tell you that He will avenge them speedily."

LUKE 18:7–8 NKJV

We pray to God to know His passion, death, and resurrection—which come from the goodness of God. We pray to God for the strength that comes from His Cross—which also comes from the goodness of God. We pray to God with all the help of the saints who have gone before us—which, again, comes from the goodness of God. All of the strength that may come through prayer comes from the goodness of God, for He is the goodness of everything. For the highest form of prayer is to the goodness of God. It comes down to us to meet our humblest needs. It gives life to our souls and makes them live and grow in grace and virtue. It is near in nature and swift in grace, for it is the same grace which our souls seek and always will.

–JULIAN OF NORWICH

 Heavenly Father, I know that all of my strength in prayer comes only from Your goodness. Your goodness meets all of my needs and gives me life. Thank You for Your goodness and grace to me. Amen.

THE PLACE OF PRAYER

They all met together continually for prayer.

ACTS 1:14 NLT

Heavenly Father, I pray today for Your Church, that it would be the prayer-filled, Spirit-led Church that You desire for it to be. Help me, as a part of Your Church, to be an effective witness for You this day. Amen.

When Christ had ascended to heaven, the disciples knew what their work was to be: continuing with one accord in prayer and supplication. This gave them power in heaven with God and on earth with men. Their duty was to wait united in prayer for the power of the Holy Spirit for their witness to Christ to the ends of the earth. The Church of Jesus Christ should be a praying, Spirit-filled church and a witnessing church to all the world.

As long as the Church maintained this character, it had power to conquer. Unfortunately, as it came under the influence of the world, it lost much of its supernatural strength and became unfaithful to its worldwide mission.

−ANDREW MURRAY

RESTING IN PRAYER

Let me dwell in Your tent forever;
Let me take refuge in the shelter of Your wings.

PSALM 61:4 NASB

I cannot help the thought which grows steadily upon me, that the better part of prayer is not the asking, but the kneeling where we can ask, the resting there, the staying there, drawing out the willing moments in heavenly communion with God, within the closet, with the night changed into the brightness of the day by the light of Him who all the night was in prayer to God. Just to be there, at leisure from ourselves, at leisure from the world, with our souls at liberty, with our spirit feeling its kinship to the Divine Spirit, with our life finding itself in the life of God—this is prayer. Would it be possible that one could be thus with God, listening to Him, speaking to Him, reposing upon His love, and not come out with a shining face, a gladdened heart, an intent more constant and more strong to give to the waiting world which so sadly needs it what has been taken from the heart of God?

—ALEXANDER MCKENZIE

Lord, as I rest in Your presence, You bring all good things to me. As I spend time with You in my prayer closet, You encourage me and strengthen me to share Your love with a lost and dying world. Amen.

THE BURDEN OF SELF

Relieve the troubles of my heart, and
bring me out of my distress.

PSALM 25:17 NRSV

*Heavenly Father, I turn all
of myself over to Your care.
You are my Creator, and I
trust You to know what is
best for me. Amen.*

The greatest burden we have to carry in life is self. The most difficult thing we have to manage is self. Our own daily living, our frames and feelings, our especial weaknesses and temptations, and our peculiar temperaments, our inward affairs of every kind—these are the things that perplex and worry us more than anything else, and that bring us oftenest into bondage and darkness. In laying off your burdens, therefore, the first one you must get rid of is yourself. You must hand yourself and all your inward experiences, your temptations, your temperament, your frames and feelings, all over into the care and keeping of your God, and leave them there. He made you and therefore He understands you, and knows how to manage you, and you must trust Him to do it.

–HANNAH WHITALL SMITH

WAITING ON GOD

...and to know this love that surpasses knowledge—that
you may be filled to the measure of all the fullness of God.

EPHESIANS 3:19

In praying, we are often occupied with ourselves, with our
own needs, and our own efforts in the presentation of them.
In waiting upon God, the first thought is of *the God upon
whom we wait*. God longs to reveal Himself, to fill us with
Himself. Waiting on God gives Him time in His own way and
divine power to come to us. Before you pray, bow quietly
before God, to remember and realize who He is, how near He
is, how certainly He can and will help. Be still before Him,
and allow His Holy Spirit to waken and stir up in your soul
the childlike disposition of absolute dependence and confident expectation. Wait on God till you know you have met
Him; prayer will then become so different. And when you are
praying, let there be intervals of silence, reverent stillness of
soul, in which you yield yourself to God, in case He may have
aught He wishes to teach you or to work in you.

–ANDREW MURRAY

*Lord, I want to focus only on You today. Cleanse
my mind of all selfish thoughts as I linger in
Your presence and yield myself to You. Amen.*

ALWAYS BE PRAYERFUL

Be glad for all God is planning for you.
Be patient in trouble, and always be prayerful.

ROMANS 12:12 NLT

Lord, it is so important that I always be prayerful, alert, and vigilant. Keep me from the temptation to shrink from my prayer life, because that is where my strength comes from. Amen.

Prayer is a preparation for danger, it is the armor for battle. Go not into the dangerous world without it. You kneel down at night to pray and drowsiness weighs down your eyelids. A hard day's work is a kind of excuse, and you shorten your prayer, and resign yourself softly to repose. The morning breaks, and it may be you rise late, and so your early devotions are not done, or done with irregular haste. It is no marvel if that day in which you suffer drowsiness to interfere with prayer be a day on which you betray Him by cowardice and soft shrinking from duty.

–FREDERICK W. ROBERTSON

ASKING IN JESUS' NAME

Now this is the confidence that we have in Him, that if
we ask anything according to His will, He hears us.

1 JOHN 5:14 NKJV

The aim of prayer is not to force God's hand or make him do our will against his own, but to deepen our knowledge of him and our fellowship with him through contemplating his glory, confessing our dependence and need, and consciously embracing his goals. Our asking therefore must be *according to God's will and in Jesus' name....*

To ask in Jesus' name is not to use a verbal spell but to base our asking on Christ's saving relationship to us through the cross; this will involve making petitions which Christ can endorse and put his name to....

Central to the life of prayer is letting ourselves be taught by Christ through his Word and Spirit what we should pray for. To the extent that we know, through the Spirit's inner witness, that we are making a request which the Lord has specifically given us to make, to that extent we *know* that we have the answer even before we see it.

−J. I. PACKER, from *Knowing God*

 Lord, I want my desires to line up with Your desires, my will to line up with Your will. When I pray in Your name, I only want to pray that Your will be done. Thank You for Your Word, Your name, and Your Spirit, which enable my prayers according to Your will. Amen.

FORGETTING TO PRAY

Pray in the Spirit at all times with all kinds of
prayers, asking for everything you need. To do this
you must always be ready and never give up.
Always pray for all God's people.

EPHESIANS 6:18 NCV

Lord, I confess this morning I remembered my breakfast, but forgot my prayers. And as I have returned no praise, so Thou mightst justly have afforded me no protection. Yet Thou hast carefully kept me to the middle of this day, [entrusting] me with a new debt before I have paid the old score. It is now noon, too late for a morning, too soon for an evening sacrifice. My corrupt heart prompts me to put off my prayers till night; but I know it too well, or rather too ill, to trust it. I fear if I defer them till night, at night I shall forget them. Be pleased, therefore, now to accept them. Lord, let not a few hours the later make a breach, especially seeing (be it spoken not to excuse my negligence, but to implore Thy pardon) a thousand years in Thy sight are but as yesterday. I promise hereafter, by Thy assistance, to bring forth fruit in due season.

–THOMAS FULLER

Lord, sometimes it is so easy to forget to pray,
but I know that You long to spend time with me,
Your child. Forgive my lapses, and help me to
remember to put You first in my day. Amen.

PRAYER AND THE MODERN WORLD

Then he said to them, "Suppose one of you has a friend, and he goes to him at midnight and says, 'Friend, lend me three loaves of bread, because a friend of mine on a journey has come to me, and I have nothing to set before him.'"

LUKE 11:5–6

Although this parable is concerned with the power of persistent prayer, it may also serve as a basis for our thought concerning many contemporary problems and the role of the church in grappling with them. It is midnight in the parable; it is also midnight in our world, and the darkness is so deep that we can hardly see which way to turn....

If the church does not participate actively in the struggle for peace and for economic and racial justice, it will forfeit the loyalty of millions and cause men everywhere to say that it has atrophied its will. But if the church will free itself from the shackles of a deadening status quo, and, recovering its great historic mission, will speak and act fearlessly and insistently in terms of justice and peace, it will enkindle the imagination of mankind and fire the souls of men, imbuing them with a glowing and ardent love for truth, justice, and peace.

–MARTIN LUTHER KING, JR

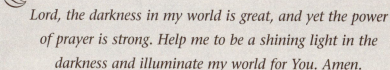

Lord, the darkness in my world is great, and yet the power of prayer is strong. Help me to be a shining light in the darkness and illuminate my world for You. Amen.

THE STRUGGLE OF PRAYER

"And he answers from within, 'Do not bother me;
the door has already been locked, and my children are
with me in bed; I cannot get up and give you anything.'"

LUKE 11:7 NRSV

Prayer, though from one standpoint the most natural thing a Christian ever does, since crying to his heavenly Father is a Spirit-wrought instinct in him, is always a battle against distractions, discouragements, and deadenings from Satan and from our own sinfulness. God may actually resist us when we pray in order that we in turn may resist and overcome his resistance, and so be led into deeper dependence on him and greater enrichment from him at the end of the day (think of wrestling Jacob, and clamoring Job, and the parable of the unjust judge). I see true prayer, like all true obedience, as a constant struggle in which you make headway by effort against what opposes, and however much you progress you are always aware of imperfection, incompleteness, and how much further you have to go.

–J. I. PACKER, from *Knowing God*

*Heavenly Father, sometimes prayer can be a real struggle.
There are so many distractions that cause my
mind and my heart to wander. Help me to stay
focused on You during my times of prayer. Amen.*

PERSEVERE

"I tell you, even though he will not get up and
give him anything because he is his friend,
yet because of his persistence he will
get up and give him as much as he needs."

LUKE 11:8 NASB

First, "Continue steadfastly in prayer." There is so much power to be had in persevering prayer. Don't forget the "importunate friend" of Luke 11:8 ("Because of his persistence he will get up and give him as much as he needs" NASB), and don't forget the parable Jesus told to the effect that we "ought always to pray and not lose heart" (Luke 18:1-8). Perseverance is the great test of genuineness in the Christian life. I praise God for Christians who have persevered in prayer sixty, seventy, or eighty years! Oh, let us be a praying people, and let this year—and all our years—be saturated with prayers to the Lord of all power and all good. It will be good to say in the end, "I have finished the race, I have kept the faith"— through prayer.

–JOHN PIPER, from *Pierced by the Word*

*Lord, I want to persevere in my prayers, to not
give up, to finish the race. Give me strength
as I continue steadfastly in prayer. Amen.*

THE SPIRIT INTERCEDES FOR US

In the same way, the Spirit helps us in our weakness.
We do not know what we ought to pray for,
but the Spirit himself intercedes for us with
groans that words cannot express.

ROMANS 8:26

If our prayer reach or move Him it is because He first reached and moved us to pray. The prayer that reached heaven began there, when Christ went forth. It began when God turned to beseech us in Christ—in the appealing Lamb slain before the foundation of the world. The Spirit went out with the power and function in it to return with our soul. Our prayer is the answer to God's.... The whole rhythm of Christ's soul, so to say, was Godhead going out and returning on itself. And so God stirs and inspires all prayer which finds and moves Him. His love provokes our sacred forwardness.... All say, "I am yours if you will"; and when we will it is prayer. Any final glory of human success or destiny rises from man being God's continual creation, and destined by Him for Him. So we pray because we were made for prayer, and God draws us out by breathing Himself in.

–P. T. FORSYTH

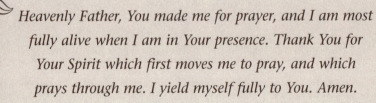

Heavenly Father, You made me for prayer, and I am most fully alive when I am in Your presence. Thank You for Your Spirit which first moves me to pray, and which prays through me. I yield myself fully to You. Amen.

SOLITUDE

[Jesus said,] "But when you pray, go away by yourself, shut the door behind you, and pray to your Father secretly. Then your Father, who knows all secrets, will reward you."

MATTHEW 6:6 NLT

Without solitude it is virtually impossible to live a spiritual life. Solitude begins with a time and place for God, and him alone. If we really believe not only that God exists but also that he is actively present in our lives—healing, teaching, and guiding—we need to set aside a time and space to give him our undivided attention....

Once we have committed ourselves to spending time in solitude, we develop an attentiveness to God's voice in us. In the beginning, during the first days, weeks, or even months, we may have the feeling that we are simply wasting our time. Time in solitude may at first seem little more than a time in which we are bombarded by thousands of thoughts and feelings that emerge from hidden areas of our mind.... At first, the many distractions keep presenting themselves. Later, as they receive less and less attention, they slowly withdraw.

–HENRI NOUWEN

 Lord, it is often so difficult to find time away from my busy schedule to spend with You. Help me learn to appreciate and even cherish times of solitude, alone in Your presence. Amen.

PRAYER FOR OTHERS

With all prayer and petition pray at all times in the Spirit,
and with this in view, be on the alert with all
perseverance and petition for all the saints.

EPHESIANS 6:18 NASB

Prayer for others is a form of petitional prayer that makes deep demands on the faith of an individualistic generation that has so largely lost its sense of inner community. Yet at no point do we touch the inner springs of prayer more vitally than here. For when we hold up the life of another before God, when we expose it to God's love, when we pray for its release from drowsiness, for the quickening of its inner health, for the power to throw off a destructive habit, for the restoration of its free and vital relationship with its fellows, for its strength to resist a temptation, for its courage to continue against sharp opposition—only then do we sense what it means to share in God's work, in His concern; only then do the walls that separate us from others go down and we sense that we are at bottom all knit together in a great and intimate family.

–DOUGLAS V. STEERE, from *Prayer and Worship*

Heavenly Father, I do not want to be selfish in my prayers, and so I lift up the needs of others to You. Through my prayers for Your people, Lord, I am privileged to share in Your work on this earth. Amen.

THE LORD'S PRAYER

[Jesus said,] "Your kingdom come, Your will be done, on earth as it is in heaven. Give us this day our daily bread. And forgive us our debts, as we also have forgiven our debtors."

MATTHEW 6:10–12 NRSV

Your will be done, on earth as it is in heaven.

May we love you with our whole heart by always thinking of you, with our whole soul by always desiring you, with our whole mind by directing all our intentions to you, and with our whole strength by spending all our energies in your service. And may we love our neighbors as ourselves....

Give us this day our daily bread.

In memory and understanding and reverence of the love which our Lord Jesus Christ has for us, revealed by his sacrifice for us on the cross, we ask for the perfect bread of his body.

And forgive us our trespasses.

We know that you forgive us, through the suffering and death of your beloved Son.

As we forgive those who trespass against us.

Enable us to forgive perfectly and without reserve any wrong that has been committed against us.

–ST. FRANCIS OF ASSISI

Lord, thank You for providing me with a model prayer to follow as I spend time in Your presence. As I pray the prayer You taught Your disciples, I am drawn closer to You and to the Father. Amen.

PRAYER FROM THE HEART

Don't worry about anything; instead, pray about everything; tell God your needs and don't forget to thank him for his answers. If you do this you will experience God's peace, which is far more wonderful than the human mind can understand. His peace will keep your thoughts and your hearts quiet and at rest as you trust in Christ Jesus.

PHILIPPIANS 4:6–7 TLB

God is a Spirit, said Jesus Christ, *and they that worship him must worship him in spirit and in truth.* Prayer then is in itself a wholly spiritual act, addressed to him who is the Supreme Spirit, the Spirit who sees all things and is present in all things and is, as St. Augustine says, more closely united to our soul than its deepest depths. If to this essential prayer we join a particular attitude of the body and certain words and outward demonstrations, all this has no significance in itself and is only pleasing to God as it expresses the feelings of the heart. To speak properly, it is the heart that prays, it is to the voice of the heart that God listens and it is the heart that he answers, and when we speak of the heart we mean the most spiritual part of us. It is indeed noteworthy that in the Scriptures prayer is always ascribed to the heart.

–JEAN-NICOLAS GROU

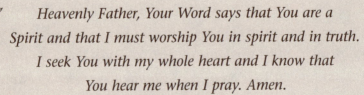

Heavenly Father, Your Word says that You are a Spirit and that I must worship You in spirit and in truth. I seek You with my whole heart and I know that You hear me when I pray. Amen.

PRAYING THE LORD'S PRAYER TODAY

He said to them, "When you pray, say: 'Father, hallowed be your name, your kingdom come.'"

LUKE 11:2

What then might it mean to pray this kingdom prayer today? It means, for a start, that as we look up into the face of our Father in heaven, and commit ourselves to the hallowing of his name, we look immediately out upon the whole world that he made, and we see it as he sees it.... It means seeing it with the love of the Creator for his spectacularly beautiful creation, and seeing it with the deep grief of the Creator for the battered and battle-scarred state in which the world now finds itself....

We are praying, as Jesus was praying and acting, for the redemption of the world.... And if we pray this way, we must of course be prepared to live this way.

So, as we pray this for the world, we also pray for the church.... Make us a community of healed healers; make us a retuned orchestra to play the kingdom-music until the world takes up the song.

–N. T. WRIGHT, from *Reflecting the Glory: Meditations for Living Christ's Life in the World*

 Father, I hallow Your name this day, and pray that Your kingdom would come on the earth. Help me to live the way You would have me to live and be a shining light for You everywhere I go. Amen.

MORNING PRAYER

Listen to my voice in the morning, LORD. Each morning
I bring my requests to you and wait expectantly.

PSALM 5:3 NLT

The entire day receives order and discipline when it acquires
unity. This unity must be sought and found in morning
prayer. It is confirmed in work. The morning prayer determines the day. Squandered time of which we are ashamed,
temptations to which we succumb, weaknesses and lack of
courage in work, disorganization and lack of discipline in our
thoughts and in our conversation with other men, all have
their origin most often in the neglect of morning prayer.

Order and distribution of our time become more firm where
they originate in prayer. Temptations which accompany the
working day will be conquered on the basis of the morning
breakthrough to God. Decisions, demanded by work, become
easier and simpler where they are made not in the fear of men
but only in the sight of God.... Even mechanical work is done
in a more patient way if it arises from the recognition of God
and his command. The powers to work take hold, therefore,
at the place where we have prayed to God.

–DIETRICH BONHOEFFER

*I seek You in the morning, Lord, when the world
is quiet, before the busy demands of the day.
I turn my schedule over to You—take my day
and live Your life through me. Amen.*

HE HEARS OUR PRAYERS

He rescued me because he delighted in me.

PSALM 18:19

When [a friend] told Jesus of the illness [of Lazarus] he said, "Lord, the one you love is sick." He doesn't base his appeal on the imperfect love of the one in need, but on the perfect love of the Savior. He doesn't say, "The one *who loves you* is sick." He says, "The one *you love* is sick." The power of the prayer, in other words, does not depend on the one who makes the prayer, but on the one who hears the prayer.

> *Lord Jesus, thank You for Your love for me, the love that enables me to come to You with all my needs. Guide me today as I lift my needs to You, Lord God. Amen.*

We can and must repeat the phrase in manifold ways. "The one you love is tired, sad, hungry, lonely, fearful, depressed." The words of the prayer vary, but the response never changes. The Savior hears the prayer.

–MAX LUCADO, from *The Great House of God*

PRAYING WITH ABANDON

Trust Him at all times, you people;
Pour out your heart before Him;
God is a refuge for us.

PSALM 62:8 NKJV

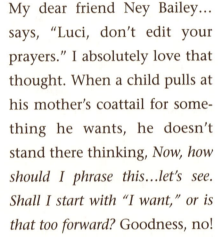

Lord, it amazes me that You are such a mighty God, and yet I can pray to You so freely. Thank You for Your love for me. I pray that You would give me a greater love for You. Amen.

My dear friend Ney Bailey... says, "Luci, don't edit your prayers." I absolutely love that thought. When a child pulls at his mother's coattail for something he wants, he doesn't stand there thinking, *Now, how should I phrase this...let's see. Shall I start with "I want," or is that too forward?* Goodness, no! The kid blurts out his thoughts spontaneously, with total abandon. The sincerity of his heart exposes his deepest desires, petitions, and longings to the parent he loves and trusts. Praying that way to our Heavenly Father fosters a bonding that's sweet and comforting.

–LUCI SWINDOLL, from *Outrageous Joy*

THE SPIRIT OF PRAYER

I will pour the spirit of grace and of supplications.

ZECHARIAH 12:10 KJV

The spirit of prayer is a holy spirit, a gracious spirit. Wherever there is a true spirit of supplication, there is the spirit of grace. The true spirit of prayer is nothing other than God's dwelling in the hearts of the saints. And as this spirit comes from God, so it naturally tends to God in holy breathings and pantings. It naturally leads to God, to converse with Him by prayer. Therefore the Spirit is said to make intercession for the saints with groanings which cannot be uttered (Romans 8:26).

The Spirit of God makes intercession for them, as it is that Spirit which in some respect incites their prayer, and leads them to pour out their souls before God. Therefore the saints are said to worship God in the Spirit. Philippians 3:3: "We are the circumcision, which worship God in the Spirit." John 4:23: "The true worshipers shall worship the Father in spirit and in truth." The truly godly have the spirit of adoption, the spirit of a child, to which it is natural to go to God and call upon Him, crying to Him as to a father.

–JONATHAN EDWARDS

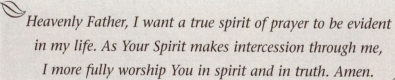
Heavenly Father, I want a true spirit of prayer to be evident in my life. As Your Spirit makes intercession through me, I more fully worship You in spirit and in truth. Amen.

A PRAYER HEARING GOD

O Thou that hearest prayer.

PSALM 65:2 KJV

It is the character of the Most High that He is a God who hears prayers.

He sometimes manifests His acceptance of prayers by special discoveries of His mercy and sufficiency which He makes in prayer, or immediately after. He gives His people special communion with Him in prayer. While they are praying, He comes to them and reveals Himself to them; gives them sweet views of His glorious grace, purity, sufficiency, and sovereignty, and enables them, with great quietness, to rest in Him, and leave themselves and prayers with Him, submit to His will and trust in His grace and faithfulness.

Such a manifestation God seems to have made of Himself in prayer to Hannah.... [S]he came and poured out her soul before God, and spoke out of the abundance of her complaint and grief; then we read that she went away and ate, and her countenance was no more sad, which seems to have been from some refreshing discoveries which God had made of Himself to her, to enable her quietly to submit to His will and trust in His mercy, whereby God manifested His acceptance of her.

–JONATHAN EDWARDS

Thank You, Lord, that You hear every prayer I make,
both spoken and unspoken. You are the God
who hears and answers prayer! Amen.

POWERFUL PRAYER

The effective, fervent prayer of a
righteous man avails much.

JAMES 5:16 NKJV

Thousands of people pray only when they are under great stress, or in danger, overcome by uncertainty. I have been in airplanes when an engine died; then people started praying. I have talked to soldiers who told me that they never prayed until they were in the midst of battle. There seems to be an instinct in man to pray in times of trouble. We know "there are no atheists in foxholes," but the kind of Christianity that fails to reach into our everyday lives will never change the world. Develop the power of prayer. The answers to all our problems can be had through contact with almighty God.

Lord God, today I choose not to rely on myself, but to commit everything to You in prayer and trust in Your strength. God, I'm in awe of Your power. Amen.

–BILLY GRAHAM, from *Day by Day with Billy Graham*

PRESSING INTO THE KINGDOM OF GOD

The law and the prophets were until John; since that time the kingdom of God is preached, and every man presseth into it.

LUKE 16:16 KJV

The kingdom of heaven should be sought, first, because of the extreme necessity we are in of getting into the kingdom of heaven. We are in a perishing necessity of it; without it we are utterly and eternally lost…. It should be sought, second, because of the shortness and uncertainty of the opportunity for getting into the kingdom…. There is much difficulty getting into the kingdom of God. Innumerable difficulties are in the way such as few conquer. Most of them who try do not have resolution, courage, earnestness, and constancy enough; but they fail, give up, and perish….

Though it is attended with so much difficulty, yet it is not an impossible thing. God is able to accomplish it, and has sufficient mercy for it; and there is sufficient provision made through Christ that God may do it consistent with the honor of His majesty, justice, and truth. It is fitting that the kingdom should be thus sought because of the great excellency of it. We are willing to seek earthly things of trifling value; it therefore certainly becomes us to seek that with great earnestness which is of infinitely greater worth and excellence.

–JONATHAN EDWARDS

Lord, my greatest desire is that Your Kingdom would come to pass on this earth. I pray for Your will to be done both in my life and in the world today. Amen.

UNION IN PRAYER

"Thus saith the Lord of hosts, It shall yet come to pass that there shall come people, and the inhabitants of many cities. And the inhabitants of one city shall go to another, saying, 'Let us go speedily to pray before the Lord, and to seek the Lord of hosts. I will go also.' Yea, many people and strong nations shall come to seek the Lord of hosts in Jerusalem, and to pray before the Lord."

ZECHARIAH 8:20–22 KJV

In this text we have an account of how the future glorious advancement of the church of God will be brought on: by multitudes in different towns and countries taking up a joint resolution, and coming into an express and visible agreement, that they will, by united and extraordinary prayer, seek that God would come and manifest Himself, and grant the tokens and fruits of His gracious presence....

The good that shall be sought by prayer, which is God Himself, is a common thing in Scripture. To "seek God" implies that God Himself is the great good desired and sought after. The blessings pursued are God's gracious presence, the blessed manifestations and communications of Himself by His Holy Spirit.

—JONATHAN EDWARDS

 I give You the sacrifice of my prayers and praise, O Lord.
I seek You and You alone, for You are the greatest good
and the source of all blessings on earth. Amen.

PRAYER BRINGS REVIVAL

"You will call upon me and come and
pray to me, and I will listen to you."

JEREMIAH 29:12

This revival will be fulfilled after this manner: first, that there shall be given much of a spirit of prayer to God's people, disposing them to come to an express agreement unitedly to pray to God in an extraordinary manner that He would appear for the help of His church and in mercy to mankind, and pour out His Spirit, revive His work, and advance His spiritual kingdom in the world as He has promised. This disposition to such prayer, and union in it, will gradually spread more and more, and increase to greater degrees, which at length will gradually introduce a revival of religion.

...The manner of prayer agreed on is literally, "Let us go in going."... When it is said, "Let us go in going, and pray before the Lord," the strength of the expression represents the earnestness of those who make the proposal, that they should be speedy, fervent, and constant in it, that it should be thoroughly performed. , from this we infer that it is a very suitable thing and well pleasing to God to pray in union.

–JONATHAN EDWARDS

Heavenly Father, I want revival to break forth in my family, my city, my nation, my world. Help me to press in to Your presence in prayer and bring Your revival to pass. Amen.

PRAYER FOR THE SPIRIT

You who call on the LORD, give yourselves no rest,
and give him no rest till he establishes Jerusalem
and makes her the praise of the earth.

ISAIAH 62:6–7

The Scriptures not only direct and encourage us to pray for the Holy Spirit above all things else, but it is the expressly revealed will of God that His church should be very much in prayer for that glorious outpouring of the Spirit that is to be in the latter days, and the things that shall be accomplished by it. God, speaking of that blessed event, says, "I will yet for this be enquired of by the house of Israel, to do it for them" (Ezekiel 36:37). This doubtless implies that it is the will of God that extraordinary prayer for this mercy should precede the bestowing of it.... And how loud is this call to the church of God to be fervent and incessant in their cries to Him for this great mercy! How wonderful are the words to be used, concerning the manner in which such worms of the dust should address the high and lofty One who inhabits eternity! And what encouragement is here to approach the mercy seat with the greatest freedom, boldness, earnestness, constancy, and full assurance of faith, to seek from God the greatest thing that can be sought in Christian prayer.

–JONATHAN EDWARDS

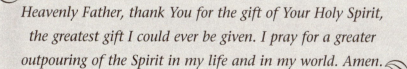

*Heavenly Father, thank You for the gift of Your Holy Spirit,
the greatest gift I could ever be given. I pray for a greater
outpouring of the Spirit in my life and in my world. Amen.*

PRAYING FOR MERCY

[Jesus said,] "If you are thirsty, come to me! If you believe
in me, come and drink! For the Scriptures declare that
rivers of living water will flow out from within."

JOHN 7:37-38 NLT

The Scriptures not only abundantly manifest it to be the duty
of God's people to be much in prayer for mercy, but it also
abounds with manifold considerations to encourage them in
it, and animate them with hopes of success. There is perhaps
no one thing that so much of the Bible is taken up in the
promises of (in order to encourage the faith, hope, and
prayers of the saints) as this, which at once affords God's
people the clearest evidences that it is their duty to be much
in prayer for this mercy (for undoubtedly that which God
abundantly makes the subject of His promises, God's people
should abundantly make the subject of their prayers), and
also affords them the strongest assurance that their prayers
shall be successful. With what confidence may we go before
God and pray for that of which we have so many exceeding
precious and glorious promises to plead!

–JONATHAN EDWARDS

 I seek Your mercy, O Lord. I am thirsty for Your Spirit,
for the rivers of living water You have promised to me.
Pour out Your Spirit in my life and let me
experience You in a fresh, new way. Amen.

FAITH AND PRAYER

"The time is fulfilled, and the kingdom of God is
at hand; repent ye, and believe the gospel."

MARK 1:15 KJV

Faith is that inward sense and act of which prayer is the expression, because in the same manner as the freedom of grace, according to the gospel covenant, is often set forth by this, that he who believes receives (Matthew 7:7-10)....

Prayer is often plainly spoken of as the expression of faith. As to its certainty, "Whosoever believeth on Him shall not be ashamed. For whosoever shall call upon the name of the Lord shall be saved" (Romans 10:11-13). Christian prayer is called the prayer of faith (James 5:15), and believing is mentioned as the life and soul of true prayer (1 Timothy 2:8; Hebrews 10:19, 22; James 1:5-6).

Faith in God is expressed in praying to God. Faith in the Lord Jesus Christ is expressed in praying to Christ, and praying in the name of Christ (John 14:13-14). And the promises are made to asking in Christ's name in the same manner as they are to believing in Christ.

–JONATHAN EDWARDS

 Lord, I believe in You; help my unbelief. I trust in You
to bring all Your promises to pass in my life. Amen.

PRAY AND PREVAIL

The earnest prayer of a righteous person
has great power and wonderful results.

JAMES 5:16 NLT

When Israel had made the golden calf, Moses returned to the Lord and said, "Alas, these people have committed a terrible sin.... But now, please forgive their sin—and if not, then blot me out of the record you are keeping" (Exodus 32:31-32). That was persistence. Moses would rather have died than not have his people forgiven.

When God had heard him and said He would send His angel with the people, Moses came again. He would not be content until, in answer to his prayer, God himself should go with them. God had said, "I will indeed do what you have asked" (Exodus 33:17). After that in answer to Moses' prayer, "Let me see your glorious presence" (Exodus 33:18), God made His goodness pass before him. Then Moses at once began pleading, "O Lord, then please go with us" (Exodus 34:9). "Moses was up on the mountain with the Lord forty days and forty nights" (Exodus 34:28).

Moses was persistent with God and prevailed....

Praise God! He still waits for us to seek Him. Faith in a prayer-hearing God will make a prayer-loving Christian.

–ANDREW MURRAY

*Heavenly Father, I want to be a person who is persistent
in prayer—and who sees results! Help me to have patience
and to press on until the victory is won. Amen.*

PERSISTENCE IN PRAYER

[Jesus said,] "You can pray for anything,
and if you believe, you will have it."

MARK 11:24 NLT

Persistence has various elements—the main ones are perseverance, determination, and intensity. It begins with the refusal to readily accept denial. This develops into a determination to persevere, to spare no time or trouble, until an answer comes. This grows in intensity until the whole being is given to God in supplication. Boldness comes to lay hold of God's strength. At one time it is quiet; at another, bold. At one point it waits in patience, but at another, it claims at once what it desires. In whatever different shape, persistence always means and knows that God hears prayer; I must be heard.

> *Lord, sometimes I get discouraged if I don't immediately see the answer to my prayer. Help me to trust in You and to persevere in prayer until I receive Your answer. Amen.*

—ANDREW MURRAY

CHRIST: THE GREATEST MIRACLE

For it pleased the Father that in Him
all the fullness should dwell.

COLOSSIANS 1:19 NKJV

Christ Himself is the greatest miracle of history. The incarnation, as the central miracle, helps us interpret the miracles done by the "I Am;" Yahweh with us....

The question is, Do miracles still happen? Yes! The miracle of life, our salvation, the transformation of personality, and specific interventions of healing and blessing. A study of the miracles leads us to an "all things are possible" kind of faith for daily living and our needs. Physical, emotional, and spiritual healings are still being done daily by the Great Physician through the Holy Spirit.

Focus on the needs of people in the context of the miraculous power available to us. Fyodor Dostoevsky was right: "Faith does not, in the realist, spring from miracles, but miracles from faith!" We believe that faith comes from the Holy Spirit focusing us on the love and forgiveness of the cross; that faith then dares to believe that as God's miracles we can expect and take special delight in the miracles He will do all around us.

–LLOYD JOHN OGILVIE

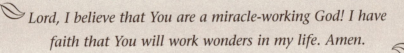

Lord, I believe that You are a miracle-working God! I have faith that You will work wonders in my life. Amen.

THE TRUE GOAL OF PRAYER

No, O people, the LORD has already told you what is
good, and this is what he requires: to do what is right,
to love mercy, and to walk humbly with your God.

MICAH 6:8 NLT

God desires to meet your needs, but His need-meeting is part of a greater process. God is always seeking to develop a closer and more intimate relationship with you. He is molding and fashioning you into the person with whom He desires to spend all eternity. He is seeking to draw you ever closer and closer to Himself.

Lord God, I have needs to bring before You today, but more than Your provision, I want to seek Your face. Draw me closer to You today, Lord God. Amen.

Many of God's delays in meeting our needs are aimed at bringing us to a place where we will turn to God, trust in God, ask of God, and rely upon God. His purpose is to teach us what it means to be in fellowship with Him and to walk closely with Him day by day.

—CHARLES STANLEY

DAILY PRAYER FOR DAILY NEEDS

Do not forget that he led you through the great and
terrifying wilderness with poisonous snakes and scorpions,
where it was so hot and dry. He gave you water from
the rock! He fed you with manna in the wilderness,
a food unknown to your ancestors.

DEUTERONOMY 8:15–16 NLT

True prayers are born out of present trials and present needs. Bread for today is enough. Bread given for today is the strongest pledge that there will be bread tomorrow. Victory today is the assurance of victory tomorrow. Our prayers need to be focused on the present. We must trust God today and leave tomorrow entirely with Him. The present is ours; the future belongs to God. Prayer is the task and duty of each new day—daily prayer for daily needs....

Today's manna is what we need; tomorrow God will see that our needs are supplied. This is the faith which God seeks to inspire.

—E. M. BOUNDS

 *Lord, as I pray, I ask You for a daily strengthening
of my faith. Thank You for meeting each
of my needs, one day at a time. Amen.*

SINGLE-MINDED

And you will seek Me and find Me,
when you search for Me with all your heart.

JEREMIAH 29:13 NKJV

God is not one among many. When we pray we are not covering our bases. Prayer is not a way of checking out a last resort of potential help. We understandably want to explore all the options: we write letters, make telephone calls, visit prospects, arrange interviews. We don't know who might be useful to us at any one time. Of course, we cultivate God. But not in prayer. We try it, but it doesn't work.

Lord God, I must confess that sometimes I ask You for help, then start thinking about what I'll do if You don't come through. God, I pray that You would develop in me a dependence on You, that I would seek You first—and only. Amen.

Prayer is exclusive. Prayer is centering.... We can't pray with one eye on the main chance and a side glance for God. Prayer trains the soul to singleness of focus: for God *alone*.

–EUGENE H. PETERSON, from *Where Your Treasure Is*

CONSTANT SURPRISES

For in Him dwells all the fullness of the Godhead bodily.

COLOSSIANS 2:9 NKJV

The second greatest miracle, next to Christ, is what happens to a person who comes to know Christ personally. When we commit our lives to Him and invite Him to live in us, our days are filled with a constant succession of surprises. He is Lord of all life, has unlimited power, and can arrange events and circumstances to bless us. Our only task is to surrender our needs to Him, and then leave the results to Him.

Christ did not use the word "miracle." He talked about the "works of God." Wherever He went, He did "works" which defied both the expected and the anticipated. The reason was that He was the power of God, the "fullness of the Godhead bodily" (Colossians 2:9 NKJV)....

Where do you need a miracle—what to you seems impossible? Persist! Don't give up. At all costs make your way to the Master. Tell Him your need, and then leave it with Him. Even greater than the miracle you seek will be the miracle you become by seeking Him, touching Him, and experiencing His matchless love.

–LLOYD JOHN OGILVIE

Lord, You are amazing. Your works are mighty
and astounding. I worship You for who You are:
a miracle-working God. Amen.

BEFORE THE DAY BEGINS

Now in the morning, having risen a long
while before daylight, He went out and departed
to a solitary place; and there He prayed.

MARK 1:35 NKJV

Personally I find it helpful to begin each day by silently committing that day into God's hands. I thank Him that I belong to Him, and I thank Him that He knows what the day holds for me. I ask Him to take my life that day and use it for His glory. I ask Him to cleanse me from anything which would hinder His work in my life. And then I step out in faith, knowing that His Holy Spirit is filling me continually as I trust in Him and obey His Word.

Lord, right now, I come to You and commit my day to You. Please guide me through today, teaching me what You want to teach me and using me to show Your grace to others. Amen.

—BILLY GRAHAM

CONFIDENCE AMIDST CRISIS

But He said to them, "Why are you fearful,
O you of little faith?"

MATTHEW 8:26 NKJV

When we are afraid, the least we can do is pray to God.... Yet our trust is only in God up to a certain point, then we turn back to the elementary panic-stricken prayers of those people who do not even know God. We come to our wits' end, showing that we don't have even the slightest amount of confidence in Him or in His sovereign control of the world. To us He seems to be asleep, and we can see nothing but giant, breaking waves on the sea ahead of us.

...And what a sharp pain will go through us when we suddenly realize that we could have produced complete and utter joy in the heart of Jesus by remaining absolutely confident in Him, in spite of what we were facing....

It is when a crisis arises that we instantly reveal upon whom we rely. If we have been learning to worship God and to place our trust in Him, the crisis will reveal that we can go to the point of breaking, yet without breaking our confidence in Him.

–OSWALD CHAMBERS

Heavenly Father, it is in times of crisis that I show my true belief in You. Help me to have faith in You, no matter the circumstances I find myself in. Amen.

GOD HAS A PLAN!

When Jesus then lifted up his eyes, and saw a great
company come unto him, he saith unto Philip, Whence
shall we buy bread, that these may eat? And this he said
to prove him: for he himself knew what he would do.

JOHN 6:5–6 KJV

At this very hour you may have to come face to face with a
most tremendous need, and Christ stands beside you looking
at it and questioning you about it. He says, in effect, "How are
you going to meet it?" He is scrutinizing you ...watching you
with a gentle tender sympathy. How many of us have failed
in the test! We have taken out our pencil and our paper and
commenced to figure out the two hundred pennyworth of
bread; or we have run off hither and thither to strong and
wealthy friends to extricate us; or we have sat down in utter
despondency; or we have murmured against Him for bringing
us into such a position. Should we not have turned a sunny
face to Christ saying: *Thou hast a plan! Thine is the responsibility, and Thou must tell me what to do. I have come so far in the
path of obedience to Thy Guiding Spirit: and now, what art Thou
going to do?*

–C. G. MOORE

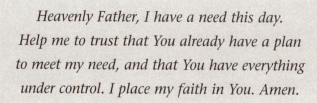

*Heavenly Father, I have a need this day.
Help me to trust that You already have a plan
to meet my need, and that You have everything
under control. I place my faith in You. Amen.*

A CHANCE TO BLESS

And they say unto him, We have here but five loaves,
and two fishes. He said, Bring them hither to me:

MATTHEW 14:17–18 KJV

*Lord, I bring my needs to
You, the Great Need-Meeter.
I give You the opportunity
to work in my life. Thank
You for Your provision and
Your care. Amen.*

Are you encompassed with needs at this very moment, and almost overwhelmed with difficulties, trials, and emergencies? These are all divinely provided vessels for the Holy Spirit to fill, and if you but rightly understood their meaning, they would become opportunities for receiving new blessings and deliverances which you can get in no other way.

Bring these vessels to God. Hold them steadily before Him in faith and prayer. Keep still, and stop your own restless working until He begins to work. Do nothing that He does not Himself command you to do. Give Him a chance to work, and He will surely do so; and the very trials that threatened to overcome you with discouragement and disaster, will become God's opportunity for the revelation of His grace and glory in your life, as you have never known Him before.

—A. B. SIMPSON

MY GRACE IS SUFFICIENT

Concerning this thing I pleaded with the Lord three times
that it might depart from me. And He said to me, "My
grace is sufficient for you, for My strength is made perfect
in weakness." Therefore most gladly I will rather boast in
my infirmities, that the power of Christ may rest upon me.

2 CORINTHIANS 12:8–9 NKJV

If you have any trial which seems intolerable, pray—pray that
it be relieved or changed. There is no harm in that. We may
pray for anything, not wrong in itself, with perfect freedom,
if we do not pray selfishly. One disabled from duty by sickness
may pray for health, that he may do his work; or one
hemmed in by internal impediments may pray for utterance,
that he may serve better the truth and the right. Or, if we
have a besetting sin, we may pray to be delivered from it, in
order to serve God and man, and not be ourselves Satans to
mislead and destroy. But the answer to the prayer may be, as
it was to Paul, not the removal of the thorn, but, instead, a
growing insight into its meaning and value. The voice of God
in our soul may show us, as we look up to Him, that His
strength is enough to enable us to bear it.

–J. F. CLARK

 *Lord, I ask You to grant me Your perspective on my trials.
I pray that Your purpose would be accomplished in my
life every day, through every circumstance. Amen.*

PRAYER AND PATIENCE

My brethren, count it all joy when you
fall into various trials, knowing that
the testing of your faith produces patience.

JAMES 1:2–3 NKJV

Lord God, even in the midst of daily frustrations and aggravations, I know that You are there and that You are in the process of molding me. I surrender my heart to You today, Lord, and ask You to perfect patience in me. Amen.

The many troubles in your household will tend to your edification, if you strive to bear them all in gentleness, patience, and kindness. Keep this ever before you, and remember constantly that God's loving eyes are upon you amid all these little worries and vexations, watching whether you take them as He would desire. Offer up all such occasions to Him, and if sometimes you are put out, and give way to impatience, do not be discouraged, but make haste to regain your lost composure.

—FRANCIS DE SALES

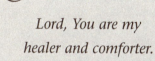

LETTING GO

Be anxious for nothing, but in everything by
prayer and supplication, with thanksgiving,
let your requests be known to God; and the
peace of God, which surpasses all understanding,
will guard your hearts and minds in Christ Jesus.

PHILIPPIANS 4:6–7 NLT

Once you have prayed, release your concerns. This doesn't mean you can't pray about the same thing again, but once you've finished a prayer, allow the issue to be surrendered into His hands so you can rest and be at peace. Don't worry about whether He heard you or if you did it right. Trust Him to take care of it. Learn to *partner* with God. "For the eyes of the LORD run to and fro throughout the whole earth, to show Himself strong on behalf of those whose heart is loyal to Him" (2 Chronicles 16:9). If you partner with God alone, you'll see more power in your prayers when you partner with others.

> *Lord, You are my
> healer and comforter.
> I bring all of my cares
> to You and lay them at
> Your feet. Amen.*

–STORMIE OMARTIAN, from *The Power of Praying Together*

APRIL 6

OUR EVER-PRESENT HELP

God is our refuge and strength,
an ever-present help in trouble.

PSALM 46:1

Lord God, thank You, again and again, that You hear my prayers. Thank You for the grace You have lavished on me by calling me Your child. And thank You for the joy of having You as my Father. Amen.

Our heavenly Father is available to us at all times. He is never too busy to hear our prayers. He is never preoccupied with other concerns to the point that He rejects our presence. Rather, He delights in having close, intimate communion with us. Whenever we are willing to spend time with Him, He is willing to spend time with us....

No matter how you may feel. No matter how you have been rejected by others. No matter how much you may hurt or how lonely you may feel, you *always* have the Lord. He is all-sufficient.

–CHARLES STANLEY

HOPE IN HIM

Great multitudes followed him, and he healed them all.

MATTHEW 12:15 KJV

What a variety of sickness must have been presented to the gaze of Jesus! Yet we do not read that He was disgusted but patiently waited on every case. What a combination of evils must have met at His feet! What sickening ulcers and putrefying sores! Yet He was ready for every new shape of the monster of evil and was victor over it in every form.... It is still the case today. Whatever my own condition may be, the beloved Physician can heal me; and whatever may be the state of others whom I may remember at this moment in prayer; I may have hope in Jesus that He will be able to heal them of their sins. My child, my friend, my dearest one—I can have hope for each, for all, when I remember the healing power of my Lord; and on my own account, however severe my struggle with sins and infirmities, I can still rejoice and be confident. He who on earth walked the hospitals still dispenses His grace and works wonders among the sons of men: Let me go to Him immediately and earnestly.

–CHARLES H. SPURGEON

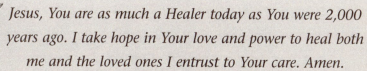

Jesus, You are as much a Healer today as You were 2,000 years ago. I take hope in Your love and power to heal both me and the loved ones I entrust to Your care. Amen.

HIS MISSION

And the whole multitude sought to touch him:
for there went virtue out of him, and healed them all.

LUKE 6:19 KJV

During His sojourn on this earth, was He not ever ready to heal diseased bodies? And do you think that He is now unwilling to minister to distressed souls? Perish the thought. He was always at the disposal of the maimed, the blind, the palsied, yes, of the repellent leper too. He was ever prepared, uncomplainingly, to relieve suffering, though it cost Him something—"there went virtue out of him" (Lk 6:19)—and though much unbelief was expressed by those He befriended. As it was then a part of His mission to heal the sick, so it is now a part of His ministry to bind up the brokenhearted. What a Saviour is ours! The almighty God, the all-tender Man. One who is infinitely above us in His original nature and present glory, yet One who became flesh and blood, lived on the same plane as we do, experienced the same troubles, and suffered as we, though far more acutely. Then how well qualified He is to supply your every need! Cast all your care upon Him, knowing that He cares for you.

—ARTHUR W. PINK

 What an amazing Savior You are, Jesus! You stand ready to heal and deliver. I cast all of my cares upon You, because I know how much You care for me. Amen.

WE LIVE

And Jesus, moved with compassion, put forth his hand,
and touched him, and saith unto him, I will; be thou
clean. And as soon as he had spoken, immediately the
leprosy departed from him, and he was cleansed.

MARK 1:41–42 KJV

It is worthy of devout notice that Jesus touched the leper. This unclean person had broken through the regulations of the ceremonial law and pressed into the house, but Jesus so far from chiding him broke through the law Himself in order to meet him. He made an interchange with the leper, for while He cleansed him, He contracted by that touch a Levitical defilement. Even so Jesus Christ was made sin for us, although in Himself He knew no sin, that we might be made the righteousness of God in Him. O that poor sinners would go to Jesus, believing in the power of His blessed substitutionary work, and they would soon learn the power of His gracious touch. That hand which multiplied the loaves, which saved sinking Peter, which upholds afflicted saints, which crowns believers, that same hand will touch every seeking sinner, and in a moment make him clean. The love of Jesus is the source of salvation. He loves, He looks, He touches us, WE LIVE.

–CHARLES H. SPURGEON

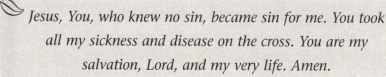

*Jesus, You, who knew no sin, became sin for me. You took
all my sickness and disease on the cross. You are my
salvation, Lord, and my very life. Amen.*

APRIL 10

HE IS THERE FOR YOU

One day He was teaching; and there were some
Pharisees and teachers of the law sitting there....
And some men were carrying on a bed a man
who was paralyzed; and they were trying to bring
him in and to set him down in front of Him.

LUKE 5:17–18 NASB

With the special gift of imagination, picture yourself
approaching the crowd around Jesus. You long to get through
to him about someone you love. Now see the crowd part and
the open corridor directly to the Lord made for you. He is
there for you. Now stand before him face to face, heart to
heart. He is waiting for you to ask for what he is ready to give.
Tell him about a person or persons on your heart. Then wait
for his answer. At this very moment you prayed, says Jesus,
my power has been released in the person for whom you
interceded. My will shall be done, in my timing, according to
my plan, and for the now and forever blessing of your loved
one. You and I are of one heart now. We both love and care.
Now go your way in faithfulness.

–LLOYD JOHN OGILVIE

 Lord, what an amazing thought: You are there for me!
You hear my prayers and answer me,
just when I need You the most. Amen.

READY TO HELP

In that same hour he cured many of their
infirmities and plagues, and of evil spirits; and
unto many that were blind he gave sight.

LUKE 7:21 KJV

Here is in this doctrine great encouragement to all persons to look to Christ under all manner of difficulties and afflictions, and that especially from what appeared in Christ when he was here. We have an account in the history of Christ of great numbers under a great variety of afflictions and difficulties, resorting to him for help. And we have no account of his rejecting one person who came to him in a friendly manner for help, under any difficulty whatever. But on the contrary, the history of his life is principally filled up with miracles that he wrought for the relief of such.... And he helped persons fully, he completely delivered them from those difficulties under which they labored. And by the doctrine of the text we learn that though he is not now upon earth, but in heaven, yet he is the same that he was then. He is as able to help, and he is as ready to help under every kind of difficulty.

–JONATHAN EDWARDS

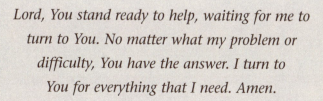

*Lord, You stand ready to help, waiting for me to
turn to You. No matter what my problem or
difficulty, You have the answer. I turn to
You for everything that I need. Amen.*

GOD-CENTERED PRAYER

To you I call, O Lord my Rock.

PSALM 28:1

Father, in this journey of prayer, sometimes I make things more about me than about You. Correct my vision, Lord, and help me see my life as centered around You. Amen.

The Psalms were not prayed by people trying to understand themselves. They are not the record of people searching for the meaning of life. They were prayed by people who understood that God had everything to do with them. God, not their feelings, was the center. God, not their souls, was the issue. God, not the meaning of life, was critical.

Feelings, souls, and meanings were not excluded—they are very much in evidence—but they are not the reason for the prayers. Human experiences might provoke the prayers, but they do not condition them *as* prayers.

–EUGENE H. PETERSON, from *Answering God*

TURN YOUR GAZE UPON HIM

As He went, the crowds were pressing against Him.

LUKE 8:42 NASB

Jesus is passing through the crowd heading for the house of Jairus, so that He might raise the ruler's dead daughter. He is so extravagant in His goodness that He works another miracle on His way there.... What delightful encouragement this truth affords us! If our Lord is so ready to heal the sick and bless the needy, then, my soul, do not be slow to put yourself in His path so that He may smile on you. Do not be lazy in asking, since He is so generous in giving. Pay careful attention to His Word now and at all times, so that Jesus may speak through it to your heart. Pitch your tent wherever He is so that you can obtain His blessing. When He is present to heal, may He not heal you? Be certain that He is present even now, for He always comes to hearts that need Him. And do you not need Him? *He* knows the extent of your need; so turn your gaze, look upon your distress, and call upon Him while He is near.

−CHARLES H. SPURGEON

Lord, I "pitch my tent" in Your presence, waiting for Your healing touch. I call upon You while You are near. Thank You for hearing my prayer. Amen.

PRAYERS OF FAITH

Such things were written in the Scriptures long ago to
teach us. They give us hope and encouragement
as we wait patiently for God's promises.

ROMANS 15:4 NLT

Have you based your faith...

on what someone else has told you God wants to do
for you?

on what you have seen Him do for another person?

on what you think is fair or loving?

on what you think would be in the best interest of those
involved?

on a doctor's recommendation for treatment?

You and I must pray in faith, or our prayer will not be pleasing to God. If your faith as you pray is based on *anything other than* faith in God's specific promise given to you in His Word, then your prayer is on a shaky foundation. So ask God to give you a promise from His Word on which you can pray in faith.

–ANNE GRAHAM LOTZ, from *Why?*

 *Lord, I want my life to be a story of Your goodness,
love, and power. Today I ask You to reveal yourself
to me, that my faith my be strengthened and that
I might know Your character better. Amen.*

NO RESERVATIONS

And when he was come into his own country, he taught them
in their synagogue.... They were offended in him.... And he
did not many mighty works there because of their unbelief.

MATTHEW 13:54,57–58 KJV

When Jesus was in Nazareth he had the same power to heal,
to change the direction of men's lives, to teach, to work miracles, as he had demonstrated in other towns in which he
sojourned. But the people in his home town were so charged
with indifference, skepticism, unbelief, that he could do no
mighty works.

It seems reasonable to suppose that God has the power to
answer prayer in our lives as he has answered it in countless
other lives. But we have the power to make his power ineffective. Praying with mental reservations is a stone wall between
the petitioner and God. To pray for a project we will not
support with our money, to pray for people with whom we
would not be willing to eat or work—such praying defeats
God's mighty works. We would
not think of withholding
cooperation from the doctor or
the lawyer, after paying them
to help us, but we hang on to
our mental reservations when
dealing with Almighty God.

—MARGUERITTE HARMON BRO

*Lord Jesus, I come to You
with no reservations. I
believe that You are able to
do mighty things in my life
when I place my trust and
faith in You. I fully
cooperate with Your will
in my life. Amen.*

APRIL 16

THE WAY IS OPEN

As he was going into a village, ten men who had leprosy met him. They stood at a distance and called out in a loud voice, "Jesus, Master, have pity on us!" When he saw them, he said, "Go, show yourselves to the priests." And as they went, they were cleansed.

LUKE 17:12-14

Leprosy is a wasting disease. It destroys the cells of the body, taking away appendages....

But perhaps the most devastating consequence of all to lepers in biblical times was that their contagiousness meant isolation. They lived in caves, huddled together, wrapped in rags, shunned by all society but each other.

No wonder Jesus had pity on the ten leprous men. No wonder he answered their prayer....

In some way, all of us are like the lepers. We all live at times with our feelings numbed by the harsh realities of life; at times we feel the wasting effects of the enemy's warfare, and at other times we feel bitterly isolated from others.

But the Lord showed us in this story that the way to his healing is open when we pray the way the Samaritan leper did: with faith to ask the Lord for what we need. Faith to listen for his instructions and follow them. And faith to return to him with gratitude in our hearts.

Lord, You reached out to me when no one else would. I have faith in You, that You will meet my every need. I wait for Your voice and trust You to do a mighty work on my behalf. Amen.

−CLAIRE CLONINGER, from *Dear Abba: A Ten-Week Journey to the Heart of God*

WHAT DO YOU WANT?

Then Jesus asked the man, "What do you want me
to do for you?" "Lord," he pleaded, "I want to see!"

LUKE 18:41 NLT

Jesus' question puzzles some people. If He's really the Messiah, then why should He have to *ask* the man what he wanted? Wouldn't it be obvious? It doesn't take a medical doctor to identify a blind beggar who for years has been crawling around, seeking handouts. Why *did* Jesus ask, "What do you want Me to do for you?"

First, we should remember that God often asks us questions, not to gain information but to get us to admit our need....

Second, the Bible makes it clear that while "all things are possible with God" (Mark 10:27,), it reminds us that we can't expect to tap into His miracle-working power without explicit prayer....

So Jesus turns to this sightless man and asks, "What do you want Me to do for you?"

The man doesn't wait to respond. He knows his need. He believes he is speaking with Israel's long-promised Messiah. And so he says simply, "Lord, that I may receive my sight."...

May we have the spiritual insight of the man *formerly* known as the blind beggar from Jericho!

–GREG LAURIE, from *Discipleship: The Next Step in Following Jesus*

Lord Jesus, I lay all of my needs before You, specifically and explicitly. I am not afraid to tell You all of my concerns, because I know that You care and long to meet my needs. I trust in You. Amen.

NO PRAYER IS WASTED

And the prayer of faith will save the sick,
and the Lord will raise him up. And if he
has committed sins, he will be forgiven.

JAMES 5:15 NKJV

Scripture tells us "the prayer of faith will save the sick" (James 5:15). Yet all of us can doubtless recall times—many times—when we prayed for a healing and it did not occur.... Does that mean that God is not listening? That your faith is too weak? Or that your prayers have not been fervent enough? I think not, but I also think it is fruitless to try to find an answer to why some people are healed and some are not.

Much of what happens on our earthly journey will remain a mystery until we get to risen life....

I do not think we can ever say prayer is wasted. Although prayer may not change a situation and give us the miracle we want, *prayer changes us*. Through prayer, we become more aware of God's presence. Through prayer, we find inner resources and strength we didn't know we had. Through prayer, we are no longer facing our fears and pain alone: God is beside us, renewing our spirit, restoring our soul, and helping us carry the burden when it becomes too heavy for us to bear alone.

–RON DELBENE WITH MARY AND HERB MONTGOMERY,
from *The Breath of Life: A Simple Way to Pray*

Lord, help me to trust in You, even when my prayers do not bring the results I seek. Help me remember that the true purpose of prayer is to bring me closer to You. Amen.

HEALING MINDS

Then they brought him a demon-possessed man
who was blind and mute, and Jesus healed him,
so that he could both talk and see.

MATTHEW 12:22

To those who saw the outward manifestations of an epileptic or some mental disorder which made a man violently destructive, it was not unnatural to think of him as possessing or being possessed by "a devil." Indeed those of us who have ever been in the presence of the violently deranged and looked into their eyes could easily agree that some evil power appears to be possessing the patient. It seems that Jesus was in many cases able to get to the storm-centre of the disturbance and resolve it with authoritative love. We do not know even yet how far the mind affects the body (or the body the mind) or how far either of them is influenced by spiritual power—by intercessory prayer, for example. We know how to "cure" certain diseases with fair accuracy, but what we are really doing is removing the obstacles which are preventing a natural ability to heal itself which both the human body and mind possess. It does not seem to me in the least unreasonable that a man of concentrated spiritual power should be able to remove these obstacles instantaneously.

—J. B. PHILLIPS

Heavenly Father, thank You for Your healing power that You have placed within both my body and my mind. Thank You that prayer can make a difference and cause true healing to take place. Amen.

APRIL 20

JESUS GIVES HOPE

This spirit had often taken control of the man. Even when he
was shackled with chains, he simply broke them and rushed out
into the wilderness, completely under the demon's power.

LUKE 8:29 NLT

This dangerous and frightening individual furnishes a picture
of Satan's ultimate goal, his "finished product." What steps
led to this state we can only imagine, but here we see "the
package deal"—sin, Satan, and death working together. The
power of Satan was so intertwined with this man that most
observers could not see the hurting soul deep inside. When
they looked at him, they saw only a crazed, suicidal maniac
roaming the graveyard.

Satan's goal was to destroy this man.

And what did Jesus do for the man? He sought him out in his
spooky little graveyard and offered him hope....

Jesus is still in the people-changing business. It thrills me to
look at some Christians and know how different they are now
from what they once were....

None of us has the power to overcome Satan in our own
strength. Neither can we count on society to give us the help
we need. But if we cry out to Jesus, He can step in and transform us—no matter what kind or how many "demons" may
torment us.

*Jesus, thank You for
Your transforming power
that can change my life.
I bring all of my "demons"
before You and ask You
to set me free. Amen.*

−GREG LAURIE, from *Discipleship:
The Next Step in Following Jesus*

IN THE WILDERNESS

Since he himself has gone through suffering
and temptation, he is able to help us
when we are being tempted.

HEBREWS 2:18 NLT

In the Jesus wilderness story our Lord learned to discern between religion that uses God and spirituality that enters into what God does, and he was thereby prepared to be our Savior, not merely our helper or adviser or entertainer.

In the David wilderness story

Lord, during those seasons of life that test my faith and strength, I sometimes get weary and want to give up. Help me remember that You use times of trial to make me holy. Amen.

we see a young man hated and hunted like an animal, ...forced to decide between a life of blasphemy and a life of prayer—and choosing prayer. In choosing prayer he entered into the practice of holiness. A very earthy holiness it was, but holiness all the same.

—EUGENE H. PETERSON, from *Leap Over a Wall*

THE PLACE OF PRAYER

The day is yours, and yours also the night.

PSALM 74:16

Dear Lord, I know that You are everywhere, even in the most mundane activities of my day. Father God, more than anything, I want my life to reflect Your presence. Please transform my "ordinary" moments into events that tell of Your glory. Amen.

David's life is the most exuberant life story in all the Scriptures, maybe the most exuberant in all world history. It is also the most extensively narrated story in our Bible. We know more about David than any other person in the biblical communities of faith....

The person in Scripture who has the most extensively told story is the same person who is shown to be most at prayer.... He was a shepherd, guerilla fighter, court musician, and politician. His entire life was lived in a sacred ordinary that we are apt, mistakenly, to call the secular. The regular place of prayer is the ordinary life.

—EUGENE H. PETERSON

PRAYER AS VOCATION

So, whether you eat or drink, or whatever you do,
do everything for the glory of God.

1 CORINTHIANS 10:31 NRSV

Jesus, we must remember, spent most of his earthly life in what we today would call a blue-collar job. He did not wait until his baptism in the Jordan to discover God. Far from it! Jesus validated the reality of God in the carpentry shop over and over before speaking of the reality of God in his ministry as a rabbi.

Many today see their vocation as a hindrance to prayer.... But prayer is not another duty to add onto an already overcommitted schedule. In Praying the Ordinary, our vocation, far from being a hindrance, is an asset.

How is this so? ...Our vocation is an asset to prayer because our work *becomes* prayer. It is prayer in action. The artist, the novelist, the surgeon, the plumber, the secretary, the lawyer, the homemaker, the farmer, the teacher—all are praying by offering their work up to God.

–RICHARD J. FOSTER, from Prayer: *Finding the Heart's True Home*

 God, I know that a thriving prayer life will flow out of an intense love for You and a desire to simply be in Your presence. Please guide me as I seek to think about Your great mercies throughout the day, and give me a greater love for You. Amen.

HANG ON

A Canaanite woman from that vicinity came to him,
crying out, "Lord, Son of David, have mercy on me!
My daughter is suffering terribly from demon-possession."

MATTHEW 15:22

At first, Jesus appears to pay no attention to her agony, and ignores her cry for relief. He gives her neither eye, nor ear, nor word. Silence, deep and chilling, greets her impassioned cry. But she is not turned aside, nor disheartened. She holds on....

This last cry won her case; her daughter was healed in the self-same hour. Hopeful, urgent, and unwearied, she stays near the master, insisting and praying until the answer is given. What a study in importunity, in earnestness, in persistence, promoted and propelled under conditions which would have disheartened any but an heroic, a constant soul....

An answer to prayer is conditional upon the amount of faith that goes to the petition. To test this, he delays the answer. The superficial pray-er subsides into silence, when the answer is delayed. But the man of prayer hangs on, and on. The Lord recognizes and honors his faith, and gives him a rich and abundant answer to his faith-evidencing, importunate prayer.

—E. M. BOUNDS

 Lord, teach me to "hang on" even when the answer to my prayer seems to be delayed. I know that in time You will honor my faith and answer my cry. Amen.

LACKiNG PRAYER

"And I begged Your disciples to cast it out,
and they could not."

LUKE 9:40 NASB

Wherein lay the difficulty with these men? They had been lax in cultivating their faith by prayer and, as a consequence, their trust utterly failed. They trusted not God, nor Christ, nor the authenticity of his mission, or their own. So has it been many a time since, in many a crisis in the church of God. Failure has resulted from a lack of trust, or from a weakness of faith, and this, in turn, from a lack of prayerfulness. Many a failure in revival efforts has been traceable to the same cause. Faith had not been nurtured and made powerful by prayer. Neglect of the inner chamber is the solution of most spiritual failure. And this is as true of our personal struggles with the devil as was the case when we went forth to attempt to cast *out* devils. To be much on our knees in private communion with God is the only surety that we shall have him with us either in our personal struggles, or in our efforts to convert sinners.

—E. M. BOUNDS

Lord, when I do not spend time with You, my faith
falters. I want to be victorious in my spiritual life,
so teach me to spend time on my knees. Amen.

TRUST HIM AT ALL TIMES

Some trust in chariots and some in horses,
but we trust in the name of the LORD our God.

PSALM 20:7

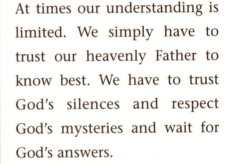

*Lord God, I know that
You are good. I know
that You hold me in Your
hand. Father, today I ask
You for a greater trust
in You. Amen.*

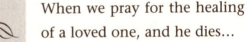

At times our understanding is limited. We simply have to trust our heavenly Father to know best. We have to trust God's silences and respect God's mysteries and wait for God's answers.

When we pray for the healing of a loved one, and he dies...

When we pray for release from a financial burden, and we go bankrupt...

When we pray for reconciliation, and we are handed divorce papers...

When we pray for our career, and we get laid off...

When we pray for protection, and we are robbed...

We just have to trust Him. Trust Him. *Trust Him!*

–ANNE GRAHAM LOTZ, from *My Heart's Cry*

YOU MUST ASK

"However, this kind does not go out
except by prayer and fasting."

MATTHEW 17:21 NKJV

This divine teacher of prayer lays himself out to make it clear and strong that God answers prayer, assuredly, certainly, inevitably; that it is the duty of the child to ask, and to press, and that the Father is obliged to answer, and to give for the asking. In Christ's teaching, prayer is no sterile, vain performance, not a mere rite, a form, but a request for an answer, a plea to gain, the seeking of a great good from God. It is a lesson of getting that for which we ask, of finding that for which we seek, and of entering the door at which we knock.

A notable occasion we have as Jesus comes down from the Mount of Transfiguration. He finds his disciples defeated, humiliated, and confused in the presence of their enemies....

Their faith had not been cultured by prayer. They failed in prayer before they failed in ability to do their work. They failed in faith because they had failed in prayer. That one thing which was necessary to do God's work was prayer. The work which God sends us to do cannot be done without prayer.

—E. M. BOUNDS

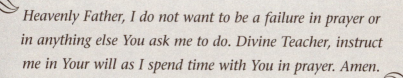

Heavenly Father, I do not want to be a failure in prayer or in anything else You ask me to do. Divine Teacher, instruct me in Your will as I spend time with You in prayer. Amen.

THE BETTER ANSWER

Jesus said to her, "I am the resurrection and the life."

JOHN 11:25

Standing at their brother's tomb, Mary and Martha grieved their loss. Martha questioned Jesus' timing. "If you had been here," Martha said, "my brother would not have died!"

But Jesus is never late. Gently he reminded Martha of his awesome power and limitless love. "I am the resurrection and the life," he said. Then he called to Lazarus, the dead man, and commanded that he come forth. And Lazarus did, still wrapped in his burial clothes.

What loss threatens to unravel your life? As you stand among the gravestones, what questions or demands do you have for the Lord? Remember, Jesus is never late. In his infinite understanding, perfect timing, and deep concern, he will hear your cry, answer your prayer, and bring life. In the meantime, keep resting in his sovereignty and trusting in his love.

–DAVE VEERMAN, from *How to Apply the Bible*

 Jesus, help me to remember that You are never late;
Your answers are always right on time. I trust You and
believe that even if the answer I seek has not yet come,
You still have all things under Your control. Amen.

HE IS NEVER LATE

Jesus said to her, "I am the resurrection and the life. He who believes in me will live, even though he dies; and whoever lives and believes in me will never die. Do you believe this?"

JOHN 11:25–26

Some prayers are followed by silence because they are wrong, others because they are bigger than we can understand. Jesus stayed where He was—a positive staying, because He loved Martha and Mary. Did they get Lazarus back? They got infinitely more; they got to know the greatest truth mortal beings ever knew—that Jesus Christ is the Resurrection and the Life. It will be a wonderful moment for some of us when we stand before God and find that the prayers we clamored for in early days and imagined were never answered, have been answered in the most amazing way, and that God's silence has been the sign of the answer.

Silence. Lord, that's the hardest answer to get from You. Teach me that even in times of silence, You are still there. Amen.

—OSWALD CHAMBERS

THE WRONG CONCLUSION

"But we were hoping that it was He who was going to
redeem Israel. Indeed, besides all this, today is
the third day since these things happened."

LUKE 24:21 NKJV

Every fact that the disciples stated was right, but the conclusions they drew from those facts were wrong. Anything that has even a hint of dejection spiritually is always wrong.... What have I been hoping or trusting God would do? Is today "the third day" and He has still not done what I expected? Am I therefore justified in being dejected and in blaming God? Whenever we insist that God should give us an answer to prayer we are off track. The purpose of prayer is that we get ahold of God, not of the answer....

We look for visions from heaven and for earth-shaking events to see God's power. Even the fact that we are dejected is proof that we do this. Yet we never realize that all the time God is at work in our everyday events and in the people around us. If we will only obey, and do the task that He has placed closest to us, we will see Him. One of the most amazing revelations of God comes to us when we learn that it is in the everyday things of life that we realize the magnificent deity of Jesus Christ.

—OSWALD CHAMBERS

 Lord, show me how You move in the everyday
events of my life, and teach me to recognize
Your loving hand all around me. Amen.

THE DOUBTER

"My Lord and my God!"

JOHN 20:28 NLT

Thomas, too, was a doubter who needed faith. Even after his best friends returned from the empty tomb and described what they had seen, Thomas refused to believe. It was only when Jesus appeared to the disciples a week later and invited Thomas to touch his wounds and satisfy his doubts that Thomas found the faith he required.

"Put your finger here; see my hands. Reach out your hand and put it into my side," the Master said. "Stop doubting and believe." And Thomas exclaimed, "My Lord and my God!" (John 20:24-28)

The Bible invites any of us who lack faith to pray in the words of the father who doubted: "I do believe; help me overcome my unbelief."

This is a prayer that God delights to answer. Faith is a gift that he delights to give. God knows what we lack and what we need. He made each of us as we are, and in our character is the raw material he will use to make us who we can become.

–CLAIRE CLONINGER, from *Dear Abba:*
A Ten-Week Journey to the Heart of God

Lord, sometimes I doubt. Sometimes I find it hard
to believe in You. Thank You for hearing my
honest prayer and helping my unbelief. Amen.

BRAND-NEW PRAYERS

As you therefore have received Christ Jesus
the Lord, so walk in Him, rooted and built up in
Him and established in the faith, as you have
been taught, abounding in it with thanksgiving.

COLOSSIANS 2:6–7 NKJV

Lord, as I sometimes stumble in my prayers, I know You hear my heart. Please hear my gratitude today, Lord God. Thank You for saving me and changing my life. Amen.

Listen to brand new Christians pray. You know, those who are fresh from birth who haven't learned "how to do it" yet, thank goodness. They talk to God like He's their friend, they use street terms anybody can understand, and they occasionally laugh or cry. It's just beautiful. Another tip that may add a new dimension to your prayer is the use of music. Sing to your God.... Occasionally, our family will spend a few minutes before supper telling one thing that happened that day, then the one who prays mentions two or three of those matters before God. The point is clear: Guard against meaningless verbiage.

–CHARLES SWINDOLL, from *Strengthening Your Grip*

SEEING IS NOT BELIEVING

Thomas said to him, "My Lord and my God!"
Then Jesus told him, "Because you have seen me,
you have believed; blessed are those who
have not seen and yet have believed."

JOHN 20:28–29

Seeing is never believing: we interpret what we see in the light of what we believe. Faith is confidence in God before you see God emerging, therefore the nature of faith is that it must be tried. To say, "Oh, yes, I believe God will triumph," may be so much credence smeared over with religious phraseology; but when you are up against things it is quite another matter to say, "I believe God will win through." The trial of our faith gives us a good banking account in the heavenly places, and when the next trial comes our wealth there will tide us over. If we have confidence in God beyond the actual earthly horizons, we shall see the lie at the heart of the fear, and our faith will win through in every detail. Jesus said that men ought always to pray and not "cave in"—"Don't look at the immediate horizon and don't take the facts you see and say they are the reality; they are actuality; the reality lies behind with God."

—OSWALD CHAMBERS

*Gracious God, thank You that the trials in my life show me
what I really believe. Help me to stand strong in my faith,
no matter what circumstances life brings my way. Amen.*

HELP IN THE HARD TIMES

The Spirit itself maketh intercession for us
with groanings which cannot be uttered.

ROMANS 8:26 KJV

Oh, the burdens that we love to bear and cannot understand! Oh, the inarticulate out-reachings of our hearts for things we cannot comprehend! And yet we know they are an echo from the throne and a whisper from the heart of God. It is often a groan rather than a song, a burden rather than a buoyant wing. But it is a blessed burden, and it is a groan whose under-tone is praise and unutterable joy. It is a groaning "which cannot be uttered." We could not ourselves express it always, and sometimes we do not understand any more than that God is praying in us, for something that needs His touch and that He understands.

And so we can just pour out the fullness of our heart, the burden of our spirit, the sorrow that crushes us, and know that He hears, He loves, He understands, He receives; and He separates from our prayer all that is imperfect, ignorant and wrong, and presents the rest, with the incense of the great High Priest, before the throne on high; and our prayer is heard, accepted and answered in His name.

−A. B. SIMPSON

Lord, at times it is hard to express what I really feel.
Thank You for Your Holy Spirit who intercedes for me,
even when I don't know what to pray. Amen.

HOPING AND PRAYING

[Jesus said,] Ask what ye will,
and it shall be done unto you.

JOHN 15:7 KJV

Let us realize that we can only fulfill our calling to bear much fruit by praying much. In Christ are all the treasures any person needs; in Him all God's children are blessed with all spiritual blessings; He is full of grace and truth. But it needs prayer, much prayer, strong believing prayer, to bring these blessings down....

Let us claim it as one of the revelations of our wonderful life in Christ: He tells us that if we ask in His name, in virtue of our union with Him, whatsoever it be, it will be given to us. Souls are perishing because there is so little prayer. God's children are feeble because there is so little prayer. The faith of this promise would make us strong to pray; let us not rest till it has entered into our very heart and drawn us in the power of Christ to continue and labor and strive in prayer until the blessing comes in power.

−ANDREW MURRAY

 Heavenly Father, I want to stand strong in You.
Teach me to strive in prayer, to reach Your heart
and draw from Your strength. Amen.

PERSISTING IN PRAYER

The fruit of the righteous is a tree of life,
and he who is wise wins souls.

PROVERBS 11:30 NASB

Every born-again Christian possesses a measure of the Spirit of Christ, enough of the Holy Spirit to lead us to true consecration and inspire us with the faith that is essential to our prevalence in prayer. Let us, then, not grieve or resist Him, but accept the commission, fully consecrate ourselves with all we have, to the saving of our great and only life work.

Let us get onto the altar, with all we have and are, and lie there and persist in prayer until we receive the provision.

Now, observe, conversion to Christ is not to be confounded with the acceptance of this commission to convert the world. The first is a personal transaction between the soul and Christ relating to its own salvation. The second is the soul's acceptance of the service in which Christ proposes to employ it. Christ does not require us to make brick without straw. To whom He gives the commission He also gives the admonition and the promise. If the commission is heartily accepted, if the promise is believed, if the admonition to wait upon the Lord until our strength is renewed be complied with, we shall receive the provision.

–CHARLES G. FINNEY

Lord, I want to be known as someone who persists in prayer, someone who stands strong until the provision comes. Thank You for giving me the measure of faith that I need. Amen.

TEACH US TO PRAY

Lord, teach us to pray.

LUKE 11:1 KJV

One day the disciples said to Jesus Christ: "Lord, teach us to pray." It was the Holy Spirit who inspired them to make this request. The Holy Spirit convinced them of their inability to pray in their own

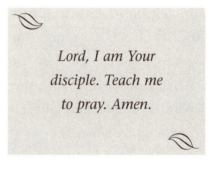

Lord, I am Your disciple. Teach me to pray. Amen.

strength, and He moved their hearts to draw near to Jesus as their only Master who could teach them how they ought to pray. It was then that Jesus taught them the Lord's Prayer.

There is no Christian who is not in the same case as the disciples.... Ah, if we were only convinced of our ignorance and of our need of a teacher like Jesus Christ! If we would only approach Him with confidence, asking Him to teach us Himself and desiring to be taught by His grace how to converse with God!

How soon we should be skilled in it and how many of its secrets we should discover. Do not let us say that we know how to pray the prayer they learned from Him. We may know the words, but without the grace we cannot understand the meaning—and we cannot ask or receive what it expresses.

–JEAN-NICOLAS GROU

THERE'S HOPE IN SILENCE

Be still and know that I am God.

PSALM 46:10 KJV

Imagine a soul so closely united to God that it has no need of outward acts to remain attentive to the inward prayer. In these moments of silence and peace when it pays no heed to what is happening within itself, it prays and prays excellently, with a simple and direct prayer that God will understand perfectly by the action of grace.

The heart will be full of aspirations toward God without any clear expression. If it is the heart that prays, it is evident that sometimes and even continuously, it can pray by itself without any help from words, spoken or not. Here is something that few people understand. Though prayers may elude our own consciousness, they will not escape the consciousness of God.

This prayer, so empty of all images and perceptions, apparently so passive and yet so active, is—so far as the limitations of this life allow—pure adoration in spirit and in truth.... This is what is called the prayer of silent or of quiet or of bare faith.

–JEAN-NICOLAS GROU

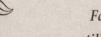
*Father, so often it is difficult to sit
still and wait quietly for Your answer.
Teach me to be still and wait on You. Amen.*

THE NECESSITY OF SILENCE

Be still in the presence of the LORD,
and wait patiently for him to act.

PSALM 37:7 NLT

Silence in prayer is not the absence of sound that occurs when we run out of things to say. It is not the embarrassing speechlessness that results from shyness. It is something positive, something fertile. It is being more interested in what God will say to me than in getting out my speech to Him. It is a preference for hearing God's word over saying my word....

Lord God, I know that true prayer is not about my words, but about having a relationship with You. Today I quiet my heart before You. Please speak to me, Lord God. Amen.

Talk in prayer is essential but it is also partial. Silence is also essential.

–EUGENE H. PETERSON, from *Where Your Treasure Is*

THE GIFT OF PRAYER

Give all your worries and cares to God,
for he cares about what happens to you.

1 PETER 5:7 NLT

There's nothing like quiet reflective moments to encourage our blood pressures to stop percolating, our hearts to fall back into rhythm, and our minds to stop gyrating. Then add to all of that the untold benefits of loving exchanges with our all-knowing, all-seeing, all-powerful God. He who assigns our days and redeems our losses has a way of calming our anxieties and even healing our infirmities....

Jesus makes our entrance to the Father possible. He knew we would need time in His presence where we could step out of the whirlwind and into His consoling company. It is there, as we lean our heads upon His breast, that we are both deeply heard and deeply understood.

–PATSY CLAIRMONT, from *Adventurous Prayer*

Lord Jesus, thank You for the privilege of coming to You in prayer. Thank You for the gift of talking to You and receiving Your blessings. Please give me a renewed desire to spend time with You, Lord. Amen.

PRAYING THE SCRIPTURE

Jesus told his disciples …that they
should always pray and not give up.

LUKE 18:1

"Praying the scripture" is a unique way of dealing with the scripture; it involves both reading and prayer. Turn to the scripture; choose some passage that is simple and fairly practical. Next, come to the Lord. Come quietly and humbly. There, before Him, read a small portion of the passage of scripture you have opened to.

Be careful as you read. Take in fully, gently, and carefully what you are reading. Taste it and digest it as you read….

Coming to the Lord by means of "praying the scripture," you do not read quickly; you read very slowly. You do not move on to the next thought until you have sensed the very heart of what you have read. You may then want to take that portion of scripture that has touched you and turn it into a prayer.

…You will be surprised to find that when your time with the Lord has ended, you will have been drawn closely to Him.

–MADAME GUYON

*Father, thank You for Your Word that brings
me life. Teach me to pray the Scriptures
so that I may draw closer to You. Amen.*

ASKING WITH HOPE

[Jesus said,] "I will do whatever you ask in my name,
so that the Son may bring glory to the Father."

JOHN 14:13

Blessed Jesus! It is You who has unlocked to Your people the gates of prayer. Without You they must have been shut up forever. It was Your atoning merit on earth that first opened them; it is Your intercessory work in heaven that keeps them open still.

How unlimited the promise—"Whatever you ask!" It is the pledge that all believers and unbelievers require. To us His faithful servants, He seems to say, "Bring your requests and under my superscription, write what you please." And then He further endorses each petition with the words, "I *will* do it!"…

Reader, do you know the blessedness of confiding your every need and every care—your every sorrow and every cross—into the ear of the Savior? He is the Wonderful Counselor. With tender sympathy, He can enter into the innermost depths of your need. That need may be great, but the everlasting arms are underneath it all.

–JOHN MACDUFF

*Jesus, You are my greatest hope, my Wonderful
Counselor, the One who cares for my every need.
Thank You for Your promise that when I ask
in Your name, You answer my prayer. Amen.*

PRAY YOUR HEART

To You, O Lord, I lift up my soul.
O my God, I trust in You.

PSALM 25:1 NKJV

Prayer is never just *asking,* nor is it *merely* a matter of asking for what I want. God is not a cosmic butler or fix-it man, and the aim of the universe is not to fulfill my desires and needs. On the other hand, I am to pray for what concerns me, and many people have found prayer impossible because they thought they should only pray for wonderful but remote needs they actually had little or no interest in or even knowledge of.

Prayer simply *dies* from efforts to pray about "good things" that honestly do not matter to us. The way to get to meaningful prayer for those good things is to start by praying for what we are truly interested in. The circle of our interests will inevitably grow in the largeness of God's love.

–DALLAS WILLARD, from *The Divine Conspiracy:*
Rediscovering Our Hidden Life in God

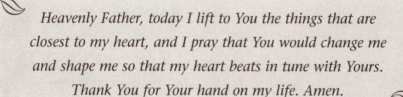

Heavenly Father, today I lift to You the things that are closest to my heart, and I pray that You would change me and shape me so that my heart beats in tune with Yours. Thank You for Your hand on my life. Amen.

HOW TO GO TO GOD

The Spirit of the Lord God is upon me.

ISAIAH 61:1 KJV

He [Brother Lawrence] discussed with me frequently, with great openness of heart, concerning his manner of going to God, to coming into His presence. To do so, there must be a hearty renunciation of everything that does not lead us to God and a continual conversation with Him, with freedom and in simplicity. We will recognize that God is intimately present with us, importuning us to address ourselves to Him, that we may beg His assistance for knowing His will in things doubtful, and for rightfully performing those which we plainly see He requires of us.

In this conversation with God, we are also employed in praising, adoring, and loving Him incessantly for His infinite goodness and perfection....

It is a great delusion to think that the times of prayer ought differ from other times. It is also a great delusion to believe that we are as strictly obliged to adhere to God by action in the time of action, as by prayer in its season.

–BROTHER LAWRENCE

 Lord, like Brother Lawrence, I want to practice Your presence every day of my life. Teach me that prayer is an ongoing conversation with You, all day long. Amen.

TOO BUSY TO PRAY

"Not by might nor by power, but by My Spirit,"
Says the LORD of hosts.

ZECHARIAH 4:6 NKJV

Prayer is a two-way conversation; it is our talking to God, and His talking to us. As a Christian, you have a Heavenly Father who hears and answers prayer. Jesus said, "All things, whatsoever ye shall ask in prayer, believing, ye shall receive." Every man or woman whose life has counted for the church and the Kingdom of God has been a person of

Lord, I know that in order to be effective in my faith, I must spend time in prayer. Please direct my thoughts toward You during the day, Lord God, and enrich my times of prayer so that I know Your heart. Amen.

prayer. You cannot afford to be too busy to pray. A prayerless Christian is a powerless Christian. Jesus Christ spent many hours in prayer. Sometimes He spent the night on a mountain-top in solitary communion with God the Father. If He felt that He had to pray, how much more do we need to pray!

–BILLY GRAHAM, from *Day by Day with Billy Graham*

HABITUAL SENSE OF GOD

Let this mind be in you, which was also in Christ Jesus.

PHILIPPIANS 2:5 KJV

Having found in many books different methods of going to God, various practices of the spiritual life, I reckoned that so much instruction only puzzled me. Simply put, all I was looking for was how to become wholly God's.

This made me resolve to give my all for His all. So, after giving myself wholly to God—that is, making satisfaction for sins by renouncing them—I renounced them for the love of Him, and I began to live as if there were none but Him and I in the world.

Sometimes I considered myself before Him as a poor criminal at the feet of his judge; at other times I beheld Him in my heart as my Father, as my God. I worshiped Him the oftenest I could, keeping my mind in His holy presence and recalling it as often as I found it wandered from Him. I found no small pain in this exercise, and yet I continued it. I made this my business, as much as all the daylong as at the appointed times of prayer. I drove away from my mind everything that was capable of interrupting my thoughts of God.

—BROTHER LAWRENCE

Heavenly Father, I want to live in a state of constant communion with You. I give myself completely over to You and Your will. Amen.

LET GOD BE GOD

The LORD your God is with you,
he is mighty to save.
He will take great delight in you,
he will quiet you with his love,
he will rejoice over you with singing.

ZEPHANIAH 3:17

God aims to exalt Himself by working for those who wait for Him. Prayer is the essential activity of waiting for God—acknowledging our helplessness and His power, calling upon Him for help, seeking His counsel. Since His purpose in the world is to be exalted for His mercy, it is evident why prayer is so often commanded by God. Prayer is the antidote for the disease of self-confidence, which opposes God's goal of getting glory by working for those who wait for Him....

God is not looking for people to work for Him, so much as He is looking for people who will let Him work for them.... The gospel commands us to give up and hang out a help-wanted sign (this is the basic meaning of prayer). Then the gospel promises that God will work for us if we do. He will not surrender the glory of being the Giver.

−JOHN PIPER, from *Desiring God*

Father God, thank You for Your heart to show yourself strong on behalf of those who wait for You. Today, Lord, I put out a "help-wanted sign" and choose to wait on You. Amen.

HOPING AND PRAYING

Prepare your minds for action.

1 PETER 1:13

It's a risky thing to pray and the danger is that our very prayers get between God and us. The great thing is not to pray but to go directly to God. There is no such thing as a kind of prayer in which you do absolutely nothing. If you are doing nothing you are not praying.

Prayer is the movement of trust, of gratitude, of adoration, or of sorrow, that places us before God, seeing both Him and ourselves in the light of His infinite truth, and moves us to ask Him for the mercy, the spiritual strength, the material help that we all need.

The man [or woman] whose prayer is so pure that he never asks God for anything does not know who God is, and does not know who he is himself: for he does not know his own need of God.

All true prayer somehow confesses our absolute dependence on the Lord of life and death. It is, therefore, a deep and vital contact with Him whom we know not only as Lord but as Father. It is when we pray truly that we really are.

–THOMAS MERTON

*Precious Lord, I bring to You all that I am
and all that I have. I am Yours alone.
Teach me to rely completely on You. Amen.*

THE CHIEF END OF PRAYER

[Jesus prayed,] Father ...glorify thy Son, that thy
Son also may glorify thee. I have glorified thee on
the earth. Glorify thou me with thine own self.

JOHN 17:1,4-5 KJV

This was Jesus' goal when He was on earth: "I seek not mine own honor: I seek the honor of Him who sent me." In such words we have the keynote of His life....

Let us make His aim ours. Let the glory of the Father be the link between our asking and His doing!

Jesus' words come indeed as a sharp two-edged sword, dividing the soul and the spirit, and quickly discerning the thoughts and intents of the heart. In His prayers on earth, His intercession in heaven, and His promise of an answer to our prayers, Jesus makes His first object the glory of His father. Is this our object, too? Or are self-interest and self-will the strongest motives urging us to pray? A distinct, conscious longing for the glory of the Father must animate our prayers. For the sake of God's glory, let us learn to pray well. When we seek our own glory among men, we make faith impossible. The surrender to God and the expectation that He will show His glory in hearing us are essential. Only he who seeks God's glory will see it in the answer to his prayer.

–ANDREW MURRAY

Heavenly Father, ultimately it is Your glory that I seek. Help me to set aside my own selfish interests and focus solely on Your will. Amen.

PRAYING WITH OUR WHOLE SELVES

Devote yourselves to prayer with
an alert mind and a thankful heart.

COLOSSIANS 4:2 NLT

Dear Heavenly Father, today I pour my heart out to You. I ask that today would be saturated in prayer and in Your Spirit. Amen.

Kingdom praying and its efficacy is entirely a matter of the innermost heart's being totally open and honest before God. It is a matter of what we are saying with our whole being, moving with resolute intent and clarity of mind into the flow of God's action. In apprenticeship to Jesus, this is one of the most important things we learn how to do. He teaches us how to be in prayer what we are in life and how to be in life what we are in prayer.

—DALLAS WILLARD, from *The Divine Conspiracy: Rediscovering Our Hidden Life in God*

A PURE HEART

Who may ascend the hill of the Lord? Who may stand in his holy place? He who has clean hands and a pure heart.

PSALM 24:3–4

If your desire and aim is to reach the destination of the path and home of true happiness, of grace and glory by a straight and safe way, then earnestly apply your mind to seek constant purity of heart, clarity of mind, and calmness of the senses. Gather up your heart's desire and fix it continually on the Lord God above. To do so, you must withdraw yourself as far as you can from friends and from everyone else and from the activities that hinder you from such a purpose....

Simplify your heart with all care, diligence, and effort so that, still and at peace, you can remain always in the Lord within, as if your mind were already in the now of eternity. In this way you will be able to commit yourself completely and fully to God in all difficulties and eventualities and be willing to submit yourself patiently to His will and good pleasure at all times.

There can be no greater happiness than to place one's all in Him who lacks nothing. Cast yourself, all of yourself, with confidence into God and He will sustain you, heal you, and make you safe.

—ALBERT THE GREAT

Lord, I pray that you would make my heart pure before You. I cast my whole being on You, for I know You will sustain me. Amen.

WAITING ON GOD

It is good that a man should both hope and
quietly wait for the salvation of the Lord.

LAMENTATIONS 3:26 KJV

Those who deal with God will find it is not in vain to trust Him;
for, one, He is good to those who do. His tender mercies are
over all his works; all His creatures taste of His goodness. But He
is in a particular manner good to those who wait for Him....

While we wait for Him by faith, we must seek Him by prayer;
our souls must seek Him, else we do not seek so as to find. Our
seeking will help to keep up our waiting. To those who thus
wait and seek, God will be gracious. He will show them His
marvelous loving-kindness.

And, two, those who do so will find it good for them. It is
good to hope and quietly wait for the salvation of the Lord;
to hope that it will come, through the difficulties that lie in
the way. To wait till it does come, though it be long delayed;
and while we wait, to be quiet and silent, not quarreling with
God, nor making ourselves uneasy.

If we call to mind, "Father, thy will be done," we may have
hope that all will end well at last.

—MATTHEW HENRY

Heavenly Father, as I wait patiently on You, I learn to trust
You more and more. I know that Your will is best for me,
and in all things, I pray that Your will be done. Amen.

THERE IS HOPE IN PRAYER

This is the confidence that we have in him, that, if
we ask any thing according to his will, he heareth us.

1 JOHN 5:14 KJV

The prayer that is answered is the prayer after God's will. And the reason for this is plain. What is God's will is God's wish. And when a man does what God wills, he does what God wishes done. Therefore God will have that done at any cost, at any sacrifice.

Thousands of prayers are never answered, simply because God does not wish them answered. If we pray for any one thing, or any number of things, we are sure God wishes to come to pass, we may be sure our prayers will be gratified. For our wishes are only the reflection of God's. And the wish in us is almost equivalent to the answer. It is the answer casting its shadow backwards. Already the thing is done in the mind of God. It casts two shadows: one backward, one forward. The backward shadow—that is the wish before the thing is done which sheds itself in prayer. The forward shadow—that is the joy after the thing is done which sheds itself in praise.

—HENRY DRUMMOND

*Lord, teach my heart that Your will is best.
When I seek my own way, show me the blessings in store
for me when I pray, "Your will be done." Amen.*

KNOWING GOD'S WILL

Don't copy the behavior and customs of this world,
but let God transform you into a new person by
changing the way you think. Then you will know
what God wants you to do, and you will know how
good and pleasing and perfect his will really is.

ROMANS 12:2 NLT

When I ask God specifically to let me know if something is right or wrong for me, He gives me an answer. If I have no answer, then I assume that I need to do a little more investigating.... Eventually I will come to a point where I *will* hear God's clear answer in my spirit: "Yes, this is something good for you," or "No, this is something to avoid."

A person who is truly seeking the Lord through daily, extensive reading of God's Word and through daily prayer and communication with the Lord—desiring to hear God's answer and to know God's definition of goodness—is going to desire and to ask God for the things that are good in His eyes.

–CHARLES STANLEY

 Lord God, I really do want to know Your will. I pray that You would guide my every step, Lord—and help me know Your heart well enough to discern Your will. Amen.

ACCORDING TO YOUR WILL

So we have continued praying for you ever since we first heard about you. We ask God to give you a complete understanding of what he wants to do in your lives, and we ask him to make you wise with spiritual wisdom.

COLOSSIANS 1:9 NLT

When I pray, in church or without, in my prayer corner at home, or on the street as I walk to and fro, I pray that God's will may be done, and I pray it especially fervently during those many times when I am not able to discern God's will. Is this man the right man for the young woman I love?

Lord, thousands of times each day, I just don't know what's best. Today I commit myself to doing Your will, and I pray that You would rule and reign in my life every day. Amen.

Or vice versa. Can this marriage be saved? Can this life be saved? Should I say yes or no to this request? Often I do not know, and so I throw myself upon God's will.

—MADELEINE L'ENGLE, from *The Rock That Is Higher*

RECOGNIZING GOD'S PRESENCE

Where can I flee from your presence?

PSALM 139:7

It is a great delusion to think that times of prayer ought to differ from other times in our day. According to him, prayer is recognizing the presence of God; it isn't different than any other time in your day. When your appointed times of prayer were past, he found no difference, because he still continued with God, praising and blessing Him with all his might, so that he passed his life in continual joy; yet he hoped that God would give him somewhat to suffer, when he should grow stronger.

That we ought, once for all, heartily to put our whole trust in God and make a total surrender of ourselves to Him, secure that He would not deceive us.

That we ought not to be weary of doing little things for the love of God, who regards not the greatness of the work, but the love with which it is performed. That we should not wonder if, in the beginning, we often failed in our endeavors, but that at last we should gain a habit, which will naturally produce its acts in us, without our care, and to our exceeding great delight.

–BROTHER LAWRENCE

As I recognize Your presence in my daily life, O Lord, draw me closer to You. I surrender myself, all day long, to Your will. Amen.

NEEDS SUPPLIED

My God shall supply all your need according
to His riches in glory by Christ Jesus.

PHILIPPIANS 4:19 NKJV

If it is a throne of grace, then all the wants of those who come
to it will be supplied. The King from off such a throne will not
say, "You must bring Me gifts; you must offer Me sacrifices."
It is not a throne for receiving tribute; it is a throne for
dispensing gifts.

Come then, you who are poor as poverty itself; come you who
have no merits and are destitute of virtues; come you who are
reduced to a beggarly bankruptcy by Adam's fall and by your
own transgressions.

…Come you, now, and receive the wine and milk, which are
freely given. Yes, come, buy wine and milk without money
and without price. All the petitioner's wants shall be supplied,
because it is a throne of grace.

And the one upon this throne is your salvation. When sinners
approach His throne, He holds out a welcoming hand and
says, "Come to me." And the Apostle Paul? He reminds you
who are here tonight, "My God shall supply all your needs."

—CHARLES H. SPURGEON

*King of Majesty, I approach Your throne with confidence,
knowing that You receive me in Your love. Thank You for meeting
all of my needs, according to Your riches in glory. Amen.*

PRAYER AND PROMISE

"I will give them an undivided heart
and put a new spirit in them."

EZEKIEL 11:19

The great promises find their fulfillment along the lines of prayer. They inspire prayer, and through prayer the promises flow out to their full realization and bear their ripest fruit....

God had promised through His prophets that the coming Messiah should have a forerunner. How many homes and wombs in Israel have longed for the coming of this great honor? How much hope was heaped on this event? Perchance Zacharias and Elizabeth were the only ones who were trying to realize by prayer this great dignity and blessing. At least we know that the angel said to Zacharias, as he announced to the old man the coming Messiah: "Your prayer is heard."

It was then that the word of the Lord, as spoken by the prophets and the prayers of an old priest and his wife, brought John the Baptist into the withered womb and into the childless home of Zacharias and Elizabeth.

God has never has put His Spirit into a human heart that hasn't ardently prayed for it.

—E. M. BOUNDS

Heavenly Father, I know that You keep all of Your promises.
I long for a new spirit, one that is pure and worships You
without restraint. As I turn myself over to You, I know
that You will create a new heart within me. Amen.

THE LIGHT OF HOPE

God is light, and in him is no darkness at all.

1 JOHN 1:5 KJV

Come to God with all your desires and instincts, all your lofty ideals, all your longing for purity and unselfishness, all your yearning to love and be true, all your aspirations after self-forgetfulness and childlikeness; come to Him with all your weaknesses, all

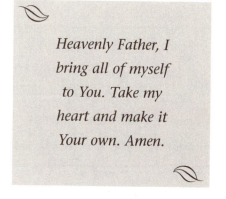

Heavenly Father, I bring all of myself to You. Take my heart and make it Your own. Amen.

your shames, all your futilities; with all your helplessness over your own thoughts.... Be sure of this, He will take you and all your misery into His care, for liberty in His limitless heart. He is light, and in Him there is no darkness at all. If he were a king, a governor, if the name that described Him were the Almighty, you may well doubt whether there could be light enough in Him for you and your darkness. But, He is your Father, and more your Father than the word can mean in any lips but His who said, "My father and your father, my God and your God."

—GEORGE MACDONALD

TURN IT ALL INTO PRAYER

Pray at all times and on every occasion in
the power of the Holy Spirit. Stay alert and be
persistent in your prayers for all Christians everywhere.

EPHESIANS 6:18 NLT

> *Lord, I know that every event is an opportunity for prayer. I know that there is nothing small in Your eyes. God, please prompt me to pray throughout the day. Amen.*

After a few introductory sentences in the Revelation, we come upon St. John in the place and practice of prayer (1:9-10)....

At the end of the book he is still praying: "Amen. Come, Lord Jesus!" (22:20). St. John listens to God, is silent before God, sings to God, asks questions of God....

St. John doesn't miss much. He reads and assimilates the Scriptures; he reads and feels the impact of the daily news. But neither ancient Scripture nor current event is left the way it arrives on his doorstep; it is all turned into prayer.

–EUGENE H. PETERSON, from *The Contemplative Pastor*

ANSWERED PRAYER

I thank God, whom I serve, as my forefathers did,
with a clear conscience, as night and day I
constantly remember you in my prayers.

2 TIMOTHY 1:3

Let me tell you how God answered the prayers of my dear mother for my conversion....

She arose from the table where she was dining with an intense yearning for the conversion of her boy. She went to her room and turned the key in the door, resolving not to leave that spot until her prayers were answered....

I, in the meantime, had been led to take up a little tract and while reading it was struck with the sentence, "The finished work of Christ." Immediately the words "It is finished" suggested themselves to my mind. What was finished?

Then it came to my mind, "If the whole work of salvation was finished and the whole debt paid, what is there left for me to do?" With this dawned the joyful conviction, as light flashed into my soul by the Holy Spirit, that there was nothing in the world to be done but to fall down on one's knees and, accepting this Savior and His salvation, to praise Him forevermore. Thus while my dear mother was praising God on her knees in her chamber, I was praising him in the old warehouse....

My dear mother assured me that it was not from any human source that she had learned about the value of hope and the power of prayer.

Lord, I lift before You all of my loved ones who do not know You. By Your Holy Spirit, draw them unto You. Help them to see their need for You. Thank You for their lives and their salvation. Amen.

—HUDSON TAYLOR

THE ABSENT BRIDEGROOM

All night long on my bed I looked for the one my heart
loves; I looked for him but did not find him.

SONG OF SONGS 3:1

The betrothed bride has learned to love her lord, and no other
companionship than his can satisfy her. His visits may be
occasional and may be brief, but they are precious times of
enjoyment. Their memory is cherished in the intervals, and
their repetition longed for. There is no real satisfaction in his
absence, and yet he comes and goes. As the ever-changing
tide, her experience is an ebbing and flowing one. It may even
be that unrest is the rule, satisfaction the exception. Is there
no help for this? Must it always continue so? Has he created
these unquenchable longings only to tantalize them? Strange
indeed it would be if this were the case.

The Bridegroom is waiting for you all the time. The conditions that prevent His approach are all of your own making.
Take the right place before Him, and He will be most ready,
most glad to satisfy your deepest longings, to meet, supply
your every need.

–HUDSON TAYLOR

 *O Great Bridegroom, I love to spend time in
Your presence. You are my joy forever! Amen.*

LOVE AND PRAYERS

[Jesus said,] "But I tell you: Love your enemies
and pray for those who persecute you."

MATTHEW 5:44

We are all selfish by nature, and our selfishness is very apt to stick to us even when we are converted. There is a tendency in us to think only of our own souls, our own spiritual conflicts, our own progress in religion, and to forget others.

Lord, take away my selfishness. Help me to focus on the needs of others as I pray. Amen.

Against this tendency, we all have need to watch and strive, and not the least in our prayers. We should try to bear in our hearts the whole world, the unbelievers, the body of true believers, the churches, the country in which we live, the congregation to which we belong, the homes in which we visit, the friends, and the relations we are connected with. For each and all of these, we should plead. This is the highest love. They love me best who love me in their prayers.

—J. C. RYLE

TALKING TO GOD

Hold fast the form of sound words, which thou hast heard
of me, in faith and love which is in Christ Jesus.

2 TIMOTHY 1:13 KJV

Sojourner Truth's mother talked to her of God. , from these conversations, her mind drew the conclusion that God was a great man and, being located high in the sky, could see all that transpired on the earth. She believed He not only saw but also noted down all her actions in a great book.

At first she heard Jesus mentioned in reading or speaking, but had received from what she heard no impression that He was any other than an eminent man, like a Washington or a Lafayette. Now He appeared to her so mild, so good, and so every way lovely, and He loved her so much! And how strange that He had always loved her and she had never known it! And how great a blessing He conferred, in that He should stand between her and God! And God was no longer a terror and a dread to her.

In the light of her great happiness, the world was clad in new beauty, the very air sparkled as with diamonds and was redolent of heaven.

–SOJOURNER TRUTH

 Jesus, because of Your life and death, I can approach the Father freely. What a joy it is to come to You! Amen.

LOVE AND SALVATION

May those who love your salvation
always say, "The Lord be exalted!"

PSALM 40:16

Will you say that you are afraid to come to God? Your fear is needless. You shall not be cast out, if you will but come in the way of faith in Christ. Our God is not an austere man. Our Father in heaven is full of mercy, love, and grace. I yield to none in desire to promote the love, mercy, and tenderness of God the Father.

We know that God is holy. We know He is just. We believe that He can be angry with them who go on still in sin. But we also believe that to those who draw near to Him in Christ Jesus, He is most merciful, most loving, most tender, and most compassionate. We tell you that the cross of Jesus Christ was the result and consequence of that love.

Draw near in faith by that living way, Christ Jesus to the Father. As the father did to the prodigal son when he ran to meet him—fell on his neck and kissed him—so will God the Father do to that soul who draws near to Him in the name of Christ.

−J. C. RYLE

 Heavenly Father, I draw near to You through Your Son, Jesus Christ. I am overwhelmed by Your love and compassion as You welcome me with open arms. Amen.

INTERCEDE IN LOVE

I exhort therefore, first of all, that supplications, prayers, intercessions, thanksgivings, be made for all men.

1 TIMOTHY 2:1 ASV

Some forget this duty of praying for others because they seldom remember to pray for themselves. Even those who are constant in praying to their Father are often so selfish in their addresses that they do not enlarge their petitions for the welfare of their fellow Christians.

Intercession will fill your hearts with love one to another. He who every day heartily intercedes at the throne of grace for all mankind cannot but in a short time be filled with love and charity to all. The frequent exercise of his love in this manner will gradually enlarge his heart. He will be filled with joy, peace, meekness, long-suffering, and all other graces of the Holy Spirit. By frequently laying his neighbor's wants before God, he will be touched with a fellow-feeling for them. Every blessing bestowed on others, instead of exciting envy in him, will be looked on as an answer to his particular intercession and fill his soul with joy unspeakable and full of glory.

–GEORGE WHITEFIELD

Lord, I lift the needs of my friends and neighbors
before You, knowing that You are the great Need-Meeter.
Thank You for Your gracious answer to my prayer. Amen.

LINGER IN THE GALLERY OF LOVE

I will make with you an everlasting covenant, my steadfast, sure love for David.

ISAIAH 55:3 NRSV

Seek feeling and you will miss it. Be content to live without it, and you will have all you require. If you are always noticing your heartbeats, you will bring on heart disease. If you are ever muffling against cold, you will become very subject to chills. If you are perpetually thinking about your health, you will induce disease. If you are always consulting your feelings, you will live in a dry and thirsty land.

Be indifferent to emotion. If it is there, be thankful. If it is absent, go on doing the will of God, counting on Him, and speaking well of Him. It is impossible to rush into God's presence, catch up anything we fancy, and run off with it. To attempt this will end in mere delusion and disappointment. Nature will not unveil her rarest beauty to the chance tourist. Pictures that are the result of a life of work do not disclose their secret loveliness to those who stroll down a gallery. And God's best cannot be ours apart from patient waiting in His holy presence.

Get into the presence of Jesus, and you will be told clearly and unmistakably His will.

—F. B. MEYER

Lord Jesus, teach me to linger in Your presence, where there is fullness of joy and life. Amen.

STANDING ON THE PROMISES OF LOVE

Has not God chosen those who are poor in the eyes of the world to be rich in faith and to inherit the kingdom he promised those who love him?

JAMES 2:5

We may lose heart and hope, our head may turn dizzy, our heart faint, and the mocking voices of our foes suggest that God has forgotten or forsaken us. But He remains faithful. He cannot deny Himself. He cannot throw aside responsibilities that He has assumed. Often I have gone to God in desperate need, aggravated by nervous depression and heart sickness, and said, "My faith is flickering out. Its hand seems paralyzed, its eye blinded, its old glad song silenced forever. But You are faithful, and I am counting on You!"

The soul loves to stand upon the promises of God. We find no difficulty in trusting our friends because we open our hearts, like south windows, to their love. Where would be our difficulty about faith if we ceased worrying about it and were occupied with the object of faith—Jesus Christ our Lord?

—F. B. MEYER

Lord, You are faithful, and I am counting on You!
Thank You for Your eternal faithfulness. Amen.

SCENE OF LOVE FROM PAUL'S JOURNEYS

After saying good-by to each other, we went
aboard the ship, and they returned home.

ACTS 21:6

Following his visit to Ephesus, Paul arrived at Tyre, where he stopped a few days. Here he found some disciples who begged Paul not to go to Jerusalem, saying through the Spirit that he should not go up to that city. But Paul adhered to his original purpose to go to Jerusalem. The account says: "But when our time was up, we left and continued on our way. All the disciples and their wives and children accompanied us out of the city, and there on the beach we knelt to pray."

What a sight to observe on that seashore! Here is a family picture of love and devotion, where husbands, wives, and even children are present, and prayer is made out in the open air. The vessel was ready to depart, but prayer must cement their affections and bless wives and children, and bless their parting—a parting which was to be final so far as this world was concerned. Never did a seashore see a grander picture or witness a lovelier sight— Paul on his knees on the sands of that shore, invoking God's blessing upon these men, women, and children.

–E. M. BOUNDS

Heavenly Father, I know that the times I spend in prayer are the loveliest times of my life. Before any venture I make in life, remind me to first spend time with You in prayer. Amen.

PLEASING THE FATHER

"Quick! Catch all the little foxes before
they ruin the vineyard of your love, for
the grapevines are all in blossom."

SONG OF SONGS 2:15 NLT

Heavenly Father, I want to please You in every aspect of my life. Do not let anything come between me and Your wonderful presence. Amen.

Are we not all too apt to seek Him rather because of our need than for His joy and pleasure? This should not be. We do not admire selfish children who only think of what they can get from their parents and are unmindful of the pleasure that they may give or the service that they may render. But are not we in danger of forgetting that pleasing God means giving Him pleasure? Some of us look back to the time when the words "to please God" meant no more than not to sin against Him and not to grieve Him. However, would the love of earthly parents be satisfied with the mere absence of disobedience? Or would a bridegroom be satisfied if his bride only sought him for the supply of her own need?

–HUDSON TAYLOR

THE FATHER'S POWERFUL LOVE

The LORD loves those who hate evil; he guards the lives of
his faithful; he rescues them from the hand of the wicked.

PSALM 97:10 NRSV

We have often walked in the field in the early morning and
have noticed how the rising sun has turned each dewdrop
into a glittering gem. One ray of its own bright light makes a
little sun of each of the million drops that hang from the
pendent leaflets and sparkle everywhere. But it is helpful to
remember that the glorious orb itself contains infinitely more
light than all the dewdrops ever did or ever will reflect.

And so of our heavenly Father. He himself is the great source
of all that is noble and true and of all that ever has been
loving and trustworthy. Each beautiful trait of each beautiful
character is but the dim reflection of some ray of His own
great perfection. And the sum total of all human goodness
and tenderness and love is but as the dewdrops to the sun.
How blessed then to confide in the infinite and changeless
love of such a father as our Father in heaven!

–HUDSON TAYLOR

*Heavenly Father, You are the greatest love
I have ever known. I worship You for
all the wonder that You are. Amen.*

AN INVITATION TO PRAYER

Call to Me, and I will answer you, and show you great
and mighty things, which you do not know.

JEREMIAH 33:3 NKJV

*Father, it amazes me that
You allow me to come to
You so freely. Thank You for
Your invitation to pray and
spend time with You. Help
me to see prayer as the
privilege that it is, and to
call to You all day. Amen.*

John says that the only reason we love God is because He first loved us. In the same way, we could not pray to our Heavenly Father if He had not first asked us to do so. "Call to me," invites our Heavenly Father. It is an invitation to pray. He has made himself available to us 24/7/365. He has put out the welcome mat. He has given us the green light. We have a direct line to His throne room. We have a permission slip, a backstage pass, an engraved invitation. He has an open door policy for all of His children. And when we do call out His name, He gives us His undivided attention.

—CHRISTA KINDE, from *Adventurous Prayer*

PERSONAL RESPONSIBILITY FOR THE LOST

For the Son of man is come to seek and
to save that which was lost.

LUKE 19:10 KJV

I have often thought that the reason why so many pray only in form and not in heart for the salvation of souls is that they lack love like God's love for the souls of the perishing....

You must see impressively that souls are precious. Without such a sense of the value of souls, you will not pray with fervent, strong desire. Without a just apprehension of their guilt, danger, and remedy, you will not pray in faith for God's interposing grace.

You need so to love the world that your love will draw you to make similar sacrifices and put forth similar labors. Love for souls, the same in kind as God had in giving up His Son to die and as Christ had in coming cheerfully down to make Himself the offering, each servant of God must have. Otherwise, your prayers will have little heart and no power with God. This love for souls is always implied in acceptable prayer, that God would send forth laborers into His harvest.

–CHARLES G. FINNEY

Lord Jesus, give me a heart for the lost people of the world.
I want to love them the way that You love them.
Send me forth as a laborer in Your harvest. Amen.

JUNE 13

A WILLING HEART

Then I heard the Lord asking, "Whom should I send
as a messenger to my people? Who will go for us?"
And I said, "Lord, I'll go! Send me."

ISAIAH 6:8 NLT

Let us bow our souls and say, "Behold the handmaid of the
Lord!" Let us lift up our hearts and ask, "Lord, what wouldst
Thou have me do?" Then light from the opened heaven shall
stream on our daily task, revealing the grains of gold, where
yesterday all seemed dust. A hand shall sustain us and our
daily burden, so that, smiling at yesterday's fears, we shall say,
"This is easy, this is light"; every "lion in the way," as we
come up to it, shall be seen chained, and leave open the gates
of the Palace Beautiful. And to us, even to us, feeble and fluc-
tuating as we are, ministries shall be assigned, and through
our hands blessings shall be conveyed in which the spirits of
just men made perfect might delight.

–ELIZABETH RUNDLE CHARLES

*Lord, I know that You can do mighty things through
ordinary servants. But I also know that I need to have a
willing heart in order to do all the things You might use
me to do. I open my heart to You today, Lord. Amen.*

LOVE CONQUERS SELFISHNESS

For God did not give us a spirit of timidity, but
a spirit of power, of love and of self-discipline.

2 TIMOTHY 1:7

Nothing but love can expel and conquer our selfishness. Self is the great curse, whether in its relationship to God or to our fellowmen or to fellow Christians. But, praise God, Christ came to redeem us from self. Deliverance from selfishness means to be a vessel overflowing with love to everybody all the day. Many people pray for the power of the Holy Spirit, and they get something but so little! They prayed for power for work and power for blessing, but they have not prayed for power for full deliverance from self. A great many of us try hard at times to love. We try to force ourselves to love, and I do not say that is wrong; it is better than nothing. But the end of it is always very sad. "I fail continually," one must confess.

And how can I learn to love? Never until the Spirit of God fills my heart with God's love, and I begin to long for God's love in a very different sense from which I have sought it so selfishly as a comfort, a joy, a happiness, and a pleasure to myself.

−ANDREW MURRAY

 Heavenly Father, so fill my heart with Your love that
nothing of my own selfishness remains. Amen.

HEALING LOVE

"If I but touch his clothes, I will be made well."

MARK 5:27–28 NRSV

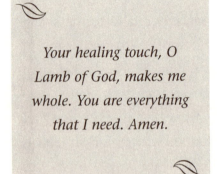

Your healing touch, O Lamb of God, makes me whole. You are everything that I need. Amen.

The God of patience, meekness, and love is the one God of my heart. The whole bent and desire of my soul is to seek for all my salvation in and through the merits and mediation of the meek, humble, patient, resigned, suffering Lamb of God. He alone has power to bring forth the blessed birth of these heavenly virtues in my soul....

What a comfort is it to think that this Lamb of God, Son of the Father, light of the world, glory of heaven, and joy of angels is as near to us—is truly in the presence of us—as He is in the presence of heaven. A desire of our heart that presses toward Him, longing to catch one small spark of His heavenly nature, is as sure of finding Him, touching Him, and drawing power from Him as the woman who was healed by longing but to touch the border of His garment.

—WILLIAM LAW

LOVING OTHERS
THROUGH PRAYER

Praise be to God, who has not rejected my
prayer or withheld his love from me!

PSALM 66:20

Are we praying as Christ did? Are our pleas and spirit the over-flow of His spirit and pleas? Does love rule the spirit—perfect love? As our great example in prayer, our Lord puts love as a primary condition—a love that has purified the heart from all the elements of hate, revenge, and ill will. Love is the supreme condition of prayer, a life inspired by love.

Answered prayer is the spring of love and is the direct encouragement to pray. A few short, feeble prayers have always been a sign of a low spiritual condition. People ought to pray much and apply themselves to it with energy and perseverance. Eminent Christians have been eminent in prayer. The deep things of God are learned nowhere else. Great things for God are done by great prayers. A person who prays much studies much, loves much, works much, and does much for God and humanity.

—E. M. BOUNDS

*Lord, I want to pray as You did, with love,
perseverance, and power. I want to be someone
who does great things through prayer! Amen.*

LOVE AND ANSWERED PRAYERS

But I pray to you, O LORD, in the time of your favor; in your great love, O God, answer me with your sure salvation.

PSALM 69:13

Almighty God is the very highest model, and to be like Him is to possess the highest character. Prayer molds us into the image of God and at the same time tends to mold others into the same image just in proportion as we pray for others. Prayer means to be Godlike, and to be Godlike is to love Christ and love God, to be one with the Father and the Son in spirit, character, and conduct.

God has much to do with believing people who have a living, transforming faith in Jesus Christ. These are God's children. A father loves his children, supplies their needs, hears their cries, and answers their requests. A child believes his father, loves him, trusts in him, and asks him for what he needs, believing without doubting that his father will hear his requests. God has everything to do with answering the prayer of His children. Their troubles concern Him, and their prayers awaken Him. Their voice is sweet to Him. He loves to hear them pray, and He is never happier than to answer their prayers.

–E. M. BOUNDS

Heavenly Father, I thank You that You love to hear my prayers to You! I am Your very precious child, and I love to spend time in Your presence. Amen.

WHY PRAY?

[Jesus said,] "'What shall we eat?' or 'What shall we drink?' or 'What shall we wear?' For the pagans run after all these things, and your heavenly Father knows that you need them."

MATTHEW 6:31–32

Some ask if God needs us as advisers. After all, if he already knows about our problems and is wise enough to know what we need, why bother to pray?…

Anyone who asks such questions does not understand why the Lord taught us to pray. It is not so much for his sake as for ours. Faithful people in the Bible were certain that God was merciful and kind. But the more they realized this, the more fervently they prayed. Elijah is one such example. He was confident that God would break a drought and send desperately needed rain. In his confidence he prayed anxiously with his face between his knees.… In no way did he doubt God would send rain. He understood that it was his duty to lay his desires before God.…

It is true that God is awake and watches over us continuously. Sometimes he will assist us even when we do not ask. But it is in our own best interest to pray constantly. When we do, we will begin to understand that it is God who is in charge. It will keep us free of evil desires because we will learn to place all our wishes in his sight. Most importantly, it will prepare us to understand that God is the giver, and we will be filled with genuine gratitude and thanksgiving.

–JOHN CALVIN

Lord, prayer does more for me than it does for You. As I spend time in Your presence, You soften my heart and turn my will to Yours. I lay all of my desires before You and submit myself to You. Amen.

THE PRAYER THAT TRANSFORMS

But we all, with unveiled face, beholding as in a mirror the
glory of the Lord, are being transformed into the same
image from glory to glory, just as by the Spirit of the Lord.

2 CORINTHIANS 3:18 NKJV

That prayer which does not succeed in moderating our wish,
in changing the passionate desire into still submission, the
anxious, tumultuous expectation into silent surrender, is no
true prayer, and proves that we have not the spirit of true
prayer. That life is most holy in which there is least of petition
and desire, and most of waiting upon God; that in which petition most often passes into thanksgiving. Pray till prayer
makes you forget your own wish, and leave it or merge it in
God's will. The Divine wisdom has given us prayer, not as a
means whereby to obtain the good things of earth, but as a
means whereby we learn to do without them; not as a means
whereby we escape evil, but as a means whereby we become
strong to meet it.

–FREDERICK W. ROBERTSON

*God, as I spend time with you in prayer,
You change me and shape me. I pray for Your
transforming power on my life today. Amen.*

NURTURING PRAYER

Very early in the morning, while it was
still dark, Jesus got up, left the house and went
off to a solitary place, where he prayed.

MARK 1:35

The proper thing is for us always to think of God and pray without ceasing. If we are not able to achieve this, we can at least set special times for prayer each day. At these designated moments we can focus entirely on God....

This is only a start, of course. We should not think of these times of prayer as a ritual. Neither do they mean we are freed from prayer at other hours of the day. Think of these moments as nothing more than a discipline for your spiritual weakness. It is a stimulation for your groggy soul. There will be times when you are under stress, times when you will be aware of others in difficulty. Immediately turn to God in prayer. Offer prayers of thanks all through the day.

When you pray, do not put any limits on God. It is not your business to tell God how to answer your prayers. This is not a time to bargain or to set conditions. Before you tell God what you want or need, ask that his will may be done. This makes your will subordinate to his.

–JOHN CALVIN

 Lord, sometimes I think my prayers should be loftier
than they are. Thank You for hearing every prayer
I make, no matter how small or simple. Amen.

JUNE 21

TEARS AND PRAYERS

The LORD says: "These people come near to me
with their mouth, and honor me with their lips,
but their hearts are far from me. Their worship
of me is made up only of rules taught by men."

ISAIAH 29:13

My mother wept faithfully to you more than mothers weep for dead children. You heard her, Lord. You heard her. Nine years were to pass. All that time this faithful widow continued her weeping and mourning. She prayed every hour. But for all her efforts, you allowed me to remain in darkness.

You gave her at least two grand assurances. In a dream, you told her that you would be with me. And through a priest, you explained to her that it was pointless to try to argue me out of my errors. I was not yet ready for instruction. I was too excited by the novelty of my heresy. "Leave him alone," he told her. "Only pray to God for him. He will discover by reading how great is his error. It is not possible that the son of these tears should perish."

—SAINT AUGUSTINE

*Lord, thank You for those who have been
faithful in prayer for me. Teach me how
to be faithful in prayer for others. Amen.*

PRAYER THAT MAKES A DIFFERENCE

I am poor and needy; may the LORD think of me. You are
my help and my deliverer; O my God, do not delay.

PSALM 40:17

If one is sure he is defenseless alone and can survive only with
God's help, that person is like the psalmist who confesses he
is poor and needy.

Make the Psalms your own. Do not sing them as verses
composed by another person. Let them be born in your own
prayers. When they come from your lips, understand that
they were not merely fulfilled temporarily when they were
first written. They are being fulfilled now in your daily life....

If you have the same attitude that the psalmist had when he
wrote or sang this poetry, you will see the meaning before you
have thought about it. The force of the words will strike you
before you have examined them with your intellect.

The Psalms express every significant religious feeling. These
words are like a mirror to our own moral experience. Once we
see this we will not hear the words nearly as much as we
perceive the meaning. Instead of being recited from memory,
they will flow from the depths of our inner being.

–JOHN CASSIAN

My pride is often in the way, Lord. I don't want to accept
assistance from anyone; I want to make it on my own.
Teach me to make the Psalms my own. Be with me as
I learn to give myself completely to You. Amen.

OBSTACLES TO PRAYER

> [Jesus said,] "Ask and it will be given to you; seek and you will find; knock and the door will be opened to you."
>
> MATTHEW 7:7

Resentment casts a cloud over your prayers. This is why Christ told us to leave our offering before the altar and first be reconciled with an enemy. If you collect injuries and resentments and think you can still pray, you would probably put water in a bucket full of holes!

Learn patience, and your prayers will be joyful....

Be careful! While attempting to heal another, you may make yourself sick. If you restrain your anger you will discover how to pray well. Anger is like an overcast day for the soul. It will destroy your prayer life.

The one who is in chains cannot run. In the same way a mind that is a slave to emotion will have a difficult time discovering genuine prayer....

When we know we are in the divine presence, negative thoughts are stilled. Our spirit is wrapped in profound tranquility. Our prayers are pure.

Much of the time, however, we struggle between prayer and disturbing thoughts. Our emotions get in the way of our prayers. Keep trying. If we knock on the door hard enough it will be opened.

−EVAGRIUS PONTICUS

I get in my own way, dear God. My emotions cloud my judgment and scatter my prayers in little pieces.
If I am not able to control myself, let Your Holy Spirit take charge. Do for me what I cannot do for myself. Amen.

THE NATURE OF PRAYER

Pray in the Spirit on all occasions
with all kinds of prayers and requests.

EPHESIANS 6:18

There are three kinds of prayer. The first is spoken prayer with a prepared text, such as the Lord's Prayer and other special prayers. It is useful to say these vocal prayers as devoutly as possible. Never say them care-

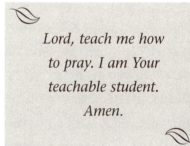

Lord, teach me how to pray. I am Your teachable student. Amen.

lessly or grudgingly. Such prayers can lift you up to God.

The second kind of prayer is spoken, but without prepared text. This is when a man or a woman feels devout and speaks to God as though they were standing together. The words match an inward stirring and reflect the various concerns of the moment. This kind of prayer pleases God. Because it comes from the heart, it never goes away without some of God's grace.

The third type of prayer is only in the heart. It is silent and brings with it great rest of body and soul. Some can pray in the heart continually, glorifying and praising God.

–WALTER HILTON

BLESSED TO BE A BLESSING

Does not the potter have the right to make
out of the same lump of clay some pottery
for noble purposes and some for common use?

ROMANS 9:21

Here is a question for the rich. How is it that you happen to be rich? Is it because God has blessed you? By what means did you receive this blessing? Is it through prayer? You prayed for riches and God gave you riches? Very well.

But answer another question. What do others, who are not rich, seek in prayer? Do they not pray the same way you do? If everyone prays for riches then it must be that your riches are not the result of your own prayers only, but also of others who have helped you pray.... It follows that since you did not receive your riches through your own prayers alone, but through the prayers of the poor, then you are obligated to relieve poverty in any way you can.

...Why does God give some a hundred and another thousands and some nothing at all? Here is the meaning. The rich are to distribute riches among the poor. Those who are rich are God's officers, God's treasurers. "It is *God,* not we, who makes things grow" (1 Corinthians 3:6, THE MESSAGE, adapted).

–HUGH LATIMER

*Lord, the problem is that none of us ever think
we are rich. But teach me to take a clear look at my
situation. Do I have anything I can share? Let me
be Your treasurer and share in Your name. Amen.*

KEEP ON PRAYING

Be joyful in hope, patient in affliction, faithful in prayer.

ROMANS 12:12

With a proper attitude toward God it will be easy to learn to persevere in prayer. We will discover ways to hold our own desires in check and wait patiently for the Lord. We can be sure he is always with us. We can be confident he actually hears our prayers even when the only immediate response is silence.

It is a mistake to be like impatient children who need instant gratification. There are times when God does not respond as quickly as we would like. This is not a time to be despondent. It does not mean that God is angry with you or indifferent toward you. This is certainly not the time to give up praying. Instead of being discouraged, keep on praying.

This perseverance in prayer is highly recommended to us in the Scripture. In Psalms we read how David and others became almost weary of praying. They complained that God was not responding to their prayers. But they understood that persistent faith was a requirement, and they continued to pray.

−JOHN CALVIN

 It may seem like a trite religious idea, Lord, but I know it is true: Sometimes Your kindest answer to my plea is "No." Or maybe, "Not yet." Thank You for whatever answer You choose to give. Amen.

SET YOUR SIGHTS HIGH

But I call to God, and the LORD saves me.

PSALM 55:16

When Jesus told us to love God with all our heart, soul, and mind, he gave us a challenging task, impossible for any of us earthlings to accomplish. Nevertheless, our Lord did tell us to love this way. His purpose (as Saint Bernard pointed out) is that we should admit our weakness and seek mercy.

When you pray, intend to make your prayer as complete and honest as you can. If you are dissatisfied with the results of your effort, do not be too angry with yourself. Do not complain that God has not given you the kind of devotion he gives others. Instead, acknowledge your weakness, consider it a valid prayer, and trust that in his mercy God will make it good....

Cry for mercy while trusting in forgiveness. There is no need to struggle. Let it go. Go on to some good work and resolve to pray better next time. Many are never able to be comfortable with the quality of their prayers. They are troubled with their thoughts for a lifetime.

—WALTER HILTON

Nothing worth doing is mastered quickly. If I want to do anything well, I must practice, practice, practice. Give me the patience to practice prayer, Lord. Keep me at it. Assure me that You are listening even when I stammer in my soul. Amen.

WHEN GOD SAYS NO

For the LORD God is our light and protector.
He gives us grace and glory.
No good thing will the LORD withhold
from those who do what is right.

PSALM 84:11 NLT

Whatsoever we ask which is not for our good, He will keep it back from us. And surely in this there is no less of love than in the granting what we desire as we ought. Will not the same love which prompts you to give a good, prompt you to keep back an evil thing? If, in our blindness, not knowing what to ask, we pray for things which would turn in our hands to sorrow and death, will not our Father, out of His very love, deny us? How awful would be our lot, if our wishes should straightway pass into realities; if we were endowed with a power to bring about all that we desire; if the inclinations of our will were followed by fulfillment of our hasty wishes, and sudden longings were always granted. One day we shall bless Him, not more for what He has granted than for what He has denied.

—H. E. MANNING

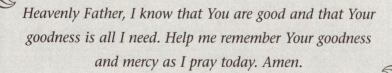

Heavenly Father, I know that You are good and that Your goodness is all I need. Help me remember Your goodness and mercy as I pray today. Amen.

ON MEDITATION

On my bed I remember you; I think of
you through the watches of the night.

PSALM 63:6

No specific rule can be given to guide everyone's meditation.
The Lord inspires a variety of meditations in a person's soul.

When one is first converted, there are strong memories of
worldly, fleshly sins.... There is a fervent seeking for mercy
and forgiveness. These sins will put a heavy weight on the
soul. A little pain here is a small price to pay for the mercy of
the Lord, who wills to forgive....

Another meditation is on the humanity of Christ.... You can
imagine being present when Jesus was arrested, bound like a
thief, beaten, and condemned to death. You can almost see
him carrying his cross. Your heart is filled with compassion....
You understand he is suffering this pain for you. Then the
Holy Spirit may open your spiritual eye and you will perceive
the divine Christ. A person ordinarily does not contemplate
Christ's divinity without first using the imagination to
perceive his humanity....

There is one thing worth doing, and that is for a person to go
into himself, to get to know his own soul and its abilities, its
fairness, and its foulness.

—WALTER HILTON

Help me to discover the reality of the spiritual life, Lord.
Show me how to clearly see my sin and Your grace
through the meditations You inspire in my soul. Amen.

LISTENING FOR GOD

It is the spirit in a man, the breath of the Almighty,
that gives him understanding.

JOB 32:8

One way God can awaken a soul is with an inner voice. This "voice" comes in many ways and is difficult to define....

There are some clues that will help you to determine if God is the source. The first and best indication is in the *power and authority* of the voice. Things are better because it was heard. Some difference is made—calmness replaces distress, for instance.

The second sign is a *peaceful tranquility* in the soul combined with an eagerness to sing praises to God.

The third sign is that the *words stick in the memory* better than ordinary conversation. There is a strong faith in the truth of what was heard....

Now if the inner voice is only the product of the imagination, none of these signs will be present. There will be no certainty, no peace, no joy.

If what you think is an "inner voice" commands an action that will have dire consequences for yourself or for others, don't do anything until you have sought competent counseling.

—TERESA OF AVILA

Let Your Holy Spirit inspire me. Make me receptive. But please, Lord God, spare me from assigning Your name to the complex thoughts, desires, and motives of my own heart. Amen.

ABUNDANT BLESSINGS

Wait for the LORD;
Be strong and take heart
and wait for the LORD.

PSALM 27:14

Dear Lord, thank You for being my Father and hearing me when I call to You. Strengthen my faith, Lord, as I seek to come to You humbly, simply needing Your provision and presence. Amen.

Our work is to lay our petitions before the Lord, and in childlike simplicity to pour out our hearts before Him, saying, "I do not deserve that You should hear me and answer my requests, but for the sake of my Precious Lord Jesus; for His sake, answer my prayer. And give me grace to wait patiently until it pleases You to grant my petition. For I believe You will do it in Your own time and way."

"For I will yet praise him" (Psalm 43:5). More prayer, more exercising of our faith, and more patient waiting leads to blessings—abundant blessings.

–L. B. COWMAN, from *Streams in the Desert*

CLEANSING PRAYER

All my longings lie open before you,
O LORD; my sighing is not hidden from you.

PSALM 38:9

Prayer is the most effective means at our disposal for the cleansing of our mind and emotions. This is because it places the mind in God's bright light and the emotions in his warm love. Prayer is like water that makes plants grow and extinguishes fires.

Best of all is silent, inward prayer, especially if it reflects upon our Lord's loving sacrifice. If you think of him frequently, he will occupy your soul. You will catch on to his manner of living and thinking. You will begin to live and think like him. It is exactly like the way children learn to talk, by listening to their mothers and then making sounds with their own voices.

There is no other way. Prayer is essential. Find an hour each day, in the morning if possible, and pray.

−FRANCIS DE SALES

 Lord, Your sacrifice has changed my life, and I pray
that You would continue that transforming work
as I pray. Please cleanse my heart and mind,
Holy Spirit, as I come to You today. Amen.

SILENT PRAYER

I will sing to the LORD all my life;
I will sing praise to my God as long as I live.
May my meditation be pleasing to him,
as I rejoice in the LORD.

PSALM 38:9

Start every prayer in the presence of God. Be strict about this and you will soon see its value. Don't rush through your prayers. The Lord's Prayer said once with comprehension is better than many prayers said in haste.

If you can do it, inward, silent prayer is best. If you are reciting a standard prayer and find your heart being drawn deeper, by all means leave the spoken prayer behind and move into silence. Don't worry about leaving your formal prayer unfinished. Your silent prayer pleases God the most, and it will be better for your soul.

Be diligent about this. Don't let a morning pass without some time in silent prayer. But if the demands of business or some other responsibility prevents it, then be sure to repair the damage that evening. Make a vow to start your regular practice of morning prayer again tomorrow.

−FRANCIS DE SALES

 Dear Lord, thank You for these thoughts on silent prayer.
Let my inner prayers take on a vibrant life. Amen.

PUTTING YOURSELF IN GOD'S PRESENCE

When Jacob awoke from his sleep, he thought, "Surely the
LORD is in this place, and I was not aware of it." He was
afraid and said, "How awesome is this place! This is none
other than the house of God; this is the gate of heaven."

GENESIS 28:16–17

Perhaps you are not able to pray silently. Many people today
are poor at this. Here is an easy way to get started. There are
several ways you can place yourself in God's presence.

Consider how God is present in all things and in all places....
Since we can't see God physically present, we need to activate
our consciousness. Before praying, we need to remind
ourselves of God's actual presence. A good way to do this is
with Bible verses. "If I go up to the heavens, you are there; if
I make my bed in the depths, you are there" (Psalm 139:8).

Remember also that God is not only where you are, he is actually in your heart, in the core of your spirit. "For in him we
live and move and have our being" (Acts 17:28)....

When you know God is present, your soul will bow before his
majesty and ask for help. "Do not cast me from your presence
or take your Holy Spirit from me" (Psalm 51:11).

–FRANCIS DE SALES

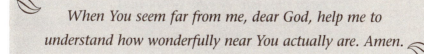

*When You seem far from me, dear God, help me to
understand how wonderfully near You actually are. Amen.*

HEAVENLY HARMONY

[Jesus prayed,] "Your kingdom come,
your will be done on earth as it is in heaven."

MATTHEW 6:10

Why did our Lord teach us to pray that? In the same way the angels in heaven live in harmony, it is desirable for us to live together. Love is shared in heaven. There is agreement. Pride does not interfere. Nothing is pretended. These are things worth praying for here and now....

"The body is a unit, though it is made up on many parts; and though all its parts are many, they form one body" (1 Corinthians 12:12). You can do your part while others perform their function. The eye sees for the entire body. The hand works and the foot walks for the whole creature. If one member suffers, all suffer.

The ones who pray, therefore, should not criticize the ones who are busy working because they are not praying. The ones who toil are not to judge the ones who are at prayer because they are not working. Let everyone do whatever they are doing for the glory of God.

—PSEUDO-MACARIUS

Spare me, dear God, from thinking that I am the only one who is doing it right. Let me value the varied contributions of others. Amen.

CHRISTIAN MEDITATION

Mary treasured up all these things and
pondered them in her heart.

LUKE 2:19

Read a passage from the Gospels. Imagine the scene as though it were actually taking place in front of you. Place yourself, for instance, at the foot of the cross. This will prevent your mind from wandering the same way a cage restricts a bird.

After your imagination has helped you prepare yourself, begin to meditate mentally. If a particular thought catches your interest, stay with it. The bees do not flit from flower to flower. They stay until they have gathered all the honey they can from each. If you find nothing after trying a particular thought, move on to the next. But don't rush the process....

Conclude your meditations with humble thanks and an offering of yourself to God. Offer prayers and then gather a devotional nosegay. Let me explain what I mean by that. When people have been strolling through a beautiful garden, they usually pick four or five flowers to take with them through the day.... When our souls have roamed in meditation through a spiritual garden, we can choose two or three ideas that seemed most helpful and think about them occasionally all day long.

−FRANCIS DE SALES

 Lord God, I know that simplicity is possible. Father, please give me a single-minded focus on You. Amen.

KEEPING PRAYER FOCUSED

"Lord, teach us to pray."

LUKE 11:1

> *Lord, I don't know what to ask of You. You know what I need. You love me better than I love myself. Give Your child what he doesn't know how to request.*
> *Amen.*

Nothing is more essential for the Christian, or more neglected, than prayer. Most people are not excited about praying. They find it a tiring ritual that they like to keep as short as possible. Even when we are led to prayer by responsibilities or anxieties, our prayers are often dull and ineffective.

Many words are unnecessary. To pray is to say, "Not my will, but yours be done" (Luke 22:42). To pray is to lift up your heart to God, to be sorry for your weakness, to regret your constant stumbling. Prayer of this kind requires no special formula. You don't even have to stop doing whatever it is that is keeping you busy. All that is needed is a movement of the heart toward God and a desire that what you are doing may be done for his glory.

–FRANÇOIS DE FÉNELON

SIMPLICITY IN PRAYER

And when you pray, do not keep on babbling
like pagans, for they think they will be heard because
of their many words. Do not be like them, for your
Father knows what you need before you ask him.

MATTHEW 6:7–8

Many words in our prayer come from our flesh. Our prayer may be long-drawn-out with many words which are not real or effective. Frequently, in our time of prayer we circle around the world several times, using up time and energy without

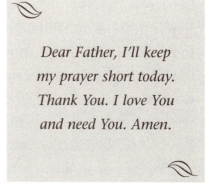

Dear Father, I'll keep my prayer short today. Thank You. I love You and need You. Amen.

obtaining any answer to real prayer. Though you have prayed much, your prayer will not be answered nor will it be effective. You simply expend your time and strength ill-advisedly. Prayer need not be too long. There is no necessity to insert many speeches into it. Be careful lest you have too much argument in your prayer. We need only to present our heart desire before God. That alone is enough. We should not add many other things to it.

–ANDREW MURRAY

WE ALL NEED PRAYER

Jehoshaphat was alarmed by this news and sought the
Lord for guidance. He also gave orders that everyone
throughout Judah should observe a fast.

LUKE 11:1

You may complain that you have little interest in prayer, that it
bores you, that your mind wanders when you attempt to pray.

It may be more difficult for those who are engaged in business
to pray and meditate than for those who live in monasteries,
but it is also far more necessary. Take some time out to be with
God. Notice how Jesus invited his disciples to a mountain
retreat after they had returned from witnessing for him in the
cities. If we live and work in a busy place where people talk
and behave as though there were no God, it is all the more
important that we return to him and restore our faith and
love. If he who was without sin prayed without ceasing, how
much more should poor sinners like us work at it?

When you pray, ask for what you will with firm faith. If you
are not confident when you pray, little will come of it. God
loves the heart that trusts in him. He will never ignore those
who place their complete trust in him. It is like a father listening to his child.

–FRANÇOIS DE FÉNELON

*Lord, sometimes it is a challenge for me to sit down to
pray. But I know that I absolutely cannot live a life that
pleases You without prayer. Increase my faith, Lord God,
and help me seek You through prayer. Amen.*

PRAYER AND THE DENIAL OF SELF

Do nothing out of selfish ambition or vain conceit,
but in humility consider others better than yourselves.

PHILIPPIANS 2:3

The self wants to be excited, entertained, gratified, coddled, reassured, rewarded, challenged, indulged. There are people on hand to manipulate and market those impulses by seduction and persuasion.

The American self characteristically chooses advertisers instead of apostles as guides. Self-assertion is, in fact, a euphemism for a way of life dominated by impulse and pressure. The self is alternately moved from within by whatever occurs in the emotions and glands, from without by whatever is presented by fashion and fad. As we become practiced in prayer we are unmoved by such bagatelles.

Lord, I know that I need Your Holy Spirit to enable me to really die to self. As I persevere in prayer, I ask You to change me, shape me, and guide me, Lord. Amen.

—EUGENE H. PETERSON, from *Where Your Treasure Is*

SHIFTING GEARS

My heart grew hot within me, and as I meditated,
the fire burned; then I spoke with my tongue:
"Show me, O LORD, my life's end and the number
of my days; let me know how fleeting is my life."

PSALM 39:3-4

After a time of meditation, immediately begin to put into practice the resolutions you have made. Don't wait another day to get started. Without this application, meditation may be useless or even detrimental. Meditate on a virtue without practicing it, and you will mislead yourself into believing that you have actually become someone you are not....

When your silent prayer is over, remain still and quiet for a few moments. Make your transition to other responsibilities gradually. Linger yet a while in the garden. Walk carefully along the path through the gate so that you won't spill the precious balm you are carrying. Don't be unnatural around other people, but keep as much prayer in you as you can.

There is an art to making the transition from prayer to earning a living. A lawyer must go from prayer to the court-room, the merchant to the store, a homemaker to appointed responsibilities with a gentle motion that will not cause distress. Both prayer and your other duties are gifts from God.

—FRANCIS DE SALES

 Someday, perhaps, O Lord, my work and my prayer life will blend. For now, I simply ask that the one will benefit the other. Amen.

CAN PRAYER BE PUT INTO WORDS?

Evening and morning and at noon I will pray,
and cry aloud, and He shall hear my voice.

PSALM 55:17 NKJV

It is best for a soul not to attempt to rise by its own efforts. If the well is dry, we are not able to put water into it. Pay attention to this. If the soul tries to go forward, it may actually go backward. The foundation for prayer is humility. The nearer we come to God, the more humility we need. There is a kind of pride that makes us want to be more spiritual. God is already doing more for us than we deserve.

When I say that people should not attempt to rise unless they are raised by God, I am using spiritual language. Some will understand me. If you can't understand what I am saying, I don't know another way to explain it.

I am sorry for those who begin with only books. There is a big difference between understanding something and knowing it through experience. I have read many religious books that deal with these matters. They explain very little. If one's soul has not already accumulated some practice in prayer, books are not much help.

—TERESA OF AVILA

My Lord, I know that You hear my words and
hear the heart behind them. I know that the "work"
of prayer is merely to direct myself toward You.
Be with me now as I sit down for prayer. Amen.

PRAYING TO OUR FATHER

Praise the LORD, I tell myself;
with my whole heart, I will praise his holy name....
The LORD is like a father to his children,
tender and compassionate to those who fear him.

PSALM 103:1, 13 NLT

Lord, I know this is the real purpose of prayer: to know You more deeply as my Father. God, please take away my anxiety about how to pray—remind me of what it means to live as Your child. Amen.

The goal of the believer is not just to be a Christian but to cultivate an intimate, devoted relationship with the heavenly Father.

God wants you to know Him; to enjoy Him; to live continually in the light of His favor, wisdom, and truth. He desires a genuine relationship with you, His child. Daily worship and prayer are the spiritual closet where you and the Father are drawn into personal intimacy. There, God's love for you and your love for Him become the bedrock of your faith.

—CHARLES STANLEY

QUIET INSPIRATION

After the earthquake came a fire, but the LORD was not
in the fire. And after the fire came a gentle whisper.

1 KINGS 19:12

The Scriptures say without hesitation that God's Spirit lives in us, gives us life, speaks to us in silence, inspires us, and that it is so much a part of us that we are *united* with the Lord in spirit. This is basic Christian teaching.

The Spirit of God is the soul of our soul! We are blind if we think that we are alone in the interior sanctuary. God is actually more present in this place than we are. We are constantly inspired, but we suppress the inspiration. God is always speaking to us, but the external noise of the world and the internal churning of our passions confuse us. We can't hear him speaking. Everything around us needs to be silent, and we must be quiet within. We need to focus our entire being to hear his soft whisper of a voice. The only ones who hear it are those who listen to nothing else.

—FRANÇOIS DE FÉNELON

I am quiet right now, Lord. Before I turn away
from this page, I pause to listen. Amen.

PRAYING THE WORD

For whatever things were written before were written
for our learning, that we through the patience and
comfort of the Scriptures might have hope.

ROMANS 15:4 NKJV

Prayer is a conversation. We speak to God in prayer then listen attentively as He speaks to us through His Word....

One major prerequisite to receiving answers to prayer is that our requests line up with God's will. How will we know what God's will is? By abiding consistently in His Word. Instead of basing our prayers on "I hope so," our prayers are based on "God says so." And if we are saturating ourselves in His Word, then His desires will be ours.

–ANNE GRAHAM LOTZ, from *My Heart's Cry*

Lord, I know the way to know Your heart is to read Your Word and pray to You. Lord, please be with me as I search the Scriptures for a word from You— and please be with me as I seek to study Your Word every day. I want to hear Your voice, Lord God. Amen.

PLEADING GOD'S PROMISES

Then King David went in and sat before the
Lord and prayed …"And now, O Lord, do as you
have promised concerning me and my family.
May it be a promise that will last forever."

1 CHRONICLES 17:1, 23 NLT

Often we ask for things that God has not specifically promised. Therefore we are not sure if our petitions are in line with His purpose, until we have persevered for some time in prayer. Yet on some occasions, and this was one in the life of David, we are fully persuaded that what we are asking is in accordance with God's will. We

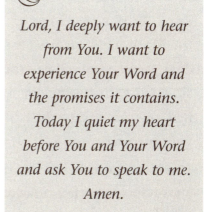

Lord, I deeply want to hear from You. I want to experience Your Word and the promises it contains. Today I quiet my heart before You and Your Word and ask You to speak to me. Amen.

feel led to select and plead a promise from the pages of Scripture, having been specially impressed that it contains a message for us. At these times, we may say with confident faith, "Do as You promised."

—L. B. COWMAN, from *Streams in the Desert*

TAKING GOD SERIOUSLY

Thou tellest my wanderings: put thou my tears
into thy bottle: are they not in thy book?

PSALM 56:8 KJV

God is in earnest with you. Why are you not so with him?
Why trifle with God? Jesus was serious in his work for us. He
was so distracted with teaching that he forgot to eat and
drink. In prayer, he continued all night. In doing good, his
friends thought he was obsessed. In suffering, he fasted forty
days, was tempted, betrayed, spit upon, buffeted, and
crowned with thorns; he sweated drops of blood, was crucified, pierced, and he died. Shouldn't you be serious in seeking
your own salvation?

The Holy Spirit is serious in wanting you to be happy. He is
always at work. He is grieved when you resist him. Shouldn't
we be serious in obeying and yielding to his motions?

God is serious in hearing our prayers and giving us his mercies.
God is afflicted with us. He regards every groan and sigh....

The servants of the world and the devil are serious and diligent.... Don't you have a better master and sweeter employment, greater encouragement and a better reward?

–RICHARD BAXTER

*Christ assures me of Your intimate interest, O God. You are
aware of falling sparrows and falling tears. Help me to respond
to Your interest in me by showing interest in You. Amen.*

CELEBRATE GOD

Enter into His gates with thanksgiving,
And into His courts with praise.
Be thankful to Him, and bless His name.
For the Lord is good;
His mercy is everlasting,
And His truth endures to all generations.

PSALM 100:4–5 NKJV

The wisdom and doctrine of Scripture teach that the experience of celebrating God is the core of worship. It is the quintessence of praise and thanksgiving—the most perfect manifestation of a heart that gratefully fellowships with the One who provides life and all the gifts of living. In fact, a grateful heart is not only the greatest virtue, it is the seed bed for all other virtues. When we are caught up in the celebration of God there is neither room nor time for the invasion of negative living. As we rejoice before the Lord, as we serve Him in the area of our calling, as we enter joyfully into our daily journey, as we give thanks to Him for His kindness and faithfulness, we celebrate God.

–LUCI SWINDOLL, from *You Bring the Confetti*

God, there is nothing in the world that warrants
a celebration more than You. Thank You for
Your saving work in my life and the world.
Thank You for Your goodness and glory. Amen.

PRAYER BEYOND PRAYER

[Jesus said,] "When you pray, don't be like those show-offs
who love to stand up and pray in the meeting places and
on the street corners. They do this just to look good.
I can assure you that they already have their reward."

MATTHEW 6:5 CEV

Whether you are praying with others or alone, try to make your prayer more than routine. Desire it to be an authentic spiritual experience. If your spirit is distracted during a time of prayer, then you are not really getting into it. You are like a business executive doing a little puttering in the garden.

Keep a tight leash on your memory when you pray. Do not allow it to suggest fanciful things to you. Let it carry an awareness of reaching out to God. Be constantly aware that your memory has a strong tendency to trouble your spirit during a time of prayer. You will recall all kinds of distressing events that will stir your passions. These passions are irrational. When they burn, you are not free to pray.

Suppose you do not have any disturbing emotions. You still may not actually engage in prayer. It is possible to have only the purest thoughts and remain far from God.

If you want to pray, you need God. God will turn ordinary prayer into exceptional prayer. He will take you beyond praising him for *what he does* to praising him for *who he is*.

–EVAGRIUS PONTICUS

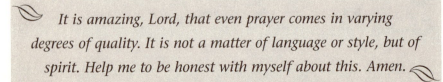

*It is amazing, Lord, that even prayer comes in varying
degrees of quality. It is not a matter of language or style, but of
spirit. Help me to be honest with myself about this. Amen.*

DEVOTIONAL DIVERSITY

There is a time for everything, and
a season for every activity under heaven.

ECCLESIASTES 3:1

Some people believe that devotion will slip away from them if they relax a little. Recreation is good for the soul. We will be stronger when we return to prayer.

Do not spend all of your time in one method of prayer. You may have found an excellent method of prayer that you really enjoy. Maybe you need a kind of Sunday. I mean a time of rest from your spiritual labor.

You think you would lose something if you stop working at prayer. My view is that your loss would be gain. Try to imagine yourself in the presence of Christ. Talk with him. Delight in him. There is no need to weary yourself by composing speeches to him.

There is a time for one thing and a time for another. The soul can become weary of eating the same food over and over again. There is a great variety of food that is wholesome and nutritious. If your spiritual palate becomes familiar with their various tastes, they will sustain the life of your soul, bringing many benefits.

—TERESA OF AVILA

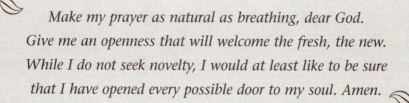

Make my prayer as natural as breathing, dear God.
Give me an openness that will welcome the fresh, the new.
While I do not seek novelty, I would at least like to be sure
that I have opened every possible door to my soul. Amen.

PRAYER IS LIFE

Pray continually.

1 THESSALONIANS 5:17

Prayer is the heart of Christian life. It is essential. Prayer is both the first step and the fulfillment of the devout life. We are directed to pray always. Particular times may be set for other acts of devotion, but for prayer there is no special time. We are to pray constantly.

Sit alone in a quiet place. Take your mind away from every earthly and vain thing. Bow your head to your chest and be attentive, not to your head, but to your heart. Observe your breathing. Let your mind find the place of the heart. At first you will be uncomfortable. If you continue without interruption, it will become a joy.

The most wonderful result of this kind of mental silence is that sinful thoughts that come knocking at the door of the mind are turned away. Pray and think what you will. Pray and do what you want. Your thoughts and activity will be purified by prayer.

–ANONYMOUS RUSSIAN

*Fully conscious, O God, let me be as aware of Your
presence as I am of the ground beneath my feet.
Let my life be continually lifted to You,
infused by You, in prayer. Amen.*

THE PRAYER OF ABBA'S CHILD

So you should not be like cowering, fearful slaves.
You should behave instead like God's very own children,
adopted into his family—calling him "Father, dear Father."
For his Holy Spirit speaks to us deep in our hearts
and tells us that we are God's children.

ROMANS 8:15–16 NLT

The prayer of the poor in spirit can simply be a single word: Abba. Yet that word can signify dynamic interaction. Imagine a little boy trying to help his father with some household work, or making his mother a gift. The help may be nothing more than getting in the way, and the gift may be totally useless, but the love behind it is simple and pure, and the loving response it evokes is virtually uncontrollable. I am sure it is this way between our Abba and us.... Our sincere desire counts far more than any specific success or failure. Thus when we try to pray and cannot, or when we fail in a sincere attempt to be compassionate, God touches us tenderly in return.

–BRENNAN MANNING, from *The Ragamuffin Gospel*

Lord, thank You that You take joy in the simple, unpolished praise and prayers of Your children. Help me rest in Your love, Lord, so that I can worship You more freely. Amen.

CONFIDENT, HUMBLE PRAYER

> [Jesus said,] "Therefore I tell you, whatever
> you ask for in prayer, believe that you have
> received it, and it will be yours."
>
> MARK 11:24

Even the humblest prayer is to be prayed with confidence that God will answer. Be sure you will succeed. There is no contradiction between humility and confidence. They are in perfect harmony with each other, like repentance and faith.

This confidence is not a soothing freedom from anxiety. The saints did their best praying when they were stimulated by difficulties and driven to despair. It is precisely when they are in turbulent times that faith comes to help them. It is while they groan in the agony of some calamity that the goodness of God shines upon them. In fearful times they trust God.

It is important, then, for a believer's prayer to be the product of both feelings....

God often declares that he will give to us in proportion to our faith. The logical conclusion is that we receive nothing without faith. Everything that results from prayer is obtained by faith.

–JOHN CALVIN

*I am sure, O God, that the faith referred to here
must be genuine faith. It is not a mere clutching
at straws, but faith that sees results. I pray that
You would nurture that faith in me. Amen.*

PRAYING NATURALLY

In all my prayers for all of you, I always pray with joy.

PHILIPPIANS 1:4

Prayer is a longing, a desire of the spirit toward God. It is like someone who is sick longing for health.

Faith prays constantly. The spirit is always attentive to the will of God and knows its own fragility. It also remembers the infirmities of others, understanding that there is no strength and no help anywhere other than in God. A neighbor's grief is no less than your own.

Suppose someone who is weak in the faith asks for your prayers. Lead such a person to the truth and promises of God. Teach that person how to trust God.

If you give me a thousand dollars and ask me to pray for you, I am no more bound than I was before. I could not pray more for you if you gave me all the world. If I see a need, I pray. I can't help praying when God's Spirit is in me.

—WILLIAM TYNDALE

Let prayer become a natural thing for me, dear God.
Let it flow like a river between us. Let it hum with
the energy of a soul that is awake. Let it glow
with the light of Your divine presence. Let it securely
anchor my life. Let it radiate to others. Amen.

PRAYING THE PSALMS

Because your love is better than life,
my lips will glorify you.

PSALM 63:3

The book of Psalms is a compilation of prayers that were meant to be prayed aloud. They are a tremendous comfort to those of you who feel you're not ready yet to open your mouth in prayer. You may feel your words won't sound good enough. You'll see that there is nothing polished or refined about the language in the Psalms prayers. They are sometimes whiny, happy, confused, faltering, repetitious, and uncertain. In other words, the Psalms use real words to express real emotion. You can literally pray the Psalms to God. Choose one, then read it aloud to God as your expression to Him. In time, doing so will not feel awkward. You will find your own spirit uniting with the spirit of the words as if you had written them yourself.

–MARILYN MEBERG, from *Assurance for a Lifetime*

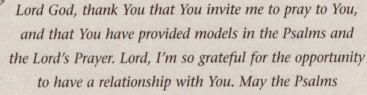

Lord God, thank You that You invite me to pray to You,
and that You have provided models in the Psalms and
the Lord's Prayer. Lord, I'm so grateful for the opportunity
to have a relationship with You. May the Psalms
draw me nearer to You today, Lord God. Amen.

MORNING PRAYER

In the morning, O LORD, you hear my voice; in the morning
I lay my requests before you and wait in expectation.

PSALM 5:3

There are some useful short kinds of prayer. One of them is morning prayer. It is a way to prepare for the day's activities. Here is how it is done.

Begin by really adoring God. Thank him for preserving you through the night. Acknowledge that this day is given to you as another opportunity to prepare for eternity.

Look for chances to serve God today.... Resolve to make the best of every opportunity to serve God and increase devotion that comes your way. Prepare carefully to avoid, resist, and overcome harmful things. It is not enough simply to resolve to do this. Make a plan of action....

Then be humble before God. Admit that you can't do any of this on your own. Offer all of your good intentions to God, as though you were holding out your heart in your hands. Ask him to be involved in your plans for the day.

These prayerful thoughts should be taken care of quickly in the morning, before you leave your bedroom. God will bless your day.

−FRANCIS DE SALES

*Lord, here is my wretched heart. With Your inspiration it
has made some good plans, but it is too weak to accomplish
what it wants. Give Your blessing through Christ, in whose name
I dedicate today and all the remaining days of my life. Amen.*

FAN THE FLAME

O God, you are my God,
earnestly I seek you;
my soul thirsts for you,
my body longs for you,
in a dry and weary land where there is no water.

PSALM 63:1

Dear Father, sometimes I get so caught up in the discipline of prayer that my heart really isn't in it. Today, I pray that You would reignite my love for You and the joy I find in Your presence. Amen.

I have a certain place where I like to pray every morning. That's the first place I go, and it is of primary importance to me that I spend time with God. But even prayer can become a work of the flesh if I pray only out of habit rather than honestly desiring God's direction.

We will miss out on an intimate relationship with God if we make prayer a work of the flesh.... We know we are being led of the Spirit when we *want* to pray, when we *want* to study the Word, and when we *want* to receive God's discipline. True joy is found when we can feel the touch of God on our plans.

–JOYCE MEYER, from *Seven Things That Steal Your Joy: Overcoming the Obstacles to Your Happiness*

LEARNING HOW TO PRAY

But you, when you pray, go into your room,
and when you have shut the door, pray to
your Father who is in the secret place; and your
Father who sees in secret will reward you openly.

MATTHEW 6:6 NKJV

Jesus …told the disciples, "When you pray, go into your room" (Matthew 6:6). He was counteracting the Pharisees' habit of praying in public for show so they would be noticed. The preface to prayer is humility. It is best when unnoticed by others.

Jesus also instructed them that words repeatedly said doesn't guarantee they are being heard (Matthew 6:7). Unrehearsed prayers tend to be more real and honest. Structure stifles spontaneity. We speak the Lord's name and come into His presence. "Your Father sees and hears your prayers and will reward you," Jesus said. When we pray, we do so in the authority of Jesus' name. We must remember that our only access in prayer is in the name of Jesus and not in the merit of the act of our praying.

–FRANKLIN GRAHAM, from *All for Jesus*

Lord Jesus, You are such a wonderful Teacher.
Thank You for teaching me to pray. Please help
me practice Your teaching today. Amen.

THIRSTING AFTER RIGHTEOUSNESS

Blessed are those who hunger and thirst for righteousness,
For they shall be filled.

MATTHEW 5:6 NKJV

Someone once said, "Any discussion on the doctrine of prayer which does not issue in the practice of prayer is not only *not* helpful, but harmful." It is true. If God is speaking to you, you must pray.

First, single out the spiritual qualities which you would like to cultivate. In reference to the Beatitudes, it may be poverty of spirit or meekness or purity of heart. Write them on your prayer list and begin to regularly pray.

Second, as you pray, pray persistently—asking, seeking, and knocking. Seek them with all your being.

Third, know this: that you *will* receive them. And they will be better than you have dreamed, because your Heavenly Father will give them to you. You will be blessed, because He will call you "blessed."

—R. KENT HUGHES, from *Blessed Are the Born Again*

Lord God, I know that You reward and answer those who diligently seek You. Today I rejoice in the confidence that You will bless me and make me what You want me to be, Lord. Amen.

THE LIMITS OF PRAYER

This is the confidence we have in approaching God: that if
we ask anything according to his will, he hears us.

1 JOHN 5:14

Our prayers are to be confined to what God permits.
Although he invites us to "pour out [our] hearts to him"
(Psalm 62:8), God does not extend it carte blanche. He does
not give us a limitless range of foolish and depraved ideas.
When he promises to give us what we wish, this does not
include nonsense and caprice.

It happens all the time. Many pray to God about frivolous
things. They have neither modesty nor reverence.... They are
so crass that they stupidly bring their follies to God when
they would blush to tell someone else what they were thinking about....

The solution to all this is for our heart to gain the same affection for God as our mind has. To help us with this, God's
Spirit guides our prayers. He can tell us what is right. He can
regulate our desires. "The Spirit helps us in our weakness. We
do not know what we ought to pray for, but the Spirit himself
intercedes for us with groans that words cannot express"
(Romans 8:26). God stimulates good prayer. Correct prayer is
a gift from God.

–JOHN CALVIN

Help me, O Lord, to pray as You
would have me to pray. Amen.

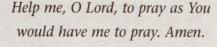

TINY PRAYERS

"Well done, my good servant!" his master replied.
"Because you have been trustworthy in a very
small matter, take charge of ten cities."

LUKE 19:17

Make frequent, short little prayers to God. Express your appreciation for his beauty. Ask him to help you. Fall at the foot of the cross. Love his goodness. Give your soul to him a thousand times a day. Stretch out your hand to him like a child. If such prayerful, intimate thoughts become habitual, you will gain a beautiful familiarity with God....

On one very clear night a devout person stood by a brook watching the sky. The stars were reflected in the water. That person said, "O my God, in the same way the stars of heaven are reflected here on earth, so are we on earth reflected in heaven." Saint Francis knelt in prayer beside such a beautiful brook and became enraptured. "God's grace flows as gently and sweetly as this little stream." Another saint watched a mother hen gather little chickens under her. He said, "Lord, keep us all under the shadow of your wings."

Many little prayers like this can make up for the lack of all other prayers. They are essential. Without them rest is mere idleness and labor is pure drudgery.

—FRANCIS DE SALES

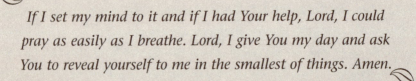

If I set my mind to it and if I had Your help, Lord, I could pray as easily as I breathe. Lord, I give You my day and ask You to reveal yourself to me in the smallest of things. Amen.

SECRET PRAYER

[Jesus said,] "When you pray, go into your room, close
the door and pray to your Father, who is unseen."

MATTHEW 6:6

Sometimes we need a place to come together for group prayer....

But we need a secret place of prayer. This will keep us from showing off. It leaves us free to use any words we please. If we want to make gestures that increase our devotion no one else will know.

Go boldly to God. He desires your prayers and has commanded you to pray. He promises to hear you, not because you are good but because he is good.

It is false prayer that Christ condemns. The tongue and the lips are busy, the body itself may be in pain, but the heart is not talking with God. It feels no sweetness at all. It has no confidence in God's promises....

There is no greater labor in the world than false prayer. When the body is compelled, and the heart unwilling, when everything is against it, then it will hurt. True prayer comforts and encourages. The body, though it were half dead, revives and is strong again. Even if many minutes pass, it seems short and easy.

—WILLIAM TYNDALE

*Alone with You, O God, I
close my mouth and listen.
Enlighten me. Inform and
edify me. Assure me that
You know what I need even
before I ask. Amen.*

A SPECIAL PRAYER

Hasten, O God, to save me; O LORD, come quickly to help me.

PSALM 70:1

This verse from Psalm 70 fits every mood and disposition of human nature. It covers every temptation and every situation. It contains an appeal to God, a plain disclosure of faith, a reverent anticipation, a contemplation on our weakness, a trusting in God's answer, and an assurance of God's providence....

Whatever the condition of our spiritual life, we need to use this verse. It reminds us that we need God to help us in both prosperity and suffering, in happiness and sorrow. Our frail nature cannot survive in either state without God's help....

I can quote this verse as an effective prayer ...for every imaginable situation. Maybe ...I am tempted to anger, selfishness, sex, pride, egotism, or criticism. To stop these devilish suggestions I can cry aloud, "Hasten, O God, to save me; O Lord, come quickly to help me!"

Pray this prayer all the time. In adversity it asks for deliverance. In prosperity it seeks security without puffed-up pride. Meditate on it. Keep it turning over in your mind. Let sleep catch you thinking about this verse until at last you pray it in your dreams.

–JOHN CASSIAN

Whatever my situation, O Lord, let me seek
Your assistance. Whether I am desperate or
comfortable, let me turn to You. Amen.

PRAYER IN A TIME OF TROUBLE

May the LORD answer you when you are in distress.

PSALM 20:1

It is important to pray in a time of extreme need. I know about this. Whenever I have prayed with passion, I have been heard. I have received more than I prayed for. Sometimes there was a delay, but the answer always came.

Prayer is a potent thing! God welcomes our prayers. There is no reason for us to hesitate. Trusting Christ's promises, we can pray with the assurance that God hears and answers.

God wants us to pray when we are in trouble. He may hide himself a little. We will have to go looking for him. Christ says, "Ask and it will be given to you; seek and you will find; knock and the door will be opened to you" (Matthew 7:7). If we intend to come to God, we must knock and then knock some more. We need to continue with much knocking at God's door.

–MARTIN LUTHER

I know I should pray all the time, giving You thanks for my blessings and remembering the needs of others. It often seems like prayer is hard work. But I am grateful to You, Lord, that when I am in difficulty, prayer comes naturally for me. It's clear I need balance in my prayer life. Give me equal fervor in every kind of prayer. Amen.

CAST YOUR BURDENS ON THE LORD

Give all your worries and cares to God,
for he cares about what happens to you.

1 PETER 5:7 NLT

Lord, thank You that You invite me to cast my burdens on You. I give You the things that are weighing on my mind today, and I ask You to take them from my hands. Amen.

Whatsoever it is that presses thee, go tell thy Father; put over the matter into His hand, and so thou shalt be freed from that dividing, perplexing care that the world is full of. When thou art either to do or suffer anything, when thou art about any purpose or business, go tell God of it, and acquaint Him with it; yea, burden Him with it, and thou hast done for the matter of caring; no more care, but quiet, sweet diligence in thy duty, and dependence on Him for the carriage of all thy matters. Roll thy cares, and thyself with them, as one burden, on thy God.

−R. LEIGHTON

REQUESTS FOR PRAYER

Jesus answered them, "It is not the healthy
who need a doctor, but the sick."

LUKE 5:31

When people ask you to remember someone in prayer, they will often say, "This is such a nice person!" That is like taking someone who is ill to the doctor and saying, "Make him well because he is so healthy!" Maybe what they mean by the "nice person" idea is that there may be a little hope for that individual's salvation.

Sometimes they will say, "Pray for so-and-so because this person has done good things on your behalf." I would prefer to pray for someone who has done me wrong. Such a person actually needs my prayers.

It is a good thing to pray for anyone who confesses and asks for forgiveness. It is even better to pray for someone who does not yet feel guilty about anything. Ask God to help them notice their sin. And pray also for those who know they are guilty but will not admit it. Maybe they are ashamed. Maybe they are actually enjoying their guilt. Ask God to help them.

–GUIGO I

Lord Jesus, You instruct us to pray for our enemies. You tell us to forgive those who have sinned against us. You want us to pray for those who persecute us. What a prayer list You give us! Here I am ready to ask for all the things I want for my loved ones. Help me to get my priorities straight. Then maybe I will be ready to love those who love me in a new light. Amen.

OFFERING OURSELVES

Joseph and Mary took [Jesus] to Jerusalem to present him to the Lord ...and to offer a sacrifice in keeping with what is said in the Law of the Lord: "a pair of doves or two young pigeons."

LUKE 2:22,24

It is only when we finally abandon ourselves to God that we realize that everything up to then was separation from God.

What will matter when I am no longer of any concern to myself? I will think less about what happens to me and more about God. His will be done. That is sufficient. If enough self-interest remains to complain about it, I have offered an incomplete sacrifice.

It isn't easy. Old ways of thinking and behaving do not vanish at once. Every now and then they spring back to life. I begin to mutter, "I didn't deserve such treatment! The charges are false and unfair! ...God is punishing me too severely! I expected some help from those good people, but they are ignoring me! God has forsaken me!"

Weak and trembling soul, soul of little faith, do you want something other than what God wills? Do you belong to him or to yourself? Renounce the miserable self in you. Cut every string. Now you are getting down to the business of sacrifice. Anything less is child's play. There is no other way your two doves can be offered to God.

O Jesus, I offer myself in order to be with You. Give me the courage I need to completely renounce myself. Lord, it is truly nothing to lose luxury, fame, money, life. Enable me to lose myself in You. Amen.

—FRANÇOIS DE FÉNELON

A DARING PRAYER

Therefore, brothers, since we have confidence to enter the
Most Holy Place by the blood of Jesus, …let us draw near
to God with a sincere heart in full assurance of faith.

HEBREWS 10:19, 22

I had some fun with God today! I dared to complain to him.
I said:

Explain to me, please, why you keep me in this miserable life.
Why do I have to put up with it? Everything here interferes
with my enjoyment of you. I have to eat and sleep and work
and talk with everyone. I do it all for the love of you, but it
torments me.

And how is it that when there is a little break and I can have
some time with you, you hide from me? … I honestly believe,
Lord, that if it were possible for me to hide from you the way
you hide from me, you would not allow it. But you are with
me and see me always. Stop this, Lord! It hurts me because I
love you so much.

I said these and other things to God. Sometimes love becomes
foolish and doesn't make a lot of sense. The Lord puts up with
it. May so good a king be praised! We wouldn't dare say these
things to earthly kings!

—TERESA OF AVILA

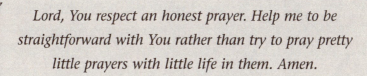

*Lord, You respect an honest prayer. Help me to be
straightforward with You rather than try to pray pretty
little prayers with little life in them. Amen.*

FACING THE DAY AHEAD

He is like the light of morning at sunrise on a cloudless morning,
like the brightness after rain that brings the grass from the earth.

2 SAMUEL 23:4

When you begin the day, think about your insensitivity to
God. Remember that he is constantly calling you and that
you need to respond.

Think about your forgetfulness of your high value to God
and how "your body is a temple of the Holy Spirit"
(1 Corinthians 6:19).

Say to your soul, "Let's get going! Follow God. Make good
plans and pursue them. Live in a manner that will please God.
Consider this day's work an assignment from God."

*Lord, distractions lie in
wait all around me, keeping
me from focusing on You.
And by the end of the day
I am tired, sometimes
battered, and always
admitting that I have had
a difficult time thinking
of Your glory and trying
to help others. Lord,
help me. Amen.*

Pray for God's help. Ask him to
give you the ability to make
the most profitable use of your
opportunities.

Begin well and go on to better.

Do everything for the glory of
God and the benefit of others.

Consider time lost if you do
not use it to at least think of
the glory of God and seek for a
way to do something for
someone else's advantage.

—JOHN BRADFORD

GLORIFYING THE FATHER

And I will do whatever you ask in my name, so that
the Son may bring glory to the Father. You may ask
me for anything in my name, and I will do it.

JOHN 14:13–14

"That the Father may be glorified in the Son": It is to this end that Jesus on His throne in glory will do everything we ask in His Name. Every answer to prayer He gives will have this as its object. When there is no prospect of this object being obtained, He will not answer. It follows as a matter of course that with us, as with Jesus, this must be the essential element in our petitions. The glory of the Father must be the aim—the very soul and life—of our prayer.

Dear Lord, it amazes me that You promise to answer prayer offered in Your name. Father, may my life and prayers never cease to glorify You. Amen.

–ANDREW MURRAY

RECOVERY

The LORD is good, a refuge in times of trouble.
He cares for those who trust in him.

NAHUM 1:7

Take your problems promptly to God. He could help you much faster if you were not so slow in turning to prayer, but you try everything else first.

Now that you have caught your breath and your trouble has passed, recuperate in God's mercies. God is near you to repair all damage and to make things better than before. Is anything too hard for God? Where is your faith? Stand strong in God. Have patience and courage. Comfort will come in time. Wait. He will come to you with healing.

Are you anxious about the future? What will that gain you but sorrow? "Do not worry about tomorrow, for tomorrow will worry about itself. Each day has enough trouble of its own" (Matthew 6:34).

Lord Jesus, You did not send Your disciples out into the world to enjoy earthly pleasures, but to do battle; not to receive honor, but to receive contempt; not to be idle, but to work; not to rest, but, in patience, to reap a harvest. Lord, give me strength to do Your will today. Amen.

…When you think you are far from God, he is really quite near. When you feel that all is lost, sometimes the greatest gain is ready to be yours. Don't judge everything by the way you feel right now. If, for a while, you feel no comfort from God, he has not rejected you. He has set you on the road to the kingdom of heaven.

—THOMAS À KEMPIS

PLANNING WITH PRAYER

Trust in the LORD with all your heart,
And lean not on your own understanding;
In all your ways acknowledge Him,
And He shall direct your paths.

PROVERBS 3:5–6 NKJV

Have you ever considered that the Lord can cause any storm in your life to blow you to the place where He intends for you to arrive? Many of us think that it is up to us to decide where we are going to be five years from now, or even that it is up to us to decide exactly what we are going to do tomorrow, next week, or next year. If we claim Jesus as our Lord, then those decisions are up to Him, not us. We can make plans, and we are wise to do so, but our plans must always be the result of prayer and made with total flexibility that if this is not what God desires for us to do, we will be quick to alter our course.

Dear Lord, there are so many things I'd like to do— and so many things I have to get done. God, as I make my plans, I pray for Your guidance, for Your blessing. I commit my way to You, O Lord. Amen.

–CHARLES STANLEY

CASTING OUR CARES

The LORD is good,
A stronghold in the day of trouble;
And He knows those who trust in Him.

NAHUM 1:7 NKJV

Did you think Jesus only cares about things like heaven and hell? About forgiveness and sin? About holiness and wickedness? About truth and lies? About salvation and judgment? Jesus does care about those things. But He also cares about your job, about whether your child makes the sports team, about your children's college tuition, about your budget now that you're unexpectedly pregnant, about the roof that leaks, about the cranky transmission in the car, and about all the other physical problems and needs we face.

Jesus cares even if the physical problem we face is largely of our own making. He cares if we are having car trouble, even if it was caused by our not having taken the time to change the oil regularly.... Jesus cares about your physical needs today.

–ANNE GRAHAM LOTZ, from *Just Give Me Jesus*

 Lord, today I'm aware of this truth: that You care for me. You know my needs, and they matter to You. Help me rest in Your love and care, confidently following You, my Shepherd. Amen.

FALSE DEVOTION

He will die for lack of discipline,
led astray by his own great folly.

PROVERBS 5:23

We are both body and spirit. God desires to be served in both. I am asking you to be careful not to think in a material way about what can only be understood spiritually.

Let me give you a simple example. What if novices read or hear about the necessity of drawing understanding into the inner self, or perhaps the importance of rising above the self. All too often this is taken literally. Abandoning humble prayer, the novices plunge into what they consider to be true spiritual exercises within their soul. This is the quickest way to physical and spiritual death. It is madness and not wisdom.

Such people do unnatural things. They put themselves into stressful situations. They ask too much of their imagination. The devil has the ability to put together false lights and sounds, trick smells and tastes, weird sensations and perceptions. Some consider this kind of illusion a serene awareness of God. They are more like sheep suffering from brain disease.

—ANONYMOUS

Spare me, Lord, from the traps of my
own understanding. Amen.

A LITTLE EFFORT–
A BIG REWARD

The LORD is near to all who call on him,
to all who call on him in truth.

PSALM 145:18

God does not lay a great burden on us—
a little thinking of him,
a little adoration,
sometimes to pray for grace,
sometimes to offer him your sorrows,
sometimes to thank him for the good things he does.

Lift up your heart to him even at meals and when you are in company. The least little remembrance will always be acceptable to him. You don't have to be loud. He is nearer to us than you think.

You don't have to be in church all the time in order to be with God. We can make a chapel in our heart where we can withdraw from time to time and converse with him in meekness, humility, and love. Everyone has the capacity for such intimate conversation with God, some more, some less. He knows what we can do. Get started. Maybe he is just waiting for one strong resolution on your part. Have courage.

–BROTHER LAWRENCE

*Can it be that if I will make a little effort, my
awareness of Your nearness will grow? How will
I know unless I try? Help me, Lord, to try. Amen.*

RIGHT WHERE WE ARE

Oh come, let us worship and bow down;
Let us kneel before the Lord our Maker....
Today, if you will hear His voice:
"Do not harden your hearts, as in the rebellion."

PSALM 95:6–8 NKJV

"How can we sing the Lord's song in a strange land?" The Israelites didn't think they could. But they did. My, how they did! How did they do it? ...They immersed themselves in torah-meditation: before they knew it they were praying. They were trees. Transplanted to Babylon they put down roots, put out leaves, and produced fruit.

Lord, Your Word teaches me about You, calling me to pray to You and seek You right where I am. God, You are good. Help me remember that today and seek You through prayer. Amen.

We all suppose that we could pray, or pray better, if we were in the right place. We put off praying until we are where we think we should be, or want to be. We let our fantasies or our circumstances distract us from attending to the word of God that is aimed right where we are, and invites our answers from that spot.

–EUGENE H. PETERSON, from *Answering God*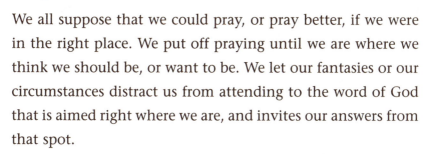

EAGER TO RECEIVE

If you believe, you will receive
whatever you ask for in prayer.

MATTHEW 21:22 NLT

When Jesus confronted a man beside the pool of Bethesda who had been paralyzed for thirty-eight years, He asked, "Do you want to get well?" (John 5:6).

At first, it must have sounded like a thoughtless question. Surely anyone who had been lying down for so long would want to get up. But Jesus knew it can be easier to lie on a cot letting people wait on you hand and foot, than to pick up all the responsibilities of life that are required when you can walk. The man answered that he did want to get well, and immediately Jesus told him to pick up his pallet, and walk. And the man did.

How do you and I show eagerness to receive all that God has promised us? One way is through persistent prayer as we ask God for change, seek His Word about the change, then persistently pray until He brings it about.

–ANNE GRAHAM LOTZ, from *God's Story*

 Father God, You know my needs. You know what's on my mind and what I'm desperately waiting for. Lord, today I seek Your promises with persistence. Amen.

SOLITUDE AND SOCIETY

Rejoice in the Lord always. I will say it again: Rejoice!
Let your gentleness be evident to all. The Lord is near.

PHILIPPIANS 4:4–5

If you are not under an obligation to mingle socially or enter-tain others in your home, remain within yourself. Entertain yourself. If visitors arrive or you are called out to someone for a good reason, go as one who is sent by God. Visit your neigh-bor with a loving heart and a good intention....

In addition to a mental solitude to which you can retreat even in the middle of a crowd, learn to love actual physical soli-tude. There is no need to go out into the desert. Simply spend some quiet time alone in your room, in a garden, or some other place. There you can think some holy thoughts or do a little spiritual reading. One of the great bishops said, "I walk alone on the beach at sunset. I use such recreation to refresh myself and shake off a little of my ordinary troubles."

Our Lord received a glowing report from his apostles about how they had preached and what a great ministry they had done. Then he said to them, "Come with me by yourselves to a quiet place and get some rest" (Mark 6:31).

−FRANCIS DE SALES

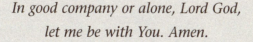

In good company or alone, Lord God,
let me be with You. Amen.

WANTING THE RIGHT THINGS

[Jesus prayed,] "Take this cup from me.
Yet not what I will, but what you will."

MARK 14:36

*Lord, show me the way
You want me to pray.
Teach me to desire the
things that You desire
for me. Amen.*

It is a mistake to ask God to give you what you want. Your desires are probably not in complete harmony with God's will. Pray instead that God will lead you to want the right things. Ask for what is good and for what is best for your soul. There is no way you could want these things for yourself more than God desires you to have them....

Relax your prayers. Do not work so hard to have your requests granted. The Lord wants to give you more than you ask. Nothing can be greater than intimate conversation with God, being absolutely preoccupied with his companionship. Prayer that is not distracted with a wish list is the highest achievement of the intellect.

–EVAGRIUS PONTICUS

ASKING FOR THE RIGHT THINGS

But when the Holy Spirit controls our lives, he will produce this kind of fruit in us: love, joy, peace, patience, kindness, goodness, faithfulness, gentleness, and self-control.

GALATIANS 5:22-23 NLT

Often when I prayed, I kept asking for things that seemed good to me. I pressured God to give me what I wanted. I did not trust God enough to allow him to provide what would be best for me. When I actually received the thing I had unreasonably sought, I would be embarrassed by my own selfish stubbornness. Ultimately, the thing would not turn out to be what I had expected....

If you would ask God for something, ask to be cleansed of your passions. Pray to be delivered from ignorance. Plead with God to free you from temptation.

In your prayers, desire justice, virtue, and spiritual knowledge. The other things will be given you as well.

If you will pray for others, you will pray like the angels.

–EVAGRIUS PONTICUS

God, I know that as much as You care about the little things in my life, You care even more about my character. Lord, today I simply ask that You make me more like You. Amen.

THE TRUE PRAYER OF FAITH

Our soul waits for the Lord;
He is our help and our shield.
For our heart shall rejoice in Him,
Because we have trusted in His holy name.

PSALM 33:20–21 NLT

Lord God, thank You for Your promises. I hold to those promises right now, Lord, and pray that You would begin the good work You began in me, that You would meet my needs according to Your riches in glory. Amen.

One may ask if it wouldn't be better to make our wishes known to God, leaving it to Him to decide what is best, without seeking to assert our wills. The answer is: *by no means*. The prayer of faith which Jesus sough to teach His disciples does not simply proclaim its desire and then leave the decision to God. That would be the prayer of submission for cases in which we cannot know God's will. But the prayer of faith, finding God's will in some promise of the Word, pleads for that promise until it comes.

—ANDREW MURRAY

STOP A WANDERING MIND

Then came Jesus forth, wearing the crown
of thorns, and the purple robe. And Pilate
saith unto them, Behold the man!

JOHN 19:5 KJV

If your mind wanders during prayer, here is a technique that will certainly help. If you are a beginner at prayer, there is no need now for subtle meditation with many mental conceptions of Jesus. Simply look at him.

If you are in trouble or sad, look at Jesus on his way to the Garden of Gethsemane. Imagine the struggle going on inside his soul. See him bending under the weight of the cross. Look at him persecuted, suffering, and deserted by his friends.

Let your prayer begin to take shape. "Lord, if you are willing to suffer such things for me, what am I suffering for you? Why should I complain? Let me imitate your way."…

You ask me how you can possibly do this, protesting that Jesus is not physically present in the world today. Listen! Anyone can make the little effort it takes to look at the Lord within. You can do this without any risk and with very little bother. If you refuse to try this, it is not likely that you would have remained at the foot of the cross either.

—TERESA OF AVILA

If I must remain a beginner at prayer, Lord God,
let me be an experienced beginner. Help me to follow
the guidance of those who know the way. Amen.

WITH JESUS IN THE GARDEN OF GETHSEMANE

He went a little farther and fell on His face, and prayed,
saying, "O My Father, if it is possible, let this cup pass
from Me; nevertheless, not as I will, but as You will."

MATTHEW 26:39 NKJV

Jesus pushes himself up from the ground and lifts his eyes towards heaven.

"Yet not what I will, but what You will."

His hands are no longer clutching the grass in despair. They are no longer clasping each other in prayer.

They are raised toward heaven.

Reaching not for bread or for fish or for any other good gifts. Not even for answers.

But reaching for the cup from His Father's hand.

And though it is a terrible cup, brimming with the wrath of God for the ferment of sin from centuries past and centuries yet to come ...and though it is a cup He fears ...He takes it.

Because more than He fears the cup, He loves the hand from which it comes.

–KEN GIRE, from *Intense Moments with the Savior*

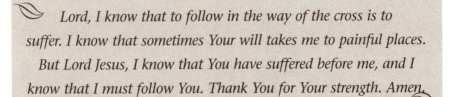

Lord, I know that to follow in the way of the cross is to suffer. I know that sometimes Your will takes me to painful places. But Lord Jesus, I know that You have suffered before me, and I know that I must follow You. Thank You for Your strength. Amen.

SURRENDER

Watch and pray, lest you enter into temptation.
The spirit indeed is willing, but the flesh is weak.

MATTHEW 26:41 NKJV

Jesus prayed, "Not My will, but Thine be done." That's the most terrifying prayer in all of Scripture. God asks some very hard things of us. He asked Abraham to sacrifice Isaac; He let Lazarus die before raising him from the dead; He did not spare His own Son. God wastes nothing. Not our joys, not our sorrows—nothing. When we offer Him the essence of ourselves and we submit to His work in our lives, His Spirit produces character in us. He knows the fragrance that comes from surrender. He knows firsthand the return from the grain of wheat that falls to the ground and dies.

I think we only get to this kind of surrender through prayer. Just as Jesus did. We bring our lives to Him and wrestle them to the ground and let them go.

–NICOLE JOHNSON, from *Fresh-Brewed Life*

Lord, prayer will make my heart soft toward You,
willing to follow You wherever You lead.
Please soften my heart as I pray right now.
Lord, I surrender my will to You. Amen.

TRUSTING GOD

This "foolish" plan of God is far wiser than the wisest
of human plans, and God's weakness is far stronger
than the greatest of human strength.

1 CORINTHIANS 1:25 NLT

*Father God, I know that
You are the God only wise.
Remind me who You are,
Lord, as I pray. Remind me
of Your greatness and
power. Amen.*

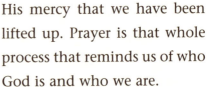

Prayer is the recognition that if God had not engaged himself in our problems, we would still be lost in the blackness. It is by His mercy that we have been lifted up. Prayer is that whole process that reminds us of who God is and who we are.

I believe there's great power in prayer. I believe God heals the wounded, and that He can raise the dead. But I don't believe we tell God what to do and when to do it.

God knows that we, with our limited vision, don't even know that for which we should pray. When we entrust our requests to Him, we trust Him to honor our prayers with holy judgment.

–MAX LUCADO, from *Walking with the Savior*

THE TERRITORY OF THE HEART

Above all else, guard your heart,
for it is the wellspring of life.

PROVERBS 4:23

O God! We don't know who you are! "The light shines in the darkness" (John 1:5) but we don't see it. Universal light! It is only because of you that we can see anything at all. Sun of the soul! You shine more brightly than the sun in the sky. You rule over everything. All I see is you. Everything else vanishes like a shadow. The one who has never seen you has seen nothing. That person lives a make-believe life, lives a dream.

But I always find you within me. You work through me in all the good I accomplish. How many times I was unable to check my emotions, resist my habits, subdue my pride, follow my reason, or stick to my plan! Without you I am "a reed swayed by the wind" (Matthew 11:7). You give me courage and everything decent that I experience. You have given me a new heart that wants nothing except what you want. I am in your hands. It is enough for me to do what you want me to do. For this purpose I was created.

–FRANÇOIS DE FÉNELON

My Creator, I close my eyes and shut out all exterior things, things that would pointlessly irritate my spirit. Thank You that in the depths of my heart, I can enjoy an intimacy with You through Jesus, Your Son. Amen.

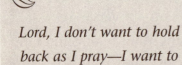

HONEST COMMUNICATION

But as for me, it is good to be near God.
I have made the sovereign LORD my refuge.

PSALM 73:28

Lord, I don't want to hold back as I pray—I want to be open and honest before You. Search my heart today, Lord God, and remind me of Your love. Amen.

I once read a greeting card with the following thoughts written on the front: "Let us live, let us love, let us share the deepest secrets of our souls...." The inside of the card read, "You go first."

How true is this impulse in developing intimacy! We don't want to be the first to bare our souls. God, however, has gone first in our relationship with Him. He initiates, He calls, He sends, He provides, He gives—all for us to know Him, to draw near to Him. Once we know and experience God as righteous, trustworthy, responsive, and our refuge, we can begin to feel comfortable with sharing our deepest secrets. David, vulnerable and honest, shows us as no other that it is permissible—even desirable—to "drop our guard" in communing with God.

–CYNTHIA HEALD, from *Intimacy with God*

STEADINESS IN PRAYER

Look to the LORD and his strength; seek his face always.

1 CHRONICLES 16:11

If we permit the love of God to replace our cares in this world, and if we give ourselves over to steady prayer and meditation, we will soon find our attitude and behavior changing. We will stop racing from one thing to another. We will rest in tranquility and peace.

A stable spiritual life requires much prayer and devout singing of psalms. Evil is only conquered by continual prayer.

Prayer can become habitual. Whether praying or meditating, it is possible to focus our attention on God. In this kind of prayer we do not think of anything in particular. Our whole will is directed toward God. The Holy Spirit burns in our soul. God is at the very heart of our being. Our prayers are made with affection and they become effective. If our prayers require words, we do not rush. We can offer almost every syllable as a prayer in itself. The love burning in us will give fiery life to our prayers.

Prayer of this kind is a delight.

–RICHARD ROLLE

 Lord, I am craving spiritual stability, to have a steady, consistent faith and relationship with You. Please fill my mind, Lord God, and give me a stability of spirit. Amen.

REALLY PRAYING THE LORD'S PRAYER

[Jesus said,] "When you pray, do not keep on babbling like pagans,
for they think they will be heard because of their many words."

MATTHEW 6:7

When I repeat the Lord's Prayer, my love causes me to desire to understand who this Father is and who this Master is who taught us the prayer.

You are wrong if you think you already know who he is. We should think of him every time we say his prayer....

Imagine that Jesus taught this prayer to each one of us individually and that he continues to explain it to us. He is always close enough to hear us. To pray the Lord's Prayer well there is one thing you need to do. Stay near the side of the Master who taught it to you....

Yes, it is a little troublesome to begin to consider Jesus when you pray the Lord's Prayer until it becomes habitual. You are right. This step turns vocal prayer into mental prayer. In my view, it is faithful vocal prayer. We need to think about who is listening to our prayers.

–TERESA OF AVILA

I am always aware that there is an edge of prayer. I come up to it, hang on to something, and peer into the unknown. But I draw back. But, Lord, I believe that You're leading me into deeper prayer. Help me really experience You, Lord God. Amen.

WHEN YOU STUMBLE

"Come now, let us reason together," says the LORD.
"Though your sins are like scarlet, they shall be as white as snow;
though they are red as crimson, they shall be like wool."

ISAIAH 1:18

You have committed a sin. It may have been from weakness or with malice. Don't panic. Go to God with humility and confidence....

Let the Lord know you are sorry. Admit it may have been worse if he had not stopped you. Thank God. Love God. He will be generous toward you. Even though what you have done is offensive to him, he will reach out to help you....

If you have really messed up, first try to regain your peace and calmness. Lift up your heart to heaven. Ask yourself whether you are really sorry for having sinned or simply afraid of being punished.

To recover the peace you have lost, forget your sin for a while and think about the love of God. He does everything possible to call sinners back to himself and to make them happy.

After this has restored peace to your soul, then you examine the motive behind your sin. Wake up your sorrow in the presence of God's love and promise to do better next time.

–LAWRENCE SCUPOLI

Kicking myself has never been very productive, Lord. Let me find rest and peace in Your support, Your forgiveness. Amen.

HUMILITY IN PRAYER

And all of you, serve each other in humility,
for "God sets himself against the proud,
but he shows favor to the humble."

1 PETER 5:5 NLT

*Humble my heart, Lord
God. Remind me of Your
greatness and my relative
smallness. Lord, I do want
to understand Your ways in
my life. Amen.*

Because humility is the opposite of pride, it is no surprise that our Lord would make it a prerequisite for prayer, for God hates pride. One verse of Scripture that speaks powerfully regarding the issue of prayer and humility is: "Then [the angel] said to me, Do not be afraid, Daniel, for from the first day that you set your heart on understanding …and on humbling yourself before your God, your words were heard, and I have come in response to your words" (Daniel 10:12 NASB). In this passage God teaches us two principles of prayer. The first is that answered prayer often comes as a result of our desire to understand, and the second is the need for our willingness to humble ourselves before God.

–LANA BATEMAN, from *The Heart of Prayer*

IGNORANCE AND WEAKNESS

[Jesus said,] "Forgive us our debts,
as we also have forgiven our debtors."

MATTHEW 6:12

There are two causes of sin. Either we don't know what we ought to do or we refuse to do what we know we should. The first cause is ignorance. The second is weakness.

O God, teach me Your law. Give me the strength to keep it. Amen.

While we can fight against both, we will certainly be defeated unless God helps us. God can teach us what is right. As our knowledge of good and evil grows, God can help us to desire the better.

When we pray for forgiveness, we need to pray also that God will lead us away from sin. The psalmist sings, "The LORD is my light and my salvation" (Psalm 27:1). With light he takes away our ignorance. With salvation he strengthens us in weakness.

−SAINT AUGUSTINE

PRAYER BEYOND PRAYER

That people may see and know, may consider and
understand, that the hand of the LORD has done this.

ISAIAH 41:20

It is possible, while you are praying the Lord's Prayer (or some
other vocal prayer), that the Lord will give you *perfect contemplation*. It turns the prayer into an actual conversation with God.
This works beyond our understanding. Words become unimpor-
tant. Anyone who experiences this will know that the divine
Master is doing the teaching without the sound of words.

The soul is aroused to love without understanding how it
loves. It understands how distinctly different this moment is
from all others. This is a gift of God. It is not earned.

This is not the equivalent of mental prayer, which is silently
thinking about what we are saying and to whom we are
saying it.

Don't think of it as something esoteric with an unusual name.
Don't let the technical term for it frighten you away.

It's like this: in regular prayer we are taking the lead with
God's help. But in the perfect contemplation described above,
God does everything. It is not easy to explain.

–TERESA OF AVILA

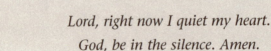

Lord, right now I quiet my heart.
God, be in the silence. Amen.

KEEPING PRAYER ON TRACK

Do not be quick with your mouth, do not be hasty in
your heart to utter anything before God. God is in heaven
and you are on earth, so let your words be few.

ECCLESIASTES 5:2

So you have difficulty with wandering thoughts in prayer!
That's nothing new! You have a lot of company.

One way to remedy this is to tell God about it. Don't use a lot
of fancy words or make your prayers too long. That in itself
will destroy your attention. Pray like a poor, paralytic beggar
before a rich man. Make it your *business* to keep your mind in
the Presence of the Lord. If you have difficulty with that,
don't fret about it. That will only make it worse. Bring your
attention back to God in tranquility.

Another way to stay with a prayer is to keep your mind from
wandering too far at other times of the day. Keep it strictly in
the Presence of God. If you think of him a lot, you will find
it easy to keep your mind calm in the time of prayer.

–BROTHER LAWRENCE

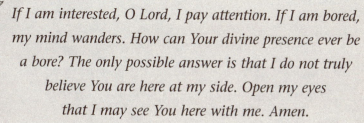

*If I am interested, O Lord, I pay attention. If I am bored,
my mind wanders. How can Your divine presence ever be
a bore? The only possible answer is that I do not truly
believe You are here at my side. Open my eyes
that I may see You here with me. Amen.*

FILLING AN EMPTINESS

> While he was blessing them, he left them
> and was taken up into heaven.
>
> LUKE 24:51

Lord, you began to perfect your apostles by taking away from them the very thing they didn't think they could do without—the actual presence of Jesus.... Once Christ was gone, you sent the Holy Spirit....

But Lord, why isn't my life filled with this Spirit? It ought to be the soul of my soul, but it isn't. I feel nothing. I see nothing. I am both physically and spiritually lazy. My feeble will is torn between you and a thousand meaningless pleasures. Where is your Spirit? Will it ever arrive and "create in me a pure heart, O God" (Psalm 51:10)? Now I understand! Your Holy Spirit desires to live in an impoverished soul.

Come, Holy Spirit! There is no place emptier than my heart.

The Holy Spirit floods the soul with light, recalling in our memory the things Jesus taught when he was on earth. We find strength and inspiration. We become one with Truth.

—FRANÇOIS DE FÉNELON

O my Love, my God! Glorify yourself in me.
My only joy in life is in You. You are everything to me.
Please breathe Your Holy Spirit in me. Amen.

PRAYING FOR THE HOLY SPIRIT

If you sinful people know how to give good gifts to your
children, how much more will your heavenly Father
give the Holy Spirit to those who ask him.

LUKE 11:13 NLT

Prayer is the key to accessing the power of the Holy Spirit within you. You open your mouth and use your words. You open your heart and reveal your concern. You unite with the Spirit in the knowledge He will answer you. In its most simplified form, that is prayer. Prayer is talking to God.

Heavenly Father, today I ask You for the guidance of Your Holy Spirit. Lord, please enable me to live the life to which You've called me. Amen.

The moment we begin talking to God and making our needs known, we are accessing the power of the Spirit. As the psalmist wrote, "When I pray, you answer me." God hears us and begins immediately to help us with the concerns in our lives.

That's why we talk to God about everything. He listens, He cares, and He works for us.

—MARILYN MEBERG, from *Assurance for a Lifetime*

GOD IN THE COMMONPLACE

Where can I go from your Spirit?
Where can I flee from your presence?

PSALM 139:7

Here are the secrets of intimacy with God:

> Renounce everything that does not lead to God.
>
> Become accustomed to a continual conversation with him in freedom and simplicity.
>
> Speak to him every moment.
>
> Ask him to tell you what to do when you are not sure.
>
> Get busy with it when you plainly see what he requires of you.
>
> Offer your activity to him even before you do it.
>
> Give God thanks when you accomplish something.

The depth of your spirituality does not depend upon *changing* the things you do but in doing for God what you ordinarily do for yourself.

The biggest mistake is to think that a time of prayer is different from any other time. It is all one. Prayer is experiencing the presence of God. There should be no change when a time of formal prayer ends. Continue with God. Praise and bless him with all your energy.

–BROTHER LAWRENCE

O my God, since You are with me, and I must now obey
Your command and apply my mind to these outward things,
I pray that You will continue to be with me. Assist me.
Receive all my labor. Possess all my affections. Amen.

PRAY AS HE PRAYED

[Jesus said,] "And whatever you ask in My name, that
I will do, that the Father may be glorified in the Son.
If you ask anything in My name, I will do it."

JOHN 14:13-14 NKJV

Christ's life and work, His suffering and death—it was all prayer, all dependence on God, trust in God, receiving from God, surrender to God. Thy redemption, O believer, is a redemption wrought out by

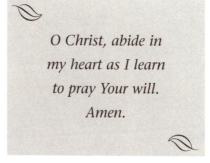

*O Christ, abide in
my heart as I learn
to pray Your will.
Amen.*

prayer and intercession: thy Christ is a praying Christ: the life
He lived for thee, the life He lives in thee, is a praying life that
delights to wait on God and receive all from Him. To pray in
His Name is to pray as He prayed. Christ is our only example
because He is our Head, our Saviour, and our Life. In virtue of
His Deity and of His Spirit He can live in us: we can pray in
His Name, because we abide in Him and He in us.

—ANDREW MURRAY

FROM THE HEART

[Jesus said,] "You may ask me for anything
in my name, and I will do it."

JOHN 14:14

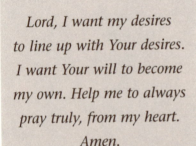

*Lord, I want my desires
to line up with Your desires.
I want Your will to become
my own. Help me to always
pray truly, from my heart.
Amen.*

True prayer is only another name for the love of God. Its excellence does not consist in the multitude of our words; for our Father knoweth what things we have need of before we ask Him. The true prayer is that of the heart, and the heart prays only for what it desires. *To pray,* then is *to desire*—but to desire what God would have us desire. He who asks what he does not from the bottom of his heart desire, is mistaken in thinking that he prays. Let him spend days in reciting prayers, in meditation or in inciting himself to pious exercises, he prays not once truly, if he really desires not the things he pretends to ask.

—FRANÇOIS FÉNELON

ASK WHAT YOU WISH

[Jesus said,] "Remain in me, and I will remain in you.
No branch can bear fruit by itself; it must remain in the
vine. Neither can you bear fruit unless you remain in me."

JOHN 15:4

So how do we pray in Jesus' name, that is, in conformity to his nature? Jesus himself says, "If you abide in me, and my words abide in you, ask for whatever you wish, and it will be done for you" (John 15:7). This "abide in me" is the all-inclusive condition for effective intercession. It is the key for prayer in the name of Jesus. We learn to become like the branch, which receives its life from the vine.... Nothing is more important to a life of prayer than learning how to become a branch.

As we live this way, we develop what Thomas à Kempis calls "a familiar friendship with Jesus." We become accustomed to his face. We distinguish the voice of the true Shepherd from that of religious hucksters in the same way professional jewelers distinguish a diamond from glass imitations—by acquaintanceship. When we have been around the genuine article long enough, the cheap and the shoddy become obvious.... We know even as we are known. This is how we pray in Jesus' name.

−RICHARD J. FOSTER, from *Prayer: Finding the Heart's True Home*

O Lord Jesus, my dearest Friend, as I abide in You,
I learn how to truly pray in Your name. Help me
to listen for Your still, small voice. Amen.

CONTENTMENT

And He said to me, "My grace is sufficient for you,
for My strength is made perfect in weakness."

2 CORINTHIANS 12:9 NKJV

Heavenly Father, You have given me so much. Lord, Your grace is truly sufficient. Thank You for saving me, for continuing to heal my life. I trust You, Father. Amen.

There are times when the one thing you want is the one thing you never get....

You pray and wait.

No answer.

You pray and wait.

May I ask a very important question? What if God says no?

What if the request is delayed or even denied? When God says no to you, how will you respond? If God says, "I've given you My grace, and that is enough," will you be content?

Content. That's the word. A state of heart in which you would be at peace if God gave you nothing more than He already has.

—MAX LUCADO, from *In the Grip of Grace*

TWO OBSTACLES TO PRAYER

[Jesus said,] "Until now you have asked nothing in My name. Ask, and you will receive, that your joy may be full."

JOHN 16:24 NKJV

There are two major obstacles to prayer. The first obstacle arises when the devil prompts you to think, "I am not yet prepared to pray. I should wait for another half-hour or another day until I have become more prepared or until I have finished taking care of this or that." Meanwhile, the devil distracts you for half an hour, so that you no longer think about prayer for the rest of the day. , from one day to the next, you are hindered and rushed with other business. This common obstacle shows us how maliciously the devil tries to trick us....

The second obstacle arises when we ask ourselves, "How can you pray to God and say the Lord's Prayer? You are too unworthy and sin every day. Wait until you are more devout...." This serious obstacle crushes us like a heavy stone. Despite our feelings of unworthiness, our hearts must struggle to remove this obstacle so that we can freely approach God and call upon him.

–MARTIN LUTHER

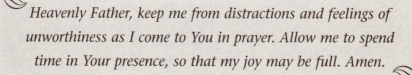

Heavenly Father, keep me from distractions and feelings of unworthiness as I come to You in prayer. Allow me to spend time in Your presence, so that my joy may be full. Amen.

THE POWER OF GOD'S LOVE

But if you do sin, there is someone to plead for you
before the Father. He is Jesus Christ, the one who pleases
God completely. He is the sacrifice for our sins.

1 JOHN 2:1–2 NLT

The only way to deal definitively with guilt is to confess the sin associated with it. A person must go to God and say, "I acknowledge this sin, and I own up to it before You, God. I ask You to forgive me for my sin and to wash this sin from my conscience and from my soul."

If you have uneasy needy feelings in your life, I encourage you to examine your past and to face any unconfessed sin. Allow God to forgive you and to free you. In receiving God's forgiveness, you are also receiving God's love, which declares you to be worthy of His forgiveness and love. Only in Christ Jesus can genuine worthiness be found.

–CHARLES STANLEY

*Lord Jesus, thank You that You have called me
Your own and made me worthy of Your love.
Please cleanse my heart as I pray, Lord, and
show me what things I need to confess. Amen.*

THE HABIT OF PRAYER

He withdrew about a stone's throw
beyond them, knelt down and prayed.

LUKE 22:41

O my brother, if thou and I would be like Jesus we must especially contemplate Jesus praying alone in the wilderness. *There is the secret of His wonderful life.* What He did and spoke to man *was first spoken and lived through with the Father.* In communion with Him, the anointing with the Holy Spirit was each day renewed. He who would be like Him in his walk and conversation must simply begin here, that he follow Jesus into solitude.... Besides the ordinary hour of prayer, he will feel at times irresistibly drawn to enter into the holy place, and not to come thence until it has been revealed anew to him that God is his portion. In his secret chamber, with closed door, or in the solitude of the wilderness, God must be found every day, and our fellowship with Him renewed. If Christ needed it, how much more we! What it was to Him it will be for us.

−ANDREW MURRAY

Father, I want to develop a habit of prayer in my life.
Give me the discipline I need to spend time in the
secret chamber with You each day. Amen.

GOING AWAY AGAIN TO PRAY

So leaving them again, he went away and prayed
for the third time, saying the same words.

MATTHEW 26:44 NRSV

It isn't wrong or unprofitable to spend much time in prayer as long as it doesn't hinder us from doing other good and necessary works duty calls us to...For to spend a long time in prayer isn't, as some think, the same thing as praying "with much speaking." Multiplied words are one thing, but the sustained warmth of desire is another. It is written that the Lord continued all night in prayers and that His prayer was prolonged when He was in agony. Isn't this an example for us from our Intercessor who, along with the Father, eternally hears our prayers? ...To talk a lot in prayer is to cheapen and overuse our words while asking for something necessary. But to prolong prayer is to have our hearts throb with continual pious emotions toward the One we pray to. In most cases, prayer consists more of groaning than of speaking, of tears rather than words. He sees our tears. Our groaning isn't hidden from Him. For He made everything by a word and doesn't need human words.

–SAINT AUGUSTINE

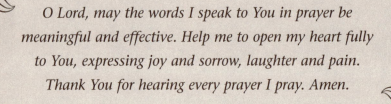

*O Lord, may the words I speak to You in prayer be
meaningful and effective. Help me to open my heart fully
to You, expressing joy and sorrow, laughter and pain.
Thank You for hearing every prayer I pray. Amen.*

THE GREATEST THING WE CAN DO

Pray without ceasing.

1 THESSALONIANS 5:17 KJV

More time and early hours for prayer would act like magic to revive and invigorate many a decayed spiritual life. More time and early hours for prayer would be manifest in holy living. A holy life would not be so rare or so difficult a thing if our devotions were not so short and hurried. A Christly temper in its sweet and passionless fragrance would not be so alien and hopeless a heritage if our closet stay were lengthened and intensified....

To pray is the greatest thing we can do: and to do it well there must be calmness, time, and deliberation; otherwise it is degraded into the littlest and meanest of things. True praying has the largest results for good; and poor praying, the least. We cannot do too much of real praying; we cannot do too little of the sham. We must learn anew the worth of prayer, enter anew the school of prayer.... We must demand and hold with iron grasp the best hours of the day for God and prayer, or there will be no praying worth the name.

—E. M. BOUNDS

 *Lord, I know that praying is the greatest thing
I can do, but sometimes distractions keep me from You.
Help me to give You the very best of my day. Amen.*

PERSEVERING PRAYER

Pray at all times and on every occasion in the power
of the Holy Spirit. Stay alert and be persistent in
your prayers for all Christians everywhere.

EPHESIANS 6:18 NLT

Of all the mysteries of the prayer world the need of persevering prayer is one of the greatest. That the Lord, who is so loving and longing to bless, should have to be supplicated time after time, sometimes year after year, before the answer comes, we cannot easily understand. It is also one of the greatest practical difficulties in the exercise of believing prayer. When, after persevering supplication, our prayer remains unanswered, it is often easiest for our slothful flesh, and it has all the appearance of pious submission, to think that we must now cease praying, because God may have His secret reason for withholding His answer to our request.

It is by faith alone that the difficulty is overcome. When once faith has taken its stand on God's word and the Name of Jesus, and has yielded itself to the leading of the Spirit to seek God's will and honor alone in its prayer, it need not be discouraged by delay. It knows from Scripture that the power of believing prayer is simply irresistible; real faith can never be disappointed.

–ANDREW MURRAY

Lord, sometimes the wait seems so long.
Keep me hanging on. Amen.

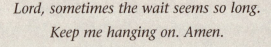

HE IS OUR EXAMPLE

Very early in the morning, while it was still dark,
Jesus got up, left the house and went off to
a solitary place, where he prayed.

MARK 1:35

Prayer alone prevails over God. But Christ has willed that it doesn't operate for evil. He gave it all its virtue when used for good. And so it knows only ...how to transform the weak, restore the sick, purge the possessed, open prison bars, and loosen the bonds of the innocent. Likewise, it washes away faults, repels temptations, extinguishes persecutions, consoles the faint-spirited, cheers the down-trodden, escorts travelers, calms waves, frightens robbers, nourishes the poor, governs the rich, raises the fallen, rescues the falling, confirms the standing. Prayer is the wall of faith. It arms us and hurls missiles against the enemy who watches us on all sides. So we never walk unarmed. By day, we are aware of our post—by night, of our vigil. Under the armor of prayer, we guard the banner of our General. We wait in prayer for the angel's trumpet.... What more do we need then, but the duty of prayer? Even the Lord Himself prayed, to whom be honor and virtue for ages and ages!

–TERTULLIAN

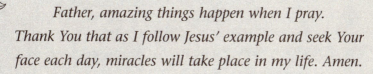
*Father, amazing things happen when I pray.
Thank You that as I follow Jesus' example and seek Your
face each day, miracles will take place in my life. Amen.*

OUR GREAT TEACHER

So He Himself often withdrew into
the wilderness and prayed.

LUKE 5:16 NKJV

The first thing the Lord teaches His disciples is that they must have a secret place for prayer. Everyone must have some solitary spot where he can be alone with his God. Every teacher must have a schoolroom. We have learned to know and accept Jesus as our only Teacher in the school of prayer. He has already taught us at Samaria that worship is no longer confined to specific times and places. Worship—true, spiritual worship—is a thing of the spirit and the life. A man's whole life must be worship in spirit and truth. But Jesus wants each one to choose for himself a fixed spot where he can meet Him daily. That inner chamber, that solitary place, is Jesus' schoolroom. That spot can be anywhere. It can even change from day to day if we're traveling. But that secret place must be somewhere with quiet time for the pupil to place himself in the Master's presence. Jesus comes there to prepare us to worship the Father.

−ANDREW MURRAY

Lord Jesus, I meet with You today to worship You.
Please teach me to pray, to live a prayerful, holy life.
Amen.

EARLY ON THEIR KNEES

And in the morning, rising up a great while
before day, he went out, and departed
into a solitary place, and there prayed.

MARK 1:35 KJV

The men who have done the most for God in this world have been early on their knees.... If God is not first in our thoughts and efforts in the morning, he will be in the last place the remainder of the day.

Behind this early rising and early praying is the ardent desire which presses us into this pursuit after God. Morning listlessness is the index to a listless heart.... Christ longed for communion with God; and so, rising a great while before day, he would go out into the mountain to pray.... We might go through the list of men who have mightily impressed the world for God, and we would find them early after God.

A desire for God which cannot break the chains of sleep is a weak thing and will do but little good for God after it has indulged itself fully. The desire for God that keeps so far behind the devil and the world at the beginning of the day will never catch up.

–FRANÇOIS FÉNELON

In the morning, O Lord, I seek Your face.
In the early hours, You will hear my prayer. Amen.

EASING OUR BURDENS

Then Jesus said, "Come to me, all of you who are weary
and carry heavy burdens, and I will give you rest. Take my
yoke upon you. Let me teach you, because I am humble
and gentle, and you will find rest for your souls."

MATTHEW 11:28–29 NLT

*Heavenly Father, praying to
You lightens my heart and
restores my joy. I know that
You hold me safely in Your
hand, and that my life has
meaning when it is used for
Your glory. Thank You for
the peace of prayer. Amen.*

At the moment we cast our
anxiety on our Heavenly
Father, believing He'll listen,
understand, care, and act on
our behalf, our burden is
lifted. Believing He truly cares
is worth a fortune in hope,
victory, and spiritual rest. And
knowing He is able to respond
to our need is a comfort
beyond all measure. I know He
can do anything, and I feel
safe and carefully tended, knowing He will accomplish what
concerns me. These precious truths are in my head, and
they've become priceless treasures buried deeply in my heart.

–LUCI SWINDOLL, from *I Married Adventure*

PETITIONARY PRAYER

The LORD has heard my cry for mercy;
the LORD accepts my prayer.

PSALM 6:9

When our asking is for ourselves it is called petition; when it is on behalf of others it is called intercession. Asking is at the heart of both experiences.

We must never negate or demean this aspect of our prayer experience. Some have suggested, for example, that while the less discerning will continue to appeal to God for aid, the real masters of the spiritual life go beyond petition to adoring God's essence with no needs or requests whatever. In this view our asking represents a more crude and naïve form of prayer, while adoration and contemplation are a more enlightened and high-minded approach, since they are free from any egocentric demands.

This, I submit to you, is a false spirituality. Petitionary Prayer remains primary throughout our lives because we are forever dependent upon God. It is something that we never really "get beyond," nor should we even want to.... The Bible itself is full of Petitionary Prayer and unabashedly recommends it to us.

–RICHARD J. FOSTER, from *Prayer: Finding the Heart's True Home*

Lord, sometimes I feel guilty for asking You for so
many things, but the truth is that I need You.
Teach me to depend on You. Amen.

BEFORE WE FINISH PRAYING

> As he was still praying, a young woman named Rebekah
> arrived with a water jug on her shoulder.... The man fell
> down to the ground and worshiped the Lord. "Praise be
> to the Lord, the God of my master, Abraham," he said.
> "The Lord has been so kind and faithful to Abraham,
> for he has led me straight to my master's relatives."
>
> GENESIS 24:15, 26–27 NLT

Every godly prayer is answered before the prayer itself is finished—"*Before* he had finished praying..." This is because Christ has pledged in His Word, "My Father will give you whatever you ask in my name" (John 16:23). When you ask in faith and in Christ's name—that is, in oneness with Him and His will—"it will be given to you" (John 15:7).

Since God's Word cannot fail, whenever we meet this simple condition, the answer to our prayer has already been granted and is complete in heaven *as we pray,* even though it may not be revealed on earth until much later. Therefore it is wise to close every prayer with praise to God for the answer He has already given.

−L. B. COWMAN, from *Streams in the Desert*

*Father God, You hear the prayers I pray even
before I finish speaking, and You graciously answer.
Today I pray in Your name, Lord Jesus, that
You would give me greater joy in You. Amen.*

SLEEPY IN PRAYER

Now it came to pass in those days that He went out to the mountain to pray, and continued all night in prayer to God.

LUKE 6:12 NKJV

Let us pray urgently and groan with continual requests. For not long ago, I was scolded in a vision because we were sleepy in our prayers and didn't pray with watchfulness. Undoubtedly, God, who "rebukes whom He loves," rebukes in order to correct and corrects to preserve. Therefore, let us break away from the bonds of sleep and pray with urgency and watchfulness. As the Apostle Paul commands us, "Continue in prayer, and watch in the same." For the apostles continually prayed day and night. Also, the Lord Jesus Himself, our teacher and example, frequently and watchfully prayed.... Certainly, what He prayed for He prayed on our behalf since He wasn't a sinner but bore the sins of others. In another place we read, "And the Lord said to Peter, 'Behold, Satan has desired to sift you as wheat: but I have prayed for thee, that thy faith fail not.'" If He labored, watched, and prayed for us and our sins, we should all the more be continually in prayer. First of all, pray and plead with the Lord. Then, through Him, be restored to God the Father!

–CYPRIAN

I long to be diligent in my prayers, O Lord.
Keep me awake and alert in You! Amen.

URGED TO PRAY

And he spake a parable unto them to this end,
that men ought always to pray, and not to faint.

LUKE 18:1 KJV

The Lord told the story of a widow who wanted justice done to her enemy. By her unceasing requests, she persuaded an evil judge to listen to her.… The story encourages us that the Lord God, who is merciful and just, pays attention to our continual prayers more than when this widow won over the indifferent, unjust, and wicked judge by her unceasing requests…The Lord gives a similar lesson in the parable of the man who had nothing to give to a traveling friend.… By his very urgent and insistent requests, he succeeded in waking the friend, who gave him as many loaves as he needed. But this friend was motivated by his wish to avoid further annoyances, not by generosity. Through this story the Lord taught that those who are asleep are compelled to give to the person who disturbs them, but those who never sleep will give with much more kindness. In fact, He even rouses us from sleep so that we can ask from Him.

−SAINT AUGUSTINE

 Lord, I know You want me to spend time in prayer.
Thank You for urging me, continually reminding
me of my need for Your presence. Amen.

PRAY DILIGENTLY

[Jesus said,] "But when you pray, go away by yourself,
shut the door behind you, and pray to your Father secretly.
Then your Father, who knows all secrets, will reward you."

MATTHEW 6:6 NLT

Prayer is a mighty weapon if it is done in the right mindset. Prayer is so strong that continual pleas have overcome shamelessness, injustice, and savage cruelty.... Let us pray diligently. Prayer is a mighty weapon if used with earnestness and sincerity, without drawing attention to ourselves. It has turned back wars and benefited an entire undeserving nation...So then, if we pray with humility, beating our chests like the tax gatherer and saying what he did, "Be merciful to me a sinner," we will obtain everything we ask for...We need much repentance, beloved, much prayer, much endurance, and much perseverance to gain the good things that have been promised to us.

My prayers are a mighty weapon in Your hands, O God. As I pray with great diligence, You work on my behalf. Amen.

–JOHN CHRYSOSTOM

STUDY AND PRAY

And they said to one another, "Did not our heart
burn within us while He talked with us on the road,
and while He opened the Scriptures to us?"

LUKE 24:32 NKJV

Your heart means far more to Christ than anything. That your heart is utterly taken with Christ is more important than any amount of service you could render or rules you could keep.... God wants to completely captivate your heart and cause it to burn with passion for Him. It is His absolute priority for you according to Mark 12:30.... Two immutable keys exist that turn our spiritual ignition and inflame godly passion. Both are tucked like rubies in the embers of Luke 24:32. "'Were not our hearts burning within us while he [1] talked with us on the road and [2] opened the Scriptures to us?'"

To me, "talked with us on the road" is a wonderfully personal and tender representation of prayer and "opened the Scriptures to us" is a perfect representation of Bible study. Beloved, we may do many other things to fan the flame of our spiritual passion for Christ, but all other efforts are in vain without the two sticks of prayer and Bible study rubbed together to ignite a fire.

–BETH MOORE, from *Praying God's Word:*
Breaking Free from Spiritual Strongholds

O God, I long to burn for You! Give me passion in
my prayers, as I talk with You along the road. Amen.

PRAYER FUEL

Man does not live on bread alone but on every
word that comes from the mouth of the LORD.

DEUTERONOMY 8:3

The Word of God is a great help in prayer. If it is lodged and written in our hearts, it will form an outflowing current of prayer, full and irresistible. Promises, stored in the heart, are to be the fuel from which prayer receives life and

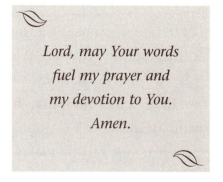

*Lord, may Your words
fuel my prayer and
my devotion to You.
Amen.*

warmth. Just as coal, which has been stored in the earth, ministers to our comfort on stormy days and wintry nights, the Word of God stored in our hearts is the food by which prayer is nourished and made strong. Prayer, like man, cannot live by bread alone, "but by every word that proceedeth out of the mouth of God" (Matthew 4:4 KJV).

Unless the vital forces of prayer are supplied by God's Word, prayer, though earnest, even vociferous in its urgency, is, in reality, flabby and void.

–E. M. BOUNDS

ANSWERED PRAYER

[Jesus said,] "But if you stay joined to me
and my words remain in you, you may ask
any request you like, and it will be granted!"

JOHN 15:7 NLT

Your father wants to answer prayer. If you are abiding in Christ, and if his Word abides in you, then you will pray in his will and he will answer. "And this is the confidence which we have before Him, that if we ask anything according to His will, He hears us" (1 John 5:14). It has well been said that prayer is not getting man's will done in heaven, but getting God's will done on earth. It is not overcoming God's reluctance but laying hold of God's willingness.

What a joy it is to have God answer prayer! What confidence it gives you to know that you can take "everything to God in prayer" and he will hear and answer! He does not always give us what we ask, but he does give us what we need, *when we need it.* This is one of the evidences of abiding.

−WARREN W. WIERSBE

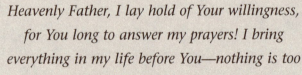

Heavenly Father, I lay hold of Your willingness,
for You long to answer my prayers! I bring
everything in my life before You—nothing is too
big or too small for Your loving care. Amen.

OUR GREAT INTERCESSOR

Therefore he is able to save completely those
who come to God through him, because
he always lives to intercede for them.

HEBREWS 7:25

One of the attributes of Jesus is that He knows the hearts of
men and understands what goes on in our spirits.... In
knowing our hearts, Jesus perceives our motivations, desires,
and yearnings as well as our inadequacies, ineptitudes, and
deficiencies. He sees what we need. Out of His deep love for
us, Jesus brings our needs to the Father.

The Father always responds to what Jesus brings to Him.
There is no prayer that Jesus prays on our behalf that goes
unheeded or unanswered by the Father. So even though we
have not brought our need to Jesus, Jesus brings our need to
the Father, and the Father takes action on our behalf, for our
good, in order to meet our need.

–CHARLES STANLEY

 Thank You, Jesus, for being my Intercessor. Thank You,
Holy Spirit, for comforting my spirit and helping me pray.
Thank You, Father, for Your wonderful love. Amen.

THE SPIRIT'S HELP

In the same way, the Spirit helps us in our weakness.
We do not know what we ought to pray for, but
the Spirit himself intercedes for us with
groans that words cannot express.

ROMANS 8:26

It is clear from what follows that Paul is speaking here about the Holy Spirit.... We do *not know how to pray as we ought* for two reasons. First, it is not yet clear what future we are hoping for or where we are heading, and second, many things in this life may seem positive but are in fact negative, and vice versa. Tribulation, for example, when it comes to a servant of God in order to test or correct him may seem futile to those who have less understanding.... But God often helps us through tribulation, and prosperity, which may be negative if it traps the soul with delight and the love of this life, is sought after in vain.

The Spirit sighs by making us sigh, arousing in us by his love a desire for the future life. The Lord your God tempts you so that he might know whether you love him, that is, to make you know, for nothing escapes God's notice.

–SAINT AUGUSTINE

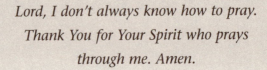

Lord, I don't always know how to pray.
Thank You for Your Spirit who prays
through me. Amen.

LET GO AND LET GOD

I do not concern myself with great matters
or things too wonderful for me.
But I have stilled and quieted my soul...
O Israel, put your hope in the LORD
both now and forevermore.

PSALM 131:1–3

In our imperfect condition both of faith and of understanding, the whole question of asking and receiving must necessarily be surrounded with mist and the possibility of mistake. It can be successfully be encountered only by the man who for himself asks and hopes. It lies in too lofty regions and involves too many unknown conditions to be reduced to formulas of ours; for God must do only the best, and man is greater and more needy than himself can know.

–GEORGE MACDONALD

*God, today I choose not to stress over what to ask,
but rather to simply lay my heart before You.
I trust You, Father, to hone and sharpen my life,
my faith—and my prayers. Thank You, Lord, that
there is such value in simply speaking to You
and directing my heart toward You. Amen.*

OUR NEED FOR PRAYER

[Jesus said,] "Ask, and it will be given to you; seek, and you will find; knock, and it will be opened to you."

MATTHEW 7:7 ESV

O God, I do not always love You as I should. Thank You for tolerating my weakness and helping me do better. Amen.

There is no better mirror in which to see your need than the Ten Commandments. In them you will find what you lack and what you should seek. You may find in them that you have a weak faith, small hope, and little love toward God. You may see that you do not praise and honor God as much as you praise and honor yourself. You may see that you do not love the Lord, your God, with all of your heart. When you see these things you should lay them before God, cry out to him and ask for help, and with all confidence expect help, believing that you are heard and that you will obtain mercy.... It is important when we have a need to go to God in prayer. I know, whenever I have prayed earnestly, that I have been heard and have obtained more than I prayed for. God sometimes delays, but He always comes.

—MARTIN LUTHER

PRAYING IN SECRET

[Jesus said,] "But you, when you pray, go into your room,
and when you have shut your door, pray to your
Father who is in the secret place; and your Father
who sees in secret will reward you openly."

MATTHEW 6:6 NKJV

When we pray, let our words and requests be disciplined, maintaining quietness and modesty. Let us consider ourselves as standing in God's sight. We must please the divine eyes both with the use of our body and with the tone of our voice. For, as it is characteristic for a shameless person to be noisy with his cries, it is fitting for the modest man to pray with calm requests. Moreover, the Lord told us to pray in secret, which is best suited to faith—in hidden and remote places and in our very bedrooms. Then we can know that God is present everywhere and hears and sees everything. In His abundant majesty, He enters even into hidden and secret places. It is written, "I am a God at hand, and not a God afar off. If a man shall hide himself in secret places, shall I not then see him? Do not I fill heaven and earth?" [Jeremiah 23:23-24]. And again: "The eyes of the Lord are in every place, beholding the evil and the good" [Proverbs 15:3].

—CYPRIAN

*Lord, I bring my requests quietly and secretly before You.
In the stillness, I listen for Your voice. Amen.*

COURAGE IN PRAYER

[Jesus said,] "For my yoke is easy, and my burden is light."

MATTHEW 11:30 NRSV

When entering the prayer chamber, we must come filled with faith and armed with courage. Nowhere else in the whole field of religious thought and activity is courage so necessary as in prayer. The successful prayer must be one without condition. We must believe that God is love and that, being love, He cannot harm us but must ever do us good. Then we must throw ourselves before Him and pray with boldness for whatever we know our good and His glory require, and the cost is no object! Whatever He in His love and wisdom would assess against us, we will accept with delight because it pleased Him. Prayers like that cannot go unanswered. The character and reputation of God guarantee their fulfillment.

We should always keep in mind the infinite loving kindness of God. No one need fear to put his life in His hands. His yoke is easy; His burden is light.

—A. W. TOZER

 Lord, I need Your courage to stand strong in my prayers. As I reflect on Your love and goodness, I have no reason to fear. Amen.

BOLDNESS IN PRAYER

Therefore, having been justified by faith, we have peace
with God through our Lord Jesus Christ, through whom
we also have access by faith into this grace in which
we stand, and rejoice in hope of the glory of God.

ROMANS 5:2 NKJV

How can we be bold in prayer? God's Word says, "Having
therefore, brethren, boldness to enter into the holiest by the
blood of Jesus..." (Hebrews 10:19 KJV). The "holiest" refers to
the sanctuary, the dwelling place of God. Only one man, one
priest, could go once a year into that room, where he could
make one offering.... Yet at Jesus' crucifixion, when the huge,
thick veil of the temple was torn in half, He made a way that
people could enter into the holiest place, the very presence of
God....

We can have boldness in prayer because of the blood of
Christ. He's the perfect Savior. He's the glorified Intercessor.
He's the reigning King. He rose from the dead, and all power
in heaven and earth are His. And He offers this power to us.

–FRANKLIN GRAHAM, from *All for Jesus*

*Lord, I am in awe that You have gone to such
great lengths to reconcile You and me. Thank You,
thank You, thank You that I can come to you
freely and with boldness. Please give me
a bold spirit today as I pray. Amen.*

THE DANGER OF PRAYERLESSNESS

[Jesus said,] "But when you pray, go into your room, close the door and pray to your Father, who is unseen. Then your Father, who sees what is done in secret, will reward you."

MATTHEW 6:6

At a subsequent meeting the opportunity was given for testimony as to what might be the sins which made the life of the church so feeble. Some began to mention failings that they had seen in other ministers, either in conduct, or in doctrine, or in service. It was soon felt that this was not the right way; each must acknowledge that in which he himself was guilty.

The Lord graciously so ordered it that we were gradually led to the sin of prayerlessness as one of the deepest roots of the evil. No one could plead himself free from this. Nothing so reveals the defective spiritual life in minister and congregation as the lack of believing and unceasing prayer. Prayer is in very deed the pulse of the spiritual life. It is the great means of bringing to minister and people the blessing and power of heaven. Persevering and believing prayer means a strong and an abundant life.

–ANDREW MURRAY

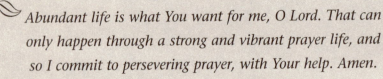
Abundant life is what You want for me, O Lord. That can only happen through a strong and vibrant prayer life, and so I commit to persevering prayer, with Your help. Amen.

THE WORD AND PRAYER

Restore my life again, just as you promised.

PSALM 119:107 NLT

Prayer and the Word of God are inseparable and should always go together. In His Word God speaks to me, and in prayer I speak to God. If there is to be true communication, God and I must both take part. If I simply pray without using God's Word, I am apt to use my own words and thoughts. Taking God's thoughts from His Word and presenting them before Him really gives prayer its power....

Through the Word the Holy Spirit shows me who God is. The Word also teaches me how sinful I am. It reveals to me all the wonders that God will do for me and the strength He will give me to do His will. The Word teaches me how to pray—with a strong desire, a firm faith, and constant perseverance. The Word teaches me not only who I am but who I may become. Above all it reminds me that Christ is the great intercessor and allows me to pray in His name.

Learn to renew your strength each day in God's Word and to pray according to His will.

—ANDREW MURRAY

As I learn Your Word, O Lord, You teach me
how to pray. Please guide me now as
I seek to pray from Your Word. Amen.

PRAYING TO A GOOD GOD

But without faith it is impossible to please Him, for he
who comes to God must believe that He is, and that
He is a rewarder of those who diligently seek Him.

HEBREWS 11:6 NKJV

So needful is prayer to the soul that the mere attitude of it may encourage a good mood. Verily to pray to that which is not, is in logic a folly; yet the good that, they say, comes of it, may rebuke the worse folly of their unbelief, for it indicates that prayer is natural, and how could it be natural if inconsistent with the very mode of our being? Theirs is a better way than that of those who, believing there is a God, but not believing that he will give any answer to their prayers, yet pray to him; that is more foolish and more immoral than praying to the No-god. Whatever the God be to whom they pray, their prayer is a mockery of him, of themselves, of the truth.

–GEORGE MACDONALD

*Lord, I know that when I come to You in prayer,
I am not coming to a capricious God, but One
who hears me and acts. Thank You, Father, for the
privilege of prayer, for the joy it brings, and for the
opportunity to have a relationship with You. Amen.*

PERSEVERING IN PRAYER

Keep on praying.

1 THESSALONIANS 5:17 NLT

One of the greatest drawbacks to the life of prayer is that the answer does not come as quickly as we expect. We are discouraged and think: "Perhaps I do not pray right." So we do not persevere. Jesus often talked about this. There may be a reason for the delay and the waiting may bring a blessing. Our desire must grow deeper and stronger, and we must ask with our whole heart. God puts us into the practicing school of persevering prayer so that our weak faith may be strengthened.

Above all God wants to draw us into closer fellowship with Him. When our prayers are not answered we learn that the fellowship and love of God are more to us than the answers of our requests, and then we continue in prayer....

Those who have persevered before God are those who have had the greatest power in prayer.

–ANDREW MURRAY

 *Heavenly Father, I often seek only answers when I pray.
Help me to learn that spending time with You is
what's important, and that Your answers
will come in Your perfect timing. Amen.*

PRAYING TO A GOD WHO ACTS

Commit your way to the LORD,
Trust also in Him,
And He shall bring it to pass.

PSALM 37:5 NKJV

To say, "Father, I should like this or that," would be enough at once, if the wish were bad, to make us know it and turn from it. Such prayer about things must of necessity help to bring the mind into true and simple relation with him; to make us remember his will even when we do not see what that will is. Surely it is better and more trusting to tell him all without fear or anxiety. Was it not thus the Lord carried himself toward his Father when he said, "If it be possible, let this cup pass from me"? ...There is no apprehension that God might be displeased with him for saying what he would like, and not leaving it all to his Father. Neither did he regard his Father's plans as necessarily so fixed that they could not be altered to his prayer.

–GEORGE MACDONALD

 Lord, when I pray what's on my heart, believing that You respond to prayer, my trust in You is renewed. God, please help me see Your will in my situation today. Amen.

PRAYER AND FASTING

Jesus told them ..."But this kind of demon
won't leave unless you have prayed and fasted."

MATTHEW 17:21 NLT

Jesus teaches us that a life of faith requires both prayer and fasting. Prayer grasps the power of heaven, fasting loosens the hold on earthly pleasure....

Abstinence from food, or moderation in taking it, helps to focus on communication with God.

Let's remember that abstinence, moderation, and self-denial are a help to the spiritual life.... To willingly sacrifice our own pleasure or enjoyment will help to focus our minds more fully on God and His priorities. The very practice needed in overcoming our own desires will give us strength to take hold of God in prayer.

Our lack of discipline in prayer comes from our fleshly desire of comfort and ease. "Those who belong to Christ Jesus have nailed the passions and desires of their sinful nature to his cross and crucified them there" (Galatians 5:24).... For the real practice of prayer—taking hold of God and having communion and fellowship with Him—it is necessary that our selfish desires be sacrificed.

Isn't it worth the trouble to deny ourselves daily in order to meet the holy God and receive His blessings?

–ANDREW MURRAY

Heavenly Father, fasting seems like such a challenge at times, but I know You want to bring maturity and discipline to my faith. Help me to deny my selfish desires and discover the power that fasting can bring to my life. Amen.

A PRAYER FOR A DEEPER WALK

Therefore we also, since we are surrounded by so great a
cloud of witnesses, let us lay aside every weight, and the
sin which so easily ensnares us, and let us run with
endurance the race that is set before us.

HEBREWS 12:1 NKJV

*Holy Father, please
remove from me the
things that keep me
from walking closely
with You. Amen.*

Lord Jesus, take from us now everything that would hinder the closest communion with God. Any wish or desire that might hamper us in prayer remove, we pray Thee. Any memory of either sorrow or care that might hinder the fixing of our affection wholly on our God, take it away now. What have we to do with idols any more? Thou hast seen and observed us. Thou knowest where the difficulty lies. Help us against it, and may we now come boldly, not into the Holy place alone, but into the Holiest of all, where we should not dare to come if our great Lord had not rent the veil, sprinkled the mercy seat with His own blood, and bidden us enter.

−CHARLES H. SPURGEON

DAY BY DAY

As the Father loved Me, I also have loved you;
abide in My love.

JOHN 15:9 NKJV

Happy is the man who has learned the secret of coming to God in daily prayer. Fifteen minutes alone with God every morning before you start the day can change circumstances and remove mountains! But all of this happiness and all of these unlimited benefits which flow from the storehouse of heaven are contingent upon our relationship to God. Absolute dependency and absolute yieldedness are the conditions of being His child. Only His children are entitled to receive those things that lend themselves to happiness; and in order to be His child, there must be the surrender of the will to Him.

Lord God, enjoying Your presence and doing Your work in the world is what makes life worth living. God, may my prayers enable me to live with You more closely and experience all that You have for me. Amen.

–BILLY GRAHAM, from *Day by Day with Billy Graham*

OCTOBER 13

MEETING THE WITH LORD

Come out from among them
And be separate, says the Lord....
I will be a Father to you,
And you shall be My sons and daughters.

2 CORINTHIANS 6:17–18 NKJV

God seemed to come to my door one day and ask if I would start walking with Him by getting up early in the morning for prayer and Bible reading. At first I thought it was something I had to do. I dragged my feet because I found I didn't want to sacrifice the extra few minutes of sleep! He was so patient as He waited for me to understand that it wasn't something I had to do; instead it was a personal time of fellowship where I could just grow in my love relationship with Him. What a difference it made in my whole attitude and approach to the early-morning hours when I became consciously aware that my heavenly Bridegroom was waiting to meet with me at that designated time!

–ANNE GRAHAM LOTZ, from *God's Story*

 Lord, You call me to You in prayer. Thank You for seeking me, for seeking a relationship with me. Lord, may I honor that privilege by spending time with You in prayer. Amen.

SETTING TIME ASIDE

But Jesus often withdrew to lonely places and prayed.

LUKE 5:16

God has so much to speak into your life. But if you don't draw apart from the busyness of your day and spend time alone with Him in quietness and solitude, you will not hear it. Jesus himself spent much time alone with God. If anyone could get away with not doing it, surely it would have been Him. How much more important must it be for us?

Lord, I know that time alone, apart, devoting my attention to You, is vital to my faith and soul. Father, be with me as I select a portion of time to spend with You. Amen.

I know finding time alone to pray can be difficult. Especially when the enemy of your soul doesn't want you to do that. But if you will make it a priority by setting a specific time to pray daily, perhaps writing it in your calendar the way you would any other important date, and determine to keep that standing appointment with God, you'll see answers to your prayers like never before.

–STORMIE OMARTIAN, from *The Power of a Praying Woman*

OCTOBER 15

THE SPIRIT OF PRAYER

For the Spirit pleads for us believers
in harmony with God's own will.

ROMANS 8:27 NLT

Prayer is not our work. It is God's work in us by His almighty power. As we pray our attitude should be one of silent expectation that the Holy Spirit will help in our weakness and pray for us with groanings that cannot be expressed.

What a thought! When I feel how imperfect my prayer is, when I have no strength of my own, I may bow in silence before God in the confidence that His Holy Spirit will teach me to pray. The Spirit is the Spirit of prayer. It is not my work, but God's work in me. The Spirit will make perfect the work even in my weakness....

The Spirit of truth will glorify Christ in us, and the Spirit of love will shed this love abroad in our hearts. And we have the Spirit of prayer, through whom our life may be one of continual prayer. Thank God that the Holy Spirit has been given to teach us to pray.

—ANDREW MURRAY

Work through me, O Lord. Pray through me,
Holy Spirit. I am Your willing vessel. Amen.

EXPERIENCING GOD'S LOVE

Now hope does not disappoint, because
the love of God has been poured out in our
hearts by the Holy Spirit who was given to us.

ROMANS 5:5 NKJV

God wants to give each of us not just fleeting impressions of His love, but a strong, settled, growing sense of it.... He wants us to enjoy a genuine, deep, constant experience of His love.

But such a relationship is ours in experience only to the degree that we get intensely involved with God. E. M. Bounds wrote that God does not reveal himself to the "hasty comer and goer." If we settle for a casual relationship we won't experience His love deeply.... His love is still just as full and flowing, just as wonderful and powerful. But we're blocking it out when we don't pursue a deeper, more constant relationship with Him.

–RUTH MYERS, from *The Perfect Love*

 Lord, I know that in order to really experience You, I need to spend time with You, allowing myself to be saturated with Your presence. Father, please make the most of my prayer times and teach me how to walk with You. Amen.

LOVE AND PRAYER

Be earnest and disciplined in your prayers. Most important
of all, continue to show deep love for each other.

1 PETER 4:7–8 NLT

Earnest prayer and fervent love are closely linked. If we pray
only for ourselves, we will not find it easy to be in the right
attitude toward God. But when our hearts are filled with love
for others, we will continue to pray for them, even for those
with whom we do not agree.

Prayer holds an important place in the life of love; they are
inseparably connected. If you want your love to increase,
forget yourself and pray for God's children. If you want to
increase in prayerfulness, spend time loving those around
you, helping to bear their burdens.

There is a great need for earnest, powerful intercessors! God
desires His children to present themselves each day before the
throne of grace to pray down the power of the Spirit upon all
believers....

As we meditate on love to those around us, we will be drawn
into fellowship with God.... Love leads to prayer—to believing prayer is given the love of God.

—ANDREW MURRAY

 *Fill my heart with Your love for others, Lord. I want to be
a burden-bearer, lifting others in prayer before You. Amen.*

UNITY THROUGH PRAYER

[Jesus prayed,] "I pray also for those who will believe in me through their message, that all of them may be one, Father, just as you are in me and I am in you. May they also be in us so that the world may believe that you have sent me."

JOHN 17:20–21

When a man prays for his fellow man, for wife or child, mother or father, sister or brother or friend, the connection between the two is so close in God, that the blessing begged may well flow to the end of the prayer. Such a one then is, in his poor, far-off way, an advocate with the Father, like his master, Jesus Christ, The Righteous. He takes his friend into the presence with him, or if not into the presence, he leaves him with but the veil between them, and they touch through the veil.

Lord God, I know that You desire unity in Your people, and I know that prayer is such a powerful connector. Today I lift up those close to me. Please meet their needs, Lord, and bring us closer together and closer to You. Amen.

–GEORGE MACDONALD

TIME FOR PRAYER

Yet no one calls on your name or pleads with you for mercy.

ISAIAH 64:7 NLT

There are earnest Christians who have just enough prayer to maintain their spiritual position but not enough to grow spiritually. Seeking to fight off temptation is a defensive attitude rather than an assertive one which reaches for higher attainment. The scriptural teaching to cry out day and night in prayer must, to some degree, become our experience if we are to be intercessors.

A man said to me, "I see the importance of much prayer, and yet my life hardly allows time for it. Am I to give up? How can I accomplish what I desire?"

I admitted that the difficulty was universal and quoted a Dutch proverb: "What is heaviest must weigh heaviest." The most important must have the first place. The law of God is unchangeable. In our communication with heaven, we only get as we give. Unless we are willing to pay the price—to sacrifice time and attention and seemingly necessary tasks for the sake of the heavenly gifts—we cannot expect much power from heaven in our work.

–ANDREW MURRAY

Heavenly Father, my life is so busy, and time with You sometimes seems like such a sacrifice. Help me to remember that You are the most important thing in my life. I put You in first place, above everything else. Amen.

THE MOST VITAL HUMAN EXPERIENCE

What is more, I consider everything a loss compared to the surpassing greatness of knowing Christ Jesus my Lord, for whose sake I have lost all things. I consider them rubbish, that I may gain Christ and be found in him.

PHILIPPIANS 3:8–9

Prayer is the most thoroughly *present* act we have as humans, and the most energetic: It sockets the immediate past into the immediate future and makes a flexible, living joint of them. The Amen gathers what has just happened into the Maranatha of the about to happen and produces a Benediction. We pay attention to God and lead others to pay attention to God. It hardly matters that so many people would rather pay attention to their standards of living, or their self-image, or their zeal to make a mark in the world.

The reality is God: worship or flee.

–EUGENE H. PETERSON, from *The Contemplative Pastor*

 Lord, today I am aware that engaging You is the most important thing I could ever do in my life. Father, please draw my eyes away from the distractions around me. I worship You today, O God. Amen.

PRAYING THROUGH

When he had gone indoors, the blind men came to him,
and he asked them, "Do you believe that I am able to do
this?" "Yes, Lord," they replied. Then he touched their eyes
and said, "According to your faith will it be done to you."

MATTHEW 9:28–29

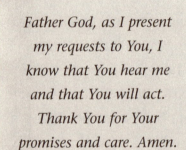

*Father God, as I present
my requests to You, I
know that You hear me
and that You will act.
Thank You for Your
promises and care. Amen.*

"Praying through" something
might be defined as follows:
"Praying your way into full
faith; coming to the point of
assurance, while still praying,
that your prayer has been
accepted and heard; and in
advance of the event, with
confident anticipation, actually becoming aware of having
received what you ask."

Let us remember that no earthly circumstances can hinder
the fulfillment of God's Word. We must look steadfastly at His
immutable Word and not at the uncertainty of this ever-
changing world. God desires for us to believe His Word
without other evidence, *and then* He is ready to do for us
"according to [our] faith" (Matthew 9:29).

–L. B. COWMAN, from *Streams in the Desert*

FAITH IN PRAYER

[Jesus told them a parable.] "Suppose you
went to a friend's house at midnight
wanting to borrow three loaves of bread."

LUKE 11:5 NLT

What the man in Luke 11 has not, another can supply. He has a rich friend nearby who will be both able and willing to give the bread. He is sure that if he only asks, he will receive. This faith makes him leave his home at midnight. If he himself has not the bread to give, he can ask another.

We need this simple, confident faith that God will give. Where that faith really exists, there will surely be no possibility of our not praying. In God's Word we have everything that can motivate and strengthen such faith in us. The heaven our natural eye sees is one great ocean of sunshine, with its light and heat giving beauty and fruitfulness to earth. In the same manner, Scripture shows us God's true heaven, which is filled with all spiritual blessings—divine light and love and life, heavenly joy and peace and power—all shining down upon us. It reveals to us our God waiting, even delighting, to bestow these blessings in answer to prayer.

—ANDREW MURRAY

*If I ask, O Lord, I will receive. If I seek, O Lord,
I will find. Thank You for hearing and
answering my prayer. Amen.*

HOLD ONTO FAITH

And the prayer that is said with faith will make the sick
person well; the Lord will heal that person. And if
the person has sinned, the sins will be forgiven.

JAMES 5:15 NCV

When you are confronted with a matter that requires immediate prayer, pray until you believe God—until with whole-
hearted sincerity you can thank Him for the answer. If you do
not see the external answer immediately, do not pray for it in
such a way that it is evident you are not definitely believing
God for it. This type of prayer will be a hindrance instead of
a help to you....

Never pray in a way that diminishes your faith. You may tell Him
you are waiting, still believing and therefore praising Him for
the answer. There is nothing that so fully solidifies faith as
being so sure of the answer that you can thank God for it.

–L. B. COWMAN, from *Streams in the Desert*

 God, I don't know what the days ahead hold in store
for me, but I believe that You answer prayer and
will meet my needs. Thank You for everything
You've done in my life until now—and thank
You for every future blessing. Amen.

PRAYING FOR BLESSING

Oh, that you would bless me and enlarge my territory!
Let your hand be with me, and keep me from
harm so that I will be free from pain.

1 CHRONICLES 4:12

When we seek God's blessing as the ultimate value in life, we are throwing ourselves entirely into the river of His will and power and purposes for us. All our other needs become secondary to what we really want—which is to become wholly immersed in what God is trying to do in us, through us, and around us for His glory.

Let me tell you a guaranteed by-product of sincerely seeking His blessing: Your life will become marked by miracles.... God's power to accomplish great things suddenly finds no obstruction in you. You're moving His direction. You're praying for exactly what God desires. Suddenly the unhindered forces of heaven can begin to accomplish God's perfect will—through you. And you will be the first to notice!

–BRUCE WILKINSON, from *The Prayer of Jabez*

 Lord, I know that You do mighty things in and through the lives of Your people. God, I pray for Your hand of blessing on my life today. Amen.

ALL WHO CALL

The Lord is near to all who call on him,
to all who call on him in truth.

PSALM 145:18

Most of our prayer lives could use a tune-up. Some prayer lives lack consistency. They're either a desert or an oasis. Long, arid, dry spells interrupted by brief plunges into the waters of communion....

Others of us need sincerity. Our prayers are a bit hollow, memorized, and rigid. More liturgy than life. And though they are daily, they are dull.

Still others lack, well, honesty. We honestly wonder if prayer makes a difference. Why on earth would God in heaven want to talk to me?...

Our prayers may be awkward. Our attempts may be feeble. But since the power of prayer is in the one who hears it and not the one who says it, our prayers do make a difference.

–MAX LUCADO, from *He Still Moves Stones*

 Dear Lord, sometimes my prayers are awkward and halting, sometimes I just don't know what to pray for, and sometimes I even pray with a wrong heart. But in Your goodness, You hear my prayers and meet me anyway. Lord, please bring my prayer life a new vitality. Amen.

A STRENGTHENING PRAYER LIFE

[Jesus said,] "Listen to me! You can pray for
anything, and if you believe, you will have it."

MARK 11:24 NLT

The consequence of sin that makes it impossible for God to give at once is a barrier on God's side as well as ours. The attempt to break through the power of sin is what makes the striving and the conflict of prayer such a reality.

Throughout history people have prayed with a sense that there were difficulties in the heavenly world to overcome. They pleaded with God for the removal of the unknown obstacles. In that persevering supplication they were brought into a state of brokenness, of entire resignation to Him, and of faith. Then the hindrances in themselves and in heaven were both overcome. As God prevails over us, we prevail with God.

God has made us so that the more clearly we see the reasonableness of a demand, the more heartily we will surrender to it. One cause of our neglecting prayer is that there appears to be something arbitrary in the call to such continued prayer. This apparent difficulty is a divine necessity and is the source of unspeakable blessing.

—ANDREW MURRAY

 As You prevail over me, O God, I will prevail with You.
Help me to submit myself to You. Amen.

PRAYER, OBEDIENCE, AND FAITH

Hear, O Israel, and be careful to obey so that it may
go well with you and that you may increase greatly
in a land flowing with milk and honey, just as
the Lord, the God of your fathers, promised you.

DEUTERONOMY 6:3

Obedience to God helps faith like no other attribute possibly can. When absolute recognition of the validity and the supremacy of the divine commands exist, faith ceases to be an almost superhuman task. It requires no straining to exercise it. Obedience to God makes it easy to believe and trust God. Where the spirit of obedience totally saturates the soul, and the will is perfectly surrendered to God, faith becomes a reality. It also does this where there is a fixed, unalterable purpose to obey God. Faith then becomes almost involuntary. After obedience it is the next natural step. It is easily and readily taken. The difficulty in prayer then is not with faith but with obedience which is faith's foundation.

—E. M. BOUNDS

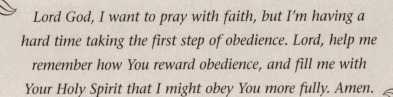

*Lord God, I want to pray with faith, but I'm having a
hard time taking the first step of obedience. Lord, help me
remember how You reward obedience, and fill me with
Your Holy Spirit that I might obey You more fully. Amen.*

DIFFICULT PRAYER

He prayed more fervently, and he was in such agony of spirit
that his sweat fell to the ground like great drops of blood.

LUKE 22:44 NLT

Have you ever noticed how much difficulties play a part in
our life? They call forth our power as nothing else can. They
strengthen character....

Imagine what the result would be if the child of God had only
to kneel down, ask, get, and go away. Loss to the spiritual life
would result. Through difficulties we discover how little we
have of God's Holy Spirit. There we learn our own weakness
and yield to the Holy Spirit to pray in us. There we take our
place in Christ Jesus and abide in Him as our only plea with
the Father. There our own will and strength are crucified.
There we rise in Christ to newness of life. Praise God for the
need and the difficulty of persistent prayer as one of His
choice means of grace.

Think what Jesus owed to the difficulties in His path. He
persevered in prayer in Gethsemane and the prince of this
world with all his temptation was overcome.

–ANDREW MURRAY

*Lord, in prayer, as in all areas of life, effort will
bring reward. Help me to persevere in prayer,
as Jesus, my blessed example, did before me. Amen.*

PRAYING TOGETHER

For where two or three come together
in my name, there am I with them.

MATTHEW 18:20

Father, as I am still in prayer, I ask You to speak to me through Your Word. Amen.

Prayer ought not be construed as an individualistic practice, in which the believer comes alone before the throne of God. Even when—especially when—the pains and struggles and hurts of life assail us, when the threats of principalities and powers and the delusions and lies of this rebellious aeon assail us, we gather with other believers who will pray when we cannot. Prayer is a communal event, in which we pray together, struggling together, bearing one another up before God, praying that God's power and sustenance will sustain, nurture, protect, and make us whole. We never pray alone, but always in communion with one another.

–LEE C. CAMP, from *Mere Discipleship: Radical Christianity in a Rebellious World*

WAITING TOGETHER

Let us not give up meeting together, as some are in the
habit of doing, but let us encourage one another—
and all the more as you see the Day approaching.

HEBREWS 10:25

The visit of Elizabeth and Mary is one of the Bible's most beautiful expressions of what it means to form community, to be together, gathered around a promise, affirming that something is really happening.

This is what prayer is all about. It is coming together around the promise. This is what celebration is all about. It is lifting up what is already there. This is what Eucharist is about. It is saying "thank you" for the seed that has been planted. It is saying, "We are waiting for the Lord, who has already come."

The whole meaning of the Christian community lies in offering a space in which we wait for that which we have already seen. Christian community is the place where we keep the flame alive among us and take it seriously, so that it can grow and become stronger in us.

–HENRI NOUWEN

Lord, as important as it is to come away alone to pray,
I know that there is nothing more refreshing and
important than coming together with others. Lord,
as I draw closer to my brothers and sisters, may
we experience You in prayer together. Amen.

OCTOBER 31

RESTING IN PRAYER

He will rejoice over you with great gladness.
With his love, he will calm all your fears.
He will exult over you by singing a happy song.

ZEPHANIAH 3:17 NLT

I believe our most honest, heartfelt prayers are the ones we pray in the middle of the night. Those prayers may not be very brave or noble or holy, but they come straight from the heart to God's ear. Lying in bed late at night with exhausted bodies and anxious minds, our usual, daily social defenses are all that's asleep. We are most open to God our Creator who knows our innermost thoughts, our most secret dreams. In the middle of the night, when we can't get off that anxious treadmill of worry and fear, the words "Please God, help!" form on our lips, take wing, and fly through the darkness.

Prayer is Sabbath. No matter what the actual content of our prayers, in prayer God calls us to trust him, to rest in him. When we pray, we lay down our burdens before the throne of Grace.... When we go into the bedroom and shut the door, we enter the Sabbath.

–HARRIET CROSBY

Lord God, praying to such a good Father is such a source of rest and contentment for my soul. I give You my burdens today and choose to rest in Your love. Amen.

PRAYERFUL DEPENDENCE

So Now I am glad to boast about my weaknesses,
so that the power of Christ may work through me.

2 CORINTHIANS 12:9 NLT

My most spectacular answers to prayers have come when I was helpless, so out of control as to be able to do nothing at all for myself....

Why would God insist on helplessness as a prerequisite to answered prayer? One obvious reason is that our human helplessness is bedrock fact. God is a realist and insists we be realists too. So long as we are deluding ourselves that human resources can supply our heart's desires, we are believing a lie....

Did Jesus have any comment on this? Yes, as always He put His finger on the very heart of the matter: "Without me ye can do nothing" (John 15:5)....

Yet not only did Jesus insist on the truth of our helplessness; He underscored it by telling us that this same helplessness applied equally to Him while He wore human flesh: "The Son can do nothing of himself, but what he seeth the Father do" (John 15:9). In this as in anything else, He was setting the pattern for imperfect humanity.

—CATHERINE MARSHALL

God, sometimes I foolishly rely on myself and my own knowledge and abilities. I know, Lord Jesus, that I can do nothing apart from You. Please be with me today, Lord. Infuse me with strength, for I am helpless without You. Amen.

THE WORK OF PRAYER

Paul and Barnabas also appointed elders in every church
and prayed for them with fasting, turning them over to
the care of the Lord, in whom they had come to trust.

ACTS 14:23 NLT

My first observation of perfectly natural and conscientious prayer came when I was a very little girl in Shanghai. One morning I went skipping along beside Dr. Hoste, at the time the director of the China Inland Mission.... He didn't turn me away, but simply said, "Edith, I am praying now, but you may come along if you wish."

I walked with him a number of times, holding his hand and being very quiet and impressed as he prayed aloud. It was his custom to walk when he prayed, and he counted it his first responsibility for the mission to pray four hours a day. He prayed for each missionary in the China Inland Mission, and for each of their children by name....

"All right, walk with me and pray," he would say in his particularly high voice. The impression that penetrates my memory is the respect I received for the *work* of prayer. I know it meant more than any series of lectures in later life could mean.

–EDITH SCHAEFFER

 *God, as I seek to do Your will in the world, I know
that prayer is more important work than anything else
I could do. Please give me wisdom for the day, Father,
and teach me to intercede for others. Amen.*

THE PRIVILEGE OF PRAYER

But as many as received Him, to them He gave the right to become children of God, to those who believe in His name.

JOHN 1:12 NKJV

Unfortunately ...for many people prayer isn't a joy but a burden. When they fail to pray, they feel guilty; when they do pray, they worry that they might not be doing it correctly. Or their prayers are wooden and lifeless, perhaps only repeating words learned in childhood but never engaging their minds or hearts.

But this is the opposite of what prayer should be. Prayer shouldn't be a *burden* but a *privilege*—a privilege God has graciously given us because He *wants* our fellowship. Remember: Jesus Christ died to destroy the barrier of sin that separates us from God, and when we give our lives to Him, we have a personal relationship with God. In fact, we have access to God in prayer only because of what Christ did for us on the cross....

Our relationship with God involves communication—not just an occasional brief chat, but a deep sharing of ourselves and our concerns with God.

–BILLY GRAHAM, from *The Journey:*
How to Live by Faith in an Uncertain World

Father God, prayer shouldn't be a chore but a delight.
Lord, today I thank You for Your goodness to me,
for reaching out and finding me. Help me see prayer
as communication with someone I love. Amen.

THANKFUL PRAYERS

> No matter what happens, always be thankful, for this
> is God's will for you who belong to Christ Jesus.
>
> 1 THESSALONIANS 5:18 NLT

True prayer begins with seeing God as He really is—and that is why *praise* should be a regular part of our prayers. When we praise God, our focus is on Him, not on ourselves. Many of the psalms are actually prayers of praise, and it is no accident that the word "praise" occurs in the book of Psalms over two hundred times. The Lord's Prayer begins with praise: "Our Father which art in heaven, Hallowed be thy name" (Matthew 6:9 KJV)....

A second dimension of prayer which helps us focus on God is *thanksgiving*....

Why should we give thanks? One reason is because everything we have comes from God: "Every good and perfect gift is from above, coming down from the Father" (James 1:17). We can't take credit for anything—even our successes. God gave us our abilities; He arranged our circumstances; He blessed our efforts.... How long has it been since you paused to thank God for all He has done for you?

–BILLY GRAHAM, from *The Journey:
How to Live by Faith in an Uncertain World*

*Father, sometimes I get so caught up with my needs
and requests that I forget to focus my prayer on You.
Today I pause to remember Your goodness and take
stock of the acts of grace You are performing in my life.
Please cultivate in me a spirit of gratitude. Amen.*

PURSUING HOLINESS THROUGH PRAYER

But you are not controlled by your sinful nature. You are controlled by the Spirit if you have the Spirit of God living in you.

ROMANS 8:9 NLT

No one overcomes the corruptions of his heart except by the enabling strength of the Spirit of God.... We express our dependence on the Holy Spirit for a holy life in two ways. The first is through *a humble and consistent intake of the Scripture.* If we truly desire to live in the realm of the Spirit we must continually feed our minds with His truth....

The second way we express our dependence on the Spirit is *to pray for holiness.* The Apostle Paul prayed continually for the working of God's Spirit in the lives of those to whom he was writing. He told the Ephesians that he prayed God would "strengthen you with power through His Spirit in your inner being" (Ephesians 3:16)....

Clearly the Apostle Paul knew we depend on the Holy Spirit for holiness, and he expressed this dependence through prayer.

−JERRY BRIDGES, from *The Pursuit of Holiness*

Lord, I desire to live a life that's worthy of the calling You've given me. Today I pray for Your Holy Spirit to continue to work in my heart, mind, and life. Amen.

FREEDOM FROM SIN

Devote yourselves to prayer with an
alert mind and a thankful heart.

COLOSSIANS 4:2 NLT

Dear Lord, I pray that You would guide me in a developing a prayer life that continues to make me holy. Amen.

Envy, jealousy, bitterness, an unforgiving and retaliatory spirit, and a critical and gossiping spirit defile us and keep us from being holy before God. They are just as evil as immorality, drunkenness, and debauchery. Therefore, we must work diligently at rooting out these sinful attitudes from our minds. Often we are not even aware our attitudes are sinful. We cloak these defiling thoughts under the guise of justice and righteous indignation. But we need to pray daily for humility and honesty to see these sinful attitudes for what they really are, and then for grace and discipline to root them out of our minds and replace them with thoughts pleasing to God.

–JERRY BRIDGES, from *The Pursuit of Holiness*

PRAYING BIG PRAYERS

Thy kingdom come. Thy will be done
in earth, as it is in heaven.

MATTHEW 6:10 KJV

Big general prayers become powerful when they are filled up with concrete, radical biblical goals for the people we are praying for.... It is mentioning these spiritual goals with passion that turns insipid generalizations into dynamite generalizations. So don't shrink back from praying huge, sweeping prayers. For example, in Ephesians 6:18 Paul says that we should be "praying at all times in the spirit, with all prayer and supplication ...for all the saints." Think of it! What an incredible breadth and generality.... Do you do that? Pray for *all* the saints? I admit I do not do it often enough. My heart is too small. But I am trying to get my heart around it. The Bible commands it.

–JOHN PIPER, from *Pierced by the Word*

Lord, sometimes when I pray for people I don't know
or for Your will to be done on earth, I lack passion.
God, I pray for a renewed sense of awe of You
and Your saving work. Let Your kingdom come,
Lord—in my life and in the world. Amen.

TOWARD TRUE WORSHIP

But the hour is coming, and now is, when the
true worshipers will worship the Father in spirit and
truth; for the Father is seeking such to worship Him.
God is Spirit, and those who worship Him
must worship in spirit and truth.

JOHN 4:23-24 NKJV

O Lord, hear our prayers not according to the poverty of our asking, but according to the richness of your grace, so that our lives may conform to those desires which accord with your will.

When our desires are amiss, may they be overruled by a power greater than ours, and by a mercy more powerful than ours....

Grant us, our Father, your grace, that, seeing ourselves in the light of your holiness, we may be cleansed of the pride and vainglory which obscure your truth; and knowing that from you no secrets are hid, we may perceive and confront those deceits and disguises by which we deceive ourselves and our fellowmen. So may we worship you in spirit and in truth and in your light, see light.

–REINHOLD NIEBUHR

Father God, again I thank You for so graciously and powerfully hearing my prayers. Lord, give me grace to worship You the way You desire to be worshipped. Amen.

PRAYER AND MEDITATION

I lie awake thinking of you,
meditating on you through the night.
I think of how you have helped me;
I sing for joy in the shadow of your protecting wings.

PSALM 63:6 NLT

Our aim in studying the Godhead must be to know God himself better.... As he is the subject of our study, and our helper in it, so he must himself be the end of it....

The rule for doing this is simple but demanding. It is that we turn each truth that we learn *about* God into matter for meditation *before* God, leading to prayer and praise *to* God....

Meditation is the activity of calling to mind, and thinking over, and dwelling on, and applying to oneself, the various things that one knows about the works and ways and promises of God. It is an activity of holy thought, consciously performed in the presence of God, under the eye of God, by the help of God, as a means of communion with God.

–J. I. PACKER, from *Knowing God*

God, prayer and meditation go hand-in-hand.
Help me pause in my words long enough to reflect
on Your character and greatness, so that
I might really know You, O Lord. Amen.

PRAYER MAKES A DIFFERENCE

And my God shall supply all your need
according to His riches in glory by Christ Jesus.

PHILIPPIANS 4:19 NKJV

In Christ we have continual peace under all trials, and through him we have power in prayer to obtain from the Lord all things necessary for this life and godliness. It has been the writer's lot to test the Lord hundreds of times about temporal needs, being driven thereto by the care of orphans and students. Prayer has many, many times brought opportune supplies and cleared away serious difficulties. I know that faith can fill a purse, provide a meal, change a hard heart, procure a site for a building, heal sickness, quiet insubordination, and stay an epidemic. Like money in the worldling's hand, faith in the hand of the man of God "answereth all things." All things in heaven, and earth, and under the earth answer to the command of prayer.... How I wish that my reader would so believe in God as to lean upon him in all the concerns of his life!

–CHARLES H. SPURGEON

Father God, I don't want my relationship with You to become only about asking and receiving. But thank You for this simple, beautiful truth that You care about Your people and hear their prayers. I leave my needs with You today. Amen.

A PRAYER OF THANKS

A single day in your courts
is better than a thousand anywhere else!

PSALM 84:10 NLT

Our Father, Thy children who know Thee delight themselves in Thy presence. We are never happier than when we are near Thee. We have found a little heaven in prayer. It has eased our load to tell Thee of its weight; it has relieved our wound to tell Thee of its smart; it has restored our spirit to confess to Thee its wanderings. No place like the mercy seat for us.

We thank Thee, Lord, that we have not only found benefit in prayer, but in the answers to it we have been greatly enriched. Thou hast opened Thy hid treasures to the voice of prayer; Thou has supplied our necessities as soon as ever we have cried unto Thee; yea, we have found it true: "Before they call I will answer, and while they are yet speaking I will hear."

We do bless Thee, Lord, for instituting the blessed ordinance of prayer.

—CHARLES H. SPURGEON

Lord, prayer is such an incredible gift.
Thank You for the peace that transcends
understanding when I pray to You. Amen.

FIRST WORDS

You look deep within the mind and heart,
O righteous God.

PSALM 7:9 NLT

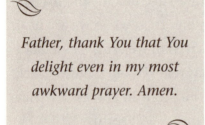

Father, thank You that You delight even in my most awkward prayer. Amen.

For many ...the main barrier to a more effective prayer life is simply a feeling that they don't know how to pray. "I know I need to pray," someone wrote recently, "but I'm not sure how. I'm afraid I might upset God."

But God delights in even our most childlike efforts. At one time you didn't know how to talk—but that didn't keep you from learning your first words and later forming a simple sentence. Few things bring greater joy to a mother or father than hearing their baby's first words—and the same is true of God. You are a child of God if you know Christ, and He *welcomes* your prayers. He is much more concerned about our hearts than our eloquence. The Bible says, "A broken and contrite heart, O God, you will not despise" (Psalm 51:17). Remember: prayer is simply talking with God.

–BILLY GRAHAM, from *The Journey:
How to Live by Faith in an Uncertain World*

THE PRAYER THAT DRAWS OTHERS TO GOD

On him we have set our hope that he will continue
to deliver us, as you help us by your prayers.

2 CORINTHIANS 1:10–11

One way is clear: the prayer will react upon the mind that prays, its light will grow, will shine the brighter, and draw and enlighten the more. But there must be more in the thing. Prayer in its perfect idea of being a rising up into the will of the Eternal, may not the help of the Father become one with the prayer of the child, and for the prayer of him he holds in his arms, go forth from him who wills not yet to be lifted to his embrace? To his bosom God himself cannot bring his children at once, and not at all except through his own suffering and theirs. But will not any good parent find some way of granting the prayer of the child who comes to him, saying, "Papa, this is my brother's birthday: I have nothing to give him, and I do love him so! could you give me something to give him, or give him something for me?"

–GEORGE MACDONALD

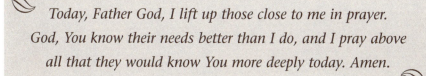

Today, Father God, I lift up those close to me in prayer.
God, You know their needs better than I do, and I pray above
all that they would know You more deeply today. Amen.

PRAYING FOR A BROKEN WORLD

*If my people, who are called by my name, will humble
themselves and pray and seek my face and turn from
their wicked ways, then will I hear from heaven and
will forgive their sin and will heal their land.*

2 CHRONICLES 7:14

God has said, "If my people ...pray ...then I will hear from
heaven." Before three thousand people were brought into the
Church on the day of Pentecost, the disciples had spent ten
days in prayer, fasting, and spiritual travail. God desires that
Christians be concerned and burdened for a lost world. If we
pray this kind of prayer, an era of peace may come to the
world and the hordes of wickedness may be turned back.

–BILLY GRAHAM, from *Day by Day with Billy Graham*

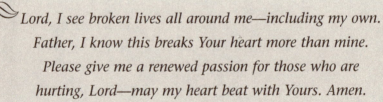

*Lord, I see broken lives all around me—including my own.
Father, I know this breaks Your heart more than mine.
Please give me a renewed passion for those who are
hurting, Lord—may my heart beat with Yours. Amen.*

ALL THINGS FOR GOOD

We know that all things work together for good for those
who love God, who are called according to his purpose.

ROMANS 8:28 NRSV

Are you ever discouraged because of an unanswered prayer? How often we think when a prayer is not answered that God has said no. Many times He has simply said, "Wait." Never doubt that God hears our prayers, even the unusual ones.

When God says, "No" or "Wait," it is because He knows what we do not know. He sees His side of the embroidery all the time. One day we will see the same side as He does. Thank Him for every answered and unanswered prayer. To those who love God, all things work together for good.

> *Lord, there are times when I wonder where You are. I wonder how what I'm facing will ever work for good. But, Father, thank You for the prayers You answer as well as the ones You don't answer. Thank You in advance that everything works together for good. Amen.*

−CORRIE TEN BOOM, from *Not I, but Christ*

WAITING

We wait in hope for the Lord;
he is our help and our shield.

PSALM 33:20

We wait hopefully—with a hope that does not disappoint (Romans 5:5)—because we know that, in his time and according to his perfect wisdom, the LORD brings all things together for good to those who love him (8:28). We often wait restlessly, so we need the community of faithful people to help us learn to abide with greater trust and confidence. The word *wait* implies absolute realization that the LORD is in control, that in his sovereignty God will accomplish his purposes, which are best for us. Therefore, thinking about the kind of God we have ...we await his perfect will. We want to want only what he wants. That causes us to depend on him, to expect his perfect timing, and thereby to act in accordance with his revelation.

–MARVA J. DAWN, from *To Walk and Not Faint*

 Lord, there are some things I've been praying about
and waiting for a long time now. But thank You
for getting me through the hard days of waiting.
Thank You for the hope that does not disappoint.
Lord, You are my hope and shield. Amen.

THE LORD'S PRAYER IN GETHSEMANE

Our Father in heaven, hallowed be your
name, your kingdom come, your will be
done on earth as it is in heaven.

MATTHEW 6:9-10

Behold: what takes place in the Garden of Gethsemane is the Lord's Prayer actually *happening,* as if the earlier words were a script and this is the drama itself:...

—Jesus pleads three times, "Remove this cup from me," the plea of the seventh petition: *Deliver us from evil.*

—But under every request of his own, he places an attitude of faithful obedience to his Father, saying, "Yet not what I will, but what thou wilt." Here is the third petition, which prepares us properly for any answer God may give all other petitions: *Thy will be done on earth as it is in heaven....*

Who can pray The Lord's Prayer now with words and not with the heart's experience?

—WALTER WANGERIN, from *Reliving the Passion*

Lord Jesus, I have sought to do the work of prayer.
But today I remember that You have gone before me,
that You have experienced each pain that I go through.
Thank You again for the gift of prayer and for teaching
me to pray. Let Your will be done in my life, Lord. Amen.

THE PRAYER OF JESUS

And do not cause us to be tempted,
but save us from the Evil One.

MATTHEW 6:13 NCV

The "Lord's Prayer," as we call it, grows directly out of what Jesus was doing in Galilee....

The prayer is therefore a way of saying to the Father: Jesus has ...caught me in the net of his good news.... I want to be part of his kingdom-movement. I find myself drawn into his heaven-on-earth way of living. I want to be part of his bread-for-the-world agenda.... I need forgiveness for myself—from sin, from debt, from every weight around my neck—and I intend to live with forgiveness in my heart in my own dealings with others.... And because I live in the real world, where evil is still powerful, I need protecting and rescuing. And, in and through it all, I acknowledge and celebrate the Father's kingdom, power, and glory.

–N. T. WRIGHT, from *Simply Christian*

 Lord Jesus, thank You again for this model of prayer.
Thank You that praying as You taught me is to
participate in Your saving work. Please continue
to heal and guide me, Lord. Amen.

HAVE MERCY ON ME

But the tax collector stood at a distance.
He would not even look up to heaven, but beat his
breast and said, "God, have mercy on me, a sinner."

LUKE 18:13

The Lord's Prayer isn't the only prayer that has formed the basis of deep and rich traditions of Christian praying. There are other prayers which have been used in similar ways through the years, either as a pattern or as something to

Lord Jesus, I do need Your mercy—every day, in every situation. Have mercy on me, Son of God. Amen.

repeat in order to go down deeper into the presence of the God we know in Jesus. Perhaps the best known of these …is the "Jesus Prayer" …: "Lord Jesus Christ, Son of the Living God, have mercy on me, a sinner."…

Praying for mercy doesn't just mean "I've done something wrong, so please forgive me." It's a much wider petition, asking that God send his merciful presence and help in a thousand and one situations, despite the fact that we don't deserve such aid and never could.

—N. T. WRIGHT, from *Simply Christian*

A PRAYER OF SURRENDER

Yet I want your will, not mine.

LUKE 22:42 NLT

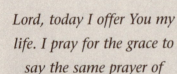

Lord, today I offer You my life. I pray for the grace to say the same prayer of surrender from my heart each day hereafter. Amen.

When Jesus prayed His prayer of surrender, "Not My will, but Yours, be done" (Luke 22:42), He set the pattern for surrender for all who would follow Him into the kingdom of heaven....

But how do we accept Christ's terms of surrender, living daily on the cross? The only way I know is by beginning each day with a prayer of surrender: "Lord, today I surrender my life to You. I choose Your will to be done, not mine. I want to be closer to You, God, than I am to myself. I accept Your terms for my life today and purpose to live personally the crucified life which I received positionally through faith in Christ. I ask You to give me grace to be a surrendered soldier of the cross today. Amen."

–DAVID JEREMIAH

OUR PROVIDER

So Abraham called that place The Lord
Will Provide. And to this day it is said,
"On the mountain of the Lord it will be provided."

GENESIS 22:14

Not only has Jehovah foreseen your need for salvation and made provision through the death and resurrection of His Son, but He also sees your day-by-day needs.... Yet, He instructs us to pray, "Give us this day our daily bread" (Matthew 6:11).

Do you feel silly asking for bread when you can get it yourself? Do you feel that it is unnecessary to come to the sovereign ruler of the universe with the seeming trivia of your individual needs? Do you wonder why God would even bother with you?

O Beloved, Jehovah-jireh is bidding us to come.... You can worship Jehovah-jireh in obedience and know that whatever you need, the Lord will provide it.

−KAY ARTHUR, from *Lord, I Want to Know You*

*Father, I give You thanks today for the
way You so abundantly meet my needs—
sometimes even before I ask. Amen.*

PRAYER BUILDS FAITH

But grow in the grace and knowledge
of our Lord and Savior Jesus Christ.

2 PETER 3:18

If we want to know what faith is, and what Christians believe, we must inquire of the Church. If we want to know what God has revealed to the believer, we must read the Scriptures, we must study those who have explained the Scriptures, and we must acquaint ourselves with the basic truths of philosophy and theology. But since faith is a gift, prayer is perhaps the most important of all the ways of seeking it from God....

Every new development of faith, every new increment of supernatural light, even though we may be working earnestly to acquire it, remains a pure gift of God.

Prayer is therefore the very heart of the life of faith.

–THOMAS MERTON

*God, if I'm going to know You, if my faith is going
to move mountains, I must persevere in prayer.
Father, direct my thoughts toward You
in prayer throughout the day. Amen.*

GOD CARES FOR YOU

Are not five sparrows sold for two pennies?
Yet not one of them is forgotten by God. Indeed,
the very hairs of your head are all numbered. Don't
be afraid; you are worth more than many sparrows.

LUKE 12:6–7

Does God care about the number of hairs in your scalp? Does He care if a sparrow falls? Yes, His Word assures us He does. Then be assured of this: He's a specialist in the things that worry you down inside. The things you dread tomorrow or this coming week. The things that make you wonder, "How can I get this together?" God's reassurance to you is, "Look, that's what I specialize in. I can take that situation you've built into a mountain, and I can bore a tunnel through it in a matter of seconds. Bring all of it to Me. Ask Me to take charge. You don't have because you don't ask."

–CHARLES SWINDOLL, from *Perfect Trust*

 Heavenly Father, thank You that You invite me to cast my burdens on You. Lord, show me what circumstances in my life need to be brought to You, and help me let go. Amen.

PRAYER AS NATURAL AS BREATHING

Friendship with the LORD is reserved
for those who fear him.
With them he shares the secrets of his covenant.

PSALM 25:14 NLT

You will never grow a close relationship with God by just attending church once a week or even having a daily quiet time. Friendship with God is built by sharing *all* of your life experiences with him....

One way is to use "breath prayers" throughout the day, as many Christians have done for centuries. You choose a brief sentence of a simple phrase that can be repeated to Jesus in one breath: "You are with me." "I receive Your grace."... You can also use a short phrase of Scripture: "For me to live is Christ." "You will never leave me." Pray it as often as possible so it is rooted deep in your heart....

Practicing the presence of God is a skill, a habit you can develop.

–RICK WARREN, from *The Purpose-Driven Life*

 Father, remind me today of Your presence—remind me that You are always with me and that You want me to recognize Your involvement in all my experiences and share them with You. Amen.

MAYDAY PRAYERS

But remember that the temptations that come into
your life are no different from what others experience.
And God is faithful. He will keep the temptation from
becoming so strong that you can't stand up against it.
When you are tempted, he will show you a way
out so that you will not give in to it.

1 CORINTHIANS 10:13 NLT

Heaven has a twenty-four-hour emergency hot line. God
wants you to ask him for assistance in overcoming temptation. He says, "Call on me in times of trouble. I will rescue
you, and you will honor me." [Psalm 50:15 GWT]

I call this a "microwave" prayer because it is quick and to the
point: Help! SOS! Mayday! When temptation strikes, you
don't have time for a long conversation with God; you simply
cry out. David, Daniel, Peter, Paul, and millions of others
have prayed this kind of instant prayer for help in trouble.

−RICK WARREN, from *The Purpose-Driven Life*

Lord Jesus, thank You again for this model of prayer.
Thank You that praying as You taught me is to
participate in Your saving work. Please continue
to heal and guide me, Lord Jesus. Amen.

GIVING ALL OF OURSELVES IN PRAYER

And do not cause us to be tempted,
but save us from the Evil One.

MATTHEW 6:13 NCV

Prayer has to do with the entire man. Prayer takes in man in his whole being, mind, soul and body. It takes the whole man to pray, and prayer affects the entire man in its gracious results. As the whole nature of man enters into prayer, so also all that belongs to man is the beneficiary of prayer. All of man receives benefits in prayer. The whole man must be given to God in praying. The largest results in praying come to him who gives himself, all of himself, all that belongs to himself, to God. This is the secret of full consecration, and this is a condition of successful praying, and the sort of praying which brings the largest fruits.

—E. M. BOUNDS

Lord God, I don't want my praying to become mere habit.
Today as I pray, I give my entire self over to You.
Please help me block out distractions, Lord,
and give You my full attention. Amen.

PRAYER MOVES GOD

This is the confidence we have in approaching God:
that if we ask anything according to his will, he hears us.
And if we know that he hears us—whatever we ask—
we know that we have what we asked of him.

1 JOHN 5:14–15

It's been said that faith may move mountains, but prayer moves God. Amazing, isn't it, that our prayers, whether grand and glorious or feeble and faint, can move the very heart of God who created the universe?...

Prayer moves God, and when God moves in your life, things get exciting! Years ago I never dreamed that God would move in my life the way He has. Even after my accident, when I signed up at the University of Maryland for art and English classes, I never realized how God would use diverse elements in my life to mold me to His will. But I sensed God was preparing me for something, and He started me out on a spiritual journey of prayer and praise that has not yet ended. You, too, have a journey through life ahead. Why not make it a journey of prayer and praise?

–JONI EARECKSON TADA, from *Seeking God*

 Lord, I'm excited, anticipating what You might do in and through me in the days to come. I praise You, Lord, for the way You move in our lives, for Your graciousness to us. I pray that You would move in my life today. Amen.

BEFORE THE THRONE

Hear, O Israel: The Lord our God, the Lord is one.
Love the Lord your God with all your heart and
with all your soul and with all your strength.

DEUTERONOMY 6:4

Lord God Almighty, before I go on in my prayers, I want to pause to remember who I'm praying to, to remember Your character. Please create in me a heart of worship, Lord. Amen.

We must remember *who* it is that we are talking with—the Almighty God. I have found it helpful to begin and end my prayers by focusing on His character traits. He is the Almighty God. He is the God who heals. He is the God of peace. He is the God who forgives. He is the God who provides, and He is the God who is in control. He knows everything that is happening. He is not caught off guard. His love is perfect.

As I consider *who* He is instead of focusing on myself or another person or my situation, I am better able to pray with faith.

—SUSAN ALEXANDER YATES, from *A House Full of Friends*

THE BASICS

Therefore, since we are surrounded by such a great cloud
of witnesses, let us throw off everything that hinders
and the sin that so easily entangles, and let us run
with perseverance the race marked out for us.

HEBREWS 12:1

In any endeavor the basics may sometimes seem boring, but practicing them is the key to victory.... When it comes to the end of earth's journey, nothing is going to satisfy but the basics.

That is why for most of my Christian life I have started each day on my knees.... My prayer is, "Lord, I want to be a suit of clothes for You today. I invite You to move around in my body as Your temple. I ask You to think with my mind, love with my heart, speak with my lips, and continue to seek and save the lost through me. Supervise and control my attitudes, my motives, my desires, my words, my actions in order to bring maximum glory to Yourself."

–BILL BRIGHT, from *The Journey Home: Finishing with Joy*

 Father, I'm seeing that prayer is so essential to a life of faith. Lord, let me not take for granted my times of prayer. And please guide my steps each day of my life. Amen.

PRAYER AND DEVOTION

Commit your way to the LORD;
trust in him and he will do this:
He will make your righteousness shine like the dawn,
the justice of your cause like the noonday sun.

PSALM 37:5–6

The root of devotion is to devote to a sacred use.… Prayer promotes the spirit of devotion, while devotion is favorable to the best praying. Devotion furthers prayer and helps to drive prayer home to the object which it seeks. Prayer thrives in the atmosphere of true devotion. It is easy to pray when in the spirit of devotion. The attitude of mind and the state of heart implied in devotion make prayer effectual in reaching the throne of grace. God dwells where the spirit of devotion resides. All the graces of the Spirit are nourished and grow well in the environment created by devotion. Indeed, these graces grow nowhere else but here.… True worship finds congeniality in the atmosphere made by a spirit of devotion. While prayer is helpful to devotion, at the same time devotion reacts on prayer, and helps us to pray.

–E. M. BOUNDS

 God, as I pray, I ask You to make me
more wholly devoted to You. Amen.

DOING GOD'S WORK

Put on the full armor of God so that you can take your
stand against the devil's schemes.... And pray in the Spirit
on all occasions with all kinds of prayers and requests.

EPHESIANS 6:11, 18

God has given us prayer to have a realistic "work" that can be done in prison, in a wheel chair, in bed in a hospital or a hovel or a palace, on the march, in the midst of battle..., or in the dark of a chalet when everyone else is asleep. We can have a practical, realistic part in the battle between God and Satan.

God, it amazes me that my prayers can make an impact for Your kingdom. Please continue to teach me to pray, Lord, so that I might take on this responsibility. Amen.

Astonishing? Unbelievable? But true. In Ephesians 6:10-20, the whole point is that the "armor of God" is needed to stand against, to wrestle against the "wiles of the devil."... Prayer is not just icing on the cake of a so-called spiritual life; prayer is warm, close communication with the living God, and also a matter of doing an active *work* on His side of the battle.

−EDITH SCHAEFFER, from *The Tapestry*

MORE THAN WE COULD EVER ASK

And God is able to make all grace abound to you,
so that in all things at all times, having all that
you need, you will abound in every good work.

2 CORINTHIANS 9:8

Prayer is sort of like an unlocked door with a giant, red-lettered sign on it that says: "Welcome. Feel Free to Take Whatever You Need." Inside is the storehouse of all that God is. He invites us to share it all. He doesn't intend for us to stay on the outside and struggle all alone with the perplexities of life, and He not only invites us to come in but to stay in, in order that His "Grace and peace be *yours in fullest measure, through the knowledge of God and Jesus our Lord*" (2 Peter 1:2 NEB, emphasis mine)....

Prayer is meant to be a part of our lives, like breathing and thinking and talking.

–GLORIA GAITHER, from *Decisions*

God, thank You that in prayer I find abundantly,
exceedingly more than I could ever ask or need.
Lord, help me rest in Your sufficiency today. Amen.

REPENTANCE

The Lord turned and looked straight at Peter. Then Peter
remembered the word the Lord had spoken to him:
"Before the rooster crows today, you will disown me
three times." And he went outside and wept bitterly.

LUKE 22:61–62

When God speaks he speaks so loudly that all the voices of
the world seem dumb. And yet when God speaks he speaks so
softly that no one hears the whisper but yourself. Today,
perhaps, the Lord is turning and looking at you. Right where
you are, your spirit is far away just now, dealing with some
sin, some unbearable weight; and God is teaching you the
lesson himself—the bitterest, yet the sweetest lesson of your
life, in heartfelt repentance. Stay right where you are. Don't
return into the hustle and bustle of life until the Lord has also
turned and looked on you again, as he looked at the thief
upon the cross, and until you have beheld the "glory of the
love of God in the face of Jesus."

–HENRY DRUMMOND

 Lord, when I stumble, help me not to rationalize or
cover it up or go through the motions of repentance.
Help me be still long enough to reconcile myself to You.
Thank You for Your unending love, O Lord. Amen.

OUR FATHER'S BUSINESS

Remain in me, and I will remain in you.
For a branch cannot produce fruit if it is severed from
the vine, and you cannot be fruitful apart from me.

JOHN 15:4 NLT

If we were to ask ourselves why we don't pray, hardly any of us could say we don't know how. I suppose if there were any reason, it would be that we are too busy.... In fact, the One who taught us to pray had a life very similar to ours.... Jesus was an extremely busy man, and He always found time to pray to His Father.

If you want the Lord's blessing on your life, there just isn't any alternative to prayer. Prayer is the way you defeat the devil, reach the lost, restore a backslider, strengthen the saints, send missionaries out, cure the sick, accomplish the impossible, and know the will of God. Prayer is the hard-work business of Christianity, and it nets amazing results.

–DAVID JEREMIAH

God, remove from me any sense of self-sufficiency.
Help me remember that I can never do Your
work without spending time in prayer. Amen.

A TWO-WAY STREET

He who belongs to God hears what God says.

JOHN 8:47

The vital connection between the Word and prayer is one of the simplest and earliest lessons of the Christian life. As that newly-converted heather put it: "I pray—I speak to my Father; I read—my Father speaks to me." Before prayer, God's Word strengthens me by giving my faith its justification and its petition. And after prayer, God's Word prepares me by revealing what the Father wants me to ask. In prayer, God's Word gives me the answer, for in it the Spirit allows me to hear the Father's voice.

Prayer is not monologue, but dialogue. Its most essential part is God's voice in response to mine. Listening to God's voice is the secret of the assurance that He will listen to mine.... My willingness to accept His words will determine the power my words have with Him. What God's words are to me is the test of what He Himself is to me. It shows the uprightness of my desire to meet Him in prayer.

−ANDREW MURRAY

Father, as I pray, I ask You to speak to me
through Your Word. Amen.

PRIVATE PRAYERS

But when you pray, go away by yourself, shut the door
behind you, and pray to your Father secretly. Then your
Father, who knows all secrets, will reward you.

MATTHEW 6:6 NLT

Have you heard and embraced Jesus' amazing promise? No
deed for God will pass by overlooked or unrewarded. Not one
cup of water, or one prayer in the middle of the night.

I visited recently with a bedridden elderly woman named
Vera. "I get so discouraged lying here all day, Dr. Wilkinson,"
she said. "I can't really *do* anything for God but pray."

"Do you pray a lot?" I asked.

Vera thought for a minute before replying. "Oh, for half of
my day, I suppose. And some of the night, too."

I encouraged Vera by reminding her that Jesus said private
prayer is so valuable to God that "your Father who sees in
secret will reward you openly" (Matthew 6:6).

–BRUCE WILKINSON, from *A Life God Rewards*

*Father, I know that the greatest work I
could ever do for You is in prayer, and that
the greatest reward of prayer is knowing You.
Father, please bless my prayers today. Amen.*

UNITED WITH CHRIST

Let the word of Christ dwell in you richly in all
wisdom, teaching and admonishing one another in
psalms and hymns and spiritual songs, singing with
grace in your hearts to the Lord. And whatever you do
in word or deed, do all in the name of the Lord Jesus,
giving thanks to God the Father through Him.

COLOSSIANS 3:16–17 NKJV

Sometimes in our despair we find it impossible to define ourselves spiritually or to reach any real levels of God-communication. Then, all of a sudden, we find ourselves in this wonderful pattern of breakthrough into the very presence of Jesus Christ. At such moments this presence becomes so real that we tremble with joy....

But union with Christ must not be restricted to those very special moments .... The best concept of union with Christ is a conscious, daily walk, fueled by the disciplines of prayer and Bible study.... Only such a constant view of union with Christ can carry us at last across the threshold of the here and now into the presence of Jesus Christ, forever.

–CALVIN MILLER, from *Loving God Up Close:*
Rekindling Your Relationship with the Holy Spirit

 Lord, thank You for exciting times in my walk with You,
but help me not to depend on spiritual highs in order
to keep seeking You. God, I pray that You would remind
me of Your presence in the day-to-day. Amen.

DRY SPELLS

And the Holy Spirit helps us in our distress. For we don't even know what we should pray for, nor how we should pray. But the Holy Spirit prays for us with groanings that cannot be expressed in words. And the Father who knows all hearts knows what the Spirit is saying, for the Spirit pleads for us believers in harmony with God's own will.

ROMANS 8:26-27 NLT

We may not know how to word our prayers. We may find ourselves too weakened by grief or depression or failure to verbalize a prayer. But the promise of the Lord is that He takes even these glances and groans toward Him and makes them into effective pleas for help and mercy….

Take heart, for even the Apostle Paul and the New Testament Christians were not on a religious high every day. In fact, they had their spiritual dry spells. This is the point of the section from Romans 8 where Paul discusses the presence of the Spirit because of the Resurrection of Jesus Christ.

You may not feel like praying. You may not sense God is real. But don't despair. Jesus is praying with you. Jesus is praying for you. Jesus is praying in you.

–WILLIAM P. BARKER, from *A Savior for All Seasons*

 Lord, there are times when I just can't seem to pray. The words don't come. My heart is tired and distracted. Thank You for meeting me here. Thank You for praying beside me and praying for me. Amen.

IN THE DESERT

Give thanks to the Lord, for he is good.
His love endures forever....
to him who led his people through the desert,
His love endures forever.

PSALM 136:1, 16

Sometimes I just don't feel spiritual. I don't feel like praying. I am in desperate need of water, yet I have little or no desire to read my Bible, which would quench my thirst....

Often it is in times like this that I find I need the Lord the most. When I *feel* like reading my Bible and praying, I probably don't need it as much as when I don't feel like it. So, discipline plays a part and although I try not to worry about my dry condition, I also try to find small springs of water: a devotional book of encouraging words, a verse to meditate upon, a quiet walk when I can talk to the Lord, honestly expressing myself...

So, in my desert I have come to accept my position in Christ as sure and secure, because it has *nothing* to do with me and *everything* to do with him.

–GIGI GRAHAM TCHIVIDJIAN, from *Coffee and Conversation with Ruth Bell Graham and Gigi Graham Tchividjian*

God, there are times when You feel far away, when I lack the desire to spend time with You. I pray that You would get me through these desert spells, Lord, and make my faith in and love for You stronger through them. Amen.

ON THE ALTAR

Submit yourselves, then, to God.
Resist the devil and he will flee from you.
Come near to God and he will come near to you.

JAMES 4:7–8

> *God, I surrender to You today. I put my prayer list aside for a moment to simply ask that Your will be done. Amen.*

"The chief act of the will is not effort but consent," says Thomas Keating, providing an axiom that serves as a key to discipleship. This is, indeed, nowhere clearer than with regard to prayer. In our consumerist, individualistic age, prayer can become yet another outlet for exercising our discretion of "choices," laying before God what we want God to do for us, telling God how we want God to run the world and fix our problems and provide simple solutions for what ails us.… But this fails to account for the true heart of prayer: laying ourselves before God, submitting our will to God's will.…

All of prayer must flow from this one starting point—that we submit ourselves and our will and our intentions to the will and intention and ways of God.

–LEE C. CAMP, from *Mere Discipleship:
Radical Christianity in a Rebellious World*

IN GOD'S GRASP

Humble yourselves, therefore, under God's
mighty hand, that he may lift you up in due time.
Cast all your anxiety on him because he cares for you.

1 PETER 5:6–7 NLT

We can easily fall into the idolatrous notion that we may possess God through praying.

We never possess God; God possesses us. We do not grasp God; God grasps us. God transcends all our human theologizing. He will not be owned; He refuses to be controlled. He allows us to know Him only when we let Him grasp and possess us.

Prayer is the process in which we learn to allow God to grasp and possess us. A life of praying is the growth of a relationship with Christ as companion. Like any friendship, this relationship grows as a result of being in communication with each other.

–WILLIAM P. BARKER, from *A Savior for All Seasons*

*Lord, I want to be possessed by You, surrendered
to Your will and used by You in Your saving work.
God, I pray that my prayer life would facilitate
that kind of loving relationship. Amen.*

PRAYER AND CONSECRATION

Joshua told the people, "Consecrate yourselves, for
tomorrow the LORD will do amazing things among you."

JOSHUA 3:5

Prayer and consecration are closely related. Prayer leads up to, and governs consecration. Prayer is precedent to consecration, accompanies it, and is a direct result of it....

Consecration is much more than a life of so-called service. It is a life of personal holiness, first of all. It is that which brings spiritual power into the heart and enlivens the entire inner man. It is a life which ever recognizes God, and a life given up to true prayer.

Full consecration is the highest type of a Christian life. It is the one divine standard of experience, of living and of service. It is the one thing at which the believer should aim. Nothing short of entire consecration must satisfy him.

Never is he to be contented till he is fully, entirely the Lord's by his own consent. His praying naturally and voluntarily leads up to this one act of his.

—E. M. BOUNDS

*Lord, I must confess that there are times when my
heart is not willing to be made completely Yours.
I pray, then, that You would make me willing, that You
would lead me to the place of consecration. Amen.*

PRAYERS OF ADORATION

Yours, O LORD, is the greatness, the power, the glory, the
victory, and the majesty. Everything in the heavens and
on earth is yours, O LORD, and this is your kingdom.
We adore you as the one who is over all things.

1 CHRONICLES 29:11 NLT

Prayer is the human *response* to the perpetual outpouring of
love by which God lays siege to every soul. When our reply to
God is most direct of all, it is called *adoration.* Adoration is the
spontaneous yearning of the heart to worship, honor,
magnify, and bless God.

In one sense adoration is not a special form of prayer, for all
true prayer is saturated with it. It is the air in which prayer
breathes, the sea in which prayer swims. In another sense,
though, it *is* distinct from other kinds of prayer, for in adoration we enter the rarefied air of selfless devotion. We ask for
nothing but to cherish him. We seek nothing but his exalta-
tion. We focus on nothing but his goodness.

—RICHARD J. FOSTER, from *Prayer: Finding the Heart's True Home*

*Lord, sometimes I neglect adoration in my prayers.
I pray that You would reawaken my love for You
and my passion to simply praise You. Amen.*

DISCIPLINE IN PRAYER

For physical training is of some value, but godliness
has value for all things, holding promise for
both the present life and the life to come.

1 TIMOTHY 4:8

Discipline in praying is essential. Without order and structure
to our prayer lives, we simply will not grow in our relationship with Jesus Christ. There is no such thing as an "instant
Christian" through the sudden emotional experience of
answering an altar call or signing a decision card. Although
an altar call or decision card may signify the start of a pilgrimage in faith as a result of Christ's call, we must undertake as
rigorous a discipline in responding to that call as an athlete or
soldier in training. In fact, the New Testament, especially
Paul's letters, consistently compares the Christian prayer life
to the rigorous and regular workouts a crack athlete must
undertake or the toughening exercises a member of an elite
military unit must constantly practice.

–WILLIAM P. BARKER, from *A Savior for All Seasons*

 Lord, today I ask You for perseverance in prayer.
I know that prayer is important, God, and that
anything important takes discipline and commitment.
Please strengthen my resolve, Father. Amen.

THE PROMISES OF JESUS

[Jesus said,] "I will do whatever you ask in my name,
so that the Father may be glorified in the Son. If in
my name you ask me for anything, I will do it."

JOHN 14:13-14 NRSV

How do we balance the practical realities of prayer with [the] promises [found in John]? It will not do simply to say that if we follow these formulas, all prayers will be answered just as they are uttered. God does not serve as our butler. On the other hand, it will not do to reject these promises altogether, as if prayer was anything more than wishful thinking. Rather, John has in mind a union, a mystical union, between our lives and the Spirit of God that will ultimately express itself in one voice…. We become one with Jesus. Our will is then transformed freely to become his will. With God's stepping so deeply inside our lives, we have utter confidence that he knows the quietest thoughts of our hearts.

–GARY M. BURGE, from *The NIV Application Commentary: John*

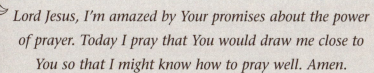

Lord Jesus, I'm amazed by Your promises about the power
of prayer. Today I pray that You would draw me close to
You so that I might know how to pray well. Amen.

NO PRAYER GOES WASTED

The righteous cry out, and the Lord hears them;
he delivers them from all their troubles.

PSALM 34:17

Lord, sometimes I'm so overwhelmed I don't know how to pray. Thank You, Lord, that You know my needs and that when I turn to You, You are an ever-present help. Amen.

Amazing things start happening when we start praying. Prayer time is never wasted time....

John Bunyan once observed, "The best prayers have often more groans than words." I experienced this kind of prayer when I had many pressing needs all around me. Honestly, I reached a point where I could hardly pray about my needs because they were so many. The only prayer I could manage was, *"Help!"* and I remember passionately praying it to God over thirty times until I experienced a breakthrough. Psalms declares, "O Lord, attend unto my cry" (17:1).... When you take one step toward God, God will take more steps toward you than you could ever count. He moved to meet my needs.

–JOHN L. MASON, from *An Enemy Called Average*

POWER TO LOVE

I pray that your love for each other will overflow
more and more, and that you will keep on growing
in your knowledge and understanding.

PHILIPPIANS 1:9

Prayer is God's appointed way to fullness of joy because it is the vent of the inward burnings of our heart for Christ.... But there is a second reason prayer leads to joy's fullness: It provides the power to do what we love to do but can't without God's help. The text says, "Ask, and you will receive, that your joy may be full." Receive what? What would bring us fullness of joy? Not a padded and protected and comfortable life. Rich people are as miserably unhappy as poor people. What we need in answer to prayer to fill our joy is the power to love.... Prayer is the fountain of joy because it is the source of power to love.

–JOHN PIPER, from *Desiring God*

 God, thank You for the many ways prayer gives me joy—
especially the way it empowers me to love others.
Through my prayers today, Lord, use me to
spread Your love to those around me. Amen.

ON ALL OCCASIONS

I urge you, brothers, by our Lord Jesus Christ
and by the love of the Spirit, to join me in
my struggle by praying to God for me.

ROMANS 15:30

We are to pray in times of adversity, lest we become faithless and unbelieving. We are to pray in times of prosperity, lest we become boastful and proud. We are to pray in times of danger, lest we become fearful and doubting. We need to pray in times of security, lest we become self-sufficient. Sinners, pray to a merciful God for forgiveness. Christians, pray for an outpouring of God's Spirit on a willful, evil, unrepentant world. Parents, pray that God may crown your home with grace and mercy. Children, pray for the salvation of your parents. Christians, saints of God, pray that the dew of heaven may fall on earth's dry thirsty ground, and that righteousness may cover the earth as the waters cover the sea.

–BILLY GRAHAM, from *Day by Day with Billy Graham*

 Heavenly Father, help me remember that prayer can change things, that I can make a difference in the lives of others by praying for them. God, please create in me a prayerful heart. Amen.

CHRIST-BASED PRAYER

Let us then approach the throne of grace with
confidence, so that we may receive mercy and
find grace to help us in our time of need.

HEBREWS 4:16

Since the true God is in truth very kind and generous, it is no wonder if those who thus reach out in his direction, ungodly though their beliefs and lives may be in all sorts of ways, find that as they pray their health improves....

Christian prayer, however, has a more solid base. Christians know the God of creation and providence as their covenant Lord, the God of saving grace, and they pray accordingly.... They claim the Father's promise to hear and answer their prayers, but their bottom line is always "thy will (not mine) be done," and they know that if through ignorance and lack of wisdom they ask for something that is not really good for them, God in love will answer by giving them something that is really better.

—J. I. PACKER

*Lord Jesus, thank You for this reminder that praying in
Your name, through Your Spirit, is a vital privilege.
Thank You for the gift of coming to You where I can
find grace to help me in my time of need. Amen.*

THE MOST PERFECT PRAYERS

Jesus replied: "'Love the Lord your God with all your
heart and with all your soul and with all your mind.'
This is the first and greatest commandment."

MATTHEW 22:37–38

God's command to "pray without ceasing" is founded on the
necessity we have of his grace to preserve the life of God in
the soul, which can no more subsist one moment without it,
than the body can without air.

Whether we think of; or speak to, God, whether we act or
suffer for him, all is prayer, when we have no other object
than his love, and the desire of pleasing him....

Prayer continues in the desire of the heart, though the understanding be employed on outward things.

In souls filled with love, the desire to please God is a continual prayer....

*God, I know that a thriving
prayer life will flow out of
an intense love for You and
a desire to simply be in
Your presence. Please guide
me as I seek to think about
Your great mercies
throughout the day, and
give me a greater love for
You. Amen.*

God only requires of his adult
children, that their hearts be
truly purified, and that they
offer him continually the
wishes and vows that naturally
spring from perfect love. For
these desires, being the
genuine fruits of love, are the
most perfect prayers that can
spring from it.

–JOHN WESLEY

DISARMING FEAR

For you did not receive a spirit that makes you a slave
again to fear, but you received the Spirit of sonship.

ROMANS 8:15

Just as the emotion of fear filters down from the mind to
cause direct psychological changes, so the act of prayer can
counter those same effects by fixing my attention away from
my body to a consciousness of soul and spirit. Prayer cuts
through the sensory overload and allows me to direct myself
to God. As I do so my body grows still, and calm. Visceral
muscles tightened by fear begin to relax. An inner peace
replaces tension.

These same results can be achieved through meditation exercises, of course, but prayer to God offers additional benefits.
It helps fight the isolation of pain by moving my focus away
from my self and my own needs as I strive to consider the
needs of others.

–PHILIP YANCEY, from *Where Is God When It Hurts?*

 *Lord, thank You for alleviating my fears as I spend time
with You. Your peace passes all understanding. Amen.*

OUR WORDLESS PRAYERS

And he who searches our hearts knows the mind
of the Spirit, because the Spirit intercedes for
the saints in accordance with God's will.

ROMANS 8:27

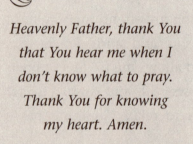

*Heavenly Father, thank You
that You hear me when I
don't know what to pray.
Thank You for knowing
my heart. Amen.*

I know well the helpless feeling of not knowing what I ought to pray, as I imagine every Christian sometimes does. How to pray for a dead-end marriage that seems to represent only stuntedness, not growth? Or for a parent of a child diagnosed with terminal cancer? Or for a Christian in Nepal imprisoned for her faith? What can we ask for? How can we pray?

Romans 8 announces the good news that we need not figure out how to pray. We need only groan. As I read Paul's words, an image comes to mind of a mother tuning in to her child's wordless cry....

The Spirit of God has resources of sensitivity beyond those of even the wisest mother.

–PHILIP YANCEY, from *Where Is God When It Hurts?*

JUST AS WE ARE

But because of his great love for us, God, who is rich in
mercy, made us alive with Christ even when we were dead
in transgressions—it is by grace you have been saved.

EPHESIANS 2:4–5

I used to think that I needed to get all my motives straightened out before I could pray, really pray….

The truth of the matter is, we all come to prayer with a tangled mass of motives—altruistic *and* selfish, merciful *and* hateful, loving *and* bitter. Frankly, this side of eternity we will *never* unravel the good from the bad, the pure from the impure. But what I have come to see is that God is big enough to receive us with all our mixture. We do not have to be bright, or pure, or filled with faith, or anything. That is what grace means, and not only are we saved by grace, we live by it as well. And we pray by it.

–RICHARD J. FOSTER, from *Prayer: Finding the Heart's True Home*

*Lord, thank You that I don't have to "clean up" to
come before You in prayer—thank You that You are
the one who purifies my heart. Today I come
before You boldly by Your grace. Amen.*

GLORIFYING GOD
IN OUR PRAYERS

Call upon Me in the day of trouble;
I will deliver you, and you shall glorify Me.

PSALM 50:15 NKJV

Without Christ, we are capable of no good....

How then do we glorify Him? Jesus gives us the answer in
John 15:7: "If you abide in me, and my words abide in you,
ask whatever you wish, and it will be done for you." We *pray!*
We ask God to do for us through Christ what we can't do for
ourselves—bear fruit. Verse 8 gives the result: "By this my
Father is glorified, that you bear much fruit." So how is God
glorified by prayer? Prayer is the open admission that without
Christ we can do nothing. And prayer is the turning away
from ourselves to God in the confidence that He will provide
the help we need. Prayer humbles us as needy and exalts God
as wealthy.

–JOHN PIPER, from *Desiring God*

 *God, I know that a thriving prayer life will flow out
of an intense love for You and a desire to simply be in
Your presence. Please guide me as I seek to think
about Your great mercies throughout the day,
and give me a greater love for You. Amen.*

A PRAYER FOR OUR LEADERS

I urge, then, first of all, that requests, prayers, intercessions
and thanksgiving be made for everyone—for kings and
all those in authority, that we may live peaceful and
quiet lives in all godliness and holiness.

1 TIMOTHY 2:1-2

O Lord our Governor, whose glory is in all the world: We commend this nation to thy merciful care, that, being guided by thy Providence, we may dwell secure in thy peace. Grant to the President of the United States, the Governor of this State (or Commonwealth),

*Father God, I lift our
leaders up to You today. I
ask You to guide and direct
them. In all things, Father,
I pray that Your kingdom
would come. Amen.*

and to all in authority, wisdom and strength to know and to do thy will. Fill them with the love of truth and righteousness, and make them ever mindful of their calling to serve this people in thy fear; through Jesus Christ our Lord, who liveth and reigneth with thee and the Holy Spirit, one God, world without end. Amen.

–THE BOOK OF COMMON PRAYER

ASKING FOR HELP

Share each other's troubles and problems,
and in this way obey the law of Christ.

GALATIANS 6:2 NLT

One of the most important things I learned about joining in prayer with another person was the need for honesty. Too often we are less than forthcoming when we share our prayer requests with another person, but honesty before both God and man is crucial....

Often people don't ask for help because they are embarrassed to admit they need it. Or they don't want to bother anyone with their problems. But there are people God has *called* to come alongside us in prayer. If we don't give them the opportunity, because either we don't ask or we don't share honestly, then we forfeit many of the blessings God has for us.

Prayer is one of the most important ways in which we can "bear one another's burdens" (Galatians 6:2).

–STORMIE OMARTIAN, from *The Power of Praying Together*

 Heavenly Father, I know how important it is to join my prayers with others'. God, I pray for the kind of relationships that allow for freedom and honesty. Give me courage to share my burdens with others, and to share others' burdens. Amen.

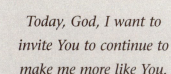

THE PRAYER THAT MOLDS US

And we, who with unveiled faces all reflect the Lord's glory, are being transformed into his likeness with ever-increasing glory, which comes from the Lord, who is Spirit.

2 CORINTHIANS 3:18

The primary purpose of prayer is to bring us into such a life of communion with the Father that, by the power of the Spirit, we are increasingly conformed to the image of the Son....

Today, God, I want to invite You to continue to make me more like You. Please purify my heart, Lord God. Amen.

When we begin to walk with God, he is gracious and marvelously answers our feeble, egocentric prayers. We think, "This is wonderful. God is real after all!" In time, however, when we try to push this button again, God says to us, "I would like to be more than your Provider. I also want to be your Teacher and Friend. Let me lead you into a more excellent way...." As we begin to follow these nudgings of the Spirit, we are changed from the inside out.

–RICHARD J. FOSTER, from *Prayer: Finding the Heart's True Home*

DECEMBER 28

LISTENING TO GOD

Listen to my cry for help, my King and my God,
for I will never pray to anyone but you.
Listen to my voice in the morning, Lord.
Each morning I bring my requests
to you and wait expectantly.

PSALM 5:2–3 NLT

Lord, I do want to hear Your voice. Help me let myself go and release myself into Your arms long enough to hear You speak. Amen.

Before I can listen to God in prayer, I must fumble through the prayers of words, of willful demands, the prayers of childish "Gimmes," of "Help mes," of "I want…" Until I tell God what I want, I have no way of knowing whether or not I truly want it. Unless I ask God for something, I do not know whether or not is something for which I ought to ask…. The prayers of words cannot be eliminated. And I must pray them daily, whether I feel like praying or not. Otherwise, when God has something to say to me, I will not know how to listen. Until I have worked through self, I will not be enabled to get out of the way.

–MADELEINE L'ENGLE, from *Glimpses of Grace: Daily Thoughts and Reflections*

THE POSSIBILITIES OF PRAYER

We have this hope as an anchor
for the soul, firm and secure.

HEBREWS 6:19

The possibilities of prayer run parallel with the promises of God. Prayer opens an outlet for the promises, removes the hindrances in the way of their execution, puts them into working order, and secures their gracious ends. More than this, prayer like faith, obtains promises, enlarges their operation, and adds to the measure of their results. God's promises were to Abraham and his seed, but many a barren womb, and many a minor obstacle stood in the way of the fulfilment of these promises; but prayer removed them all, made a highway for the promises, added the facility and speediness to their realization, and by prayer the promise shone bright and perfect in its execution.

The possibilities of prayer are found in its allying itself with the purposes of God, for God's purposes and man's praying are the combination of all potent and omnipotent forces.

–E. M. BOUNDS

 God, when I'm discouraged in prayer, remind me of the power of prayer combined with Your promises. Amen.

NOT ALONE

Therefore he is able to save completely those
who come to God through him, because
he always lives to intercede for them.

HEBREWS 7:25

Lord God, thank You for reminding me that You continually help me along. God, please continue to teach me to pray. Amen.

While we are full participants in the grace-filled work of prayer, the work of prayer does not depend on us....

We do not have to have everything perfect when we pray. The Spirit reshapes, refines, and reinterprets our feeble, ego-driven prayers. We can rest in this work of the Spirit on our behalf.

But it gets even better. The writer to the Hebrews reminds us that Jesus Christ is our great High Priest.... Do we realize what this means? ...Continual prayer is being offered at the throne of God on our behalf by none other than the eternal Son.... We can rest in this work of the Son on our behalf.

–RICHARD J. FOSTER, from *Prayer: Finding the Heart's True Home*

PRAYER IN THE YEAR TO COME

Continue in prayer.

COLOSSIANS 4:2 KJV

Hast thou no mercy to ask of God? Then may the Lord's mercy show thee thy misery! A prayerless soul is a Christless soul. Prayer is the lisping of the believing infant, the shout of the fighting believer, the requiem of the dying saint falling asleep in Jesus. It is the breath, the watchword, the comfort, the strength, the honour of a Christian. If thou be a child of God, thou wilt seek thy Father's face, and live in thy Father's love. Pray that this year thou mayst be holy, humble, zealous, and patient; have closer communion with Christ, and enter oftener into the banqueting-house of His love. Pray that thou mayst be an example and a blessing unto others—and that thou mayst live more to the glory of thy Master. The motto for this year must be, "Continue in prayer."

–CHARLES H. SPURGEON

 Heavenly Father, my time spent with You is precious.
As the year draws to a close, help me to remember
Your instruction: "Continue in prayer." Amen.

Scripture Index

Genesis
22:14 — November 21
24:15, 26-27 — September 21
28:16 — January 27, July 4
28:17 — July 4

Exodus
32:31-32 — March 23
33:17 — March 23
33:18 — March 23
34:9 — March 23
34:28 — March 23

Deuteronomy
6:3 — October 27
6:4 — November 28
8:3 — September 26
8:15-16 — March 27

Joshua
3:5 — December 12

1 Samuel
12:23 — February 14

2 Samuel
23:4 — August 8

1 Kings
19:12 — July 14

1 Chronicles
4:12 — October 24
16:11 — August 27
17:1, 23 — July 16
29:11 — December 13

2 Chronicles
7:14 — November 14
16:9 — April 5

Job
27:10 — January 9
32:8 — June 30

Psalms
4:8 — January 10
5:2-3 — December 28
5:3 — March 11, July 26
6:9 — January 2, September 20

7:9 — November 12
13:1 — February 5
13:3 — February 17
17:1 — January 7, December 16
18:19 — March 12
20:1 — August 3
20:7 — April 26
24:3-4 — May 21
25:1 — May 13
25:14 — November 24
25:17 — February 26
27:1 — August 31
27:14 — July 1
28:1 — April 12
28:2 — January 16
32:6-7 — February 16
33:20 — November 16
33:20-21 — August 20
34:17 — December 16
37:5 — October 9
37:5-6 — November 30
37:7 — May 9
38:9 — July 3
39:3-4 — July 11
40:16 — June 4
40:17 — June 22
43:5 — July 1
46:1 — April 6
46:10 — May 8
50:15 — December 24, November 25
51:10 — January 20, September 3
51:11 — July 4
51:17 — November 12
55:16 — June 27
55:17 — July 12
55:22 — January 14
56:8 — July 17
61:4 — February 25
62:8 — March 13, July 30
63:1 — February 7, July 27
63:3 — July 25

63:6 — June 29, November 9
65:2 — March 15
66:20 — June 16
69:3 — January 26
69:13 — June 17
70:1 — August 2
73:28 — August 26
74:16 — April 22
84:11 — June 28
95:6-8 — August 15
97:10 — June 10
100:4-5 — July 18
103:1, 13 — July 13
103:13 — January 24, February 1
119:107 — October 6
131:1-3 — September 30
131:2 — January 31
136:1, 16 — December 9
138:9 — July 2
139:7 — May 26, September 5
139:8 — January 3, July 4
139:23-24 — January 17
142 — February 16
145:18 — January 21, August 14, October 25

Proverbs
3:5-6 — August 11
4:23 — August 25
5:23 — August 13
11:30 — May 6
15:3 — October 2
15:8 — January 26
24:16 — February 20

Ecclesiastes
3:1 — July 20
5:2 — September 2

Song of Songs
2:15 — June 9
3:1 — June 1

Isaiah
1:18 — August 29
6:8 — June 13
29:13 — June 21
40:31 — January 4
41:20 — September 1
55:3 — June 6
61:1 — May 14
62:6-7 — March 20
64:7 — October 19, February 2

Jeremiah
23:23-24 — October 2
29:12 — March 19
29:13 — March 28
33:3 — June 11

Lamentations
3:26 — May 22

Ezekiel
11:19 — May 28
36:37 — March 20

Zephaniah
3:17 — May 17, October 31

Zechariah
4:6 — May 15
12:10 — March 14
8:20-22 — March 18

Matthew
4:4 — September 26
5:6 — July 29
5:9 — January 8
5:44 — June 2
6:5 — July 19
6:6 — January 24, March 6, September 24, October 2, October 5, December 6
6:7 — July 28, August 28
6:7-8 — July 8
6:9 — February 10, March 22, November 4
6:10 — July 5, November 7
6:9-10 — February 12, November 17
6:10-12 — March 8
6:11 — November 21
6:12 — August 31

6:13	November 18, November 26	5:17-18	April 10
6:31-32	June 18	5:31	August 5
6:34	August 10	6:12	September 22
7:7	June 23, August 3, October 1	6:19	April 8
		7:21	April 11
		8:29	April 20
		8:42	April 13
7:7-8	February 9	9:40	April 25
8:26	March 31	11:1	May 7, July 7, July 9
9:20-22	January 16		
9:28-29	October 21	11:2	March 10
11:7	August 25	11:5	October 22
11:28-29	September 19	11:5-6	March 2
11:30	October 3	11:7	March 3
12:15	April 7	11:8	January 29, January 30, March 4
12:22	April 19		
13:54, 57-58	April 15		
14:17-18	April 2	11:9	February 3
15:22	April 24	11:10	February 4
17:21	April 27, October 10	11:13	September 4
		12:6-7	November 23
18:20	October 29	16:16	March 17
21:22	August 16	17:12-14	April 16
22:37-38	December 20	18:1-8	February 9, March 4
23:37	February 1		
26:39	August 22	18:1	February 19, February 20, May 11, September 23
26:41	August 23		
26:44	September 13		

Mark

1:15	March 22	18:2-3	February 20
1:30	January 11	18:4-5	February 21
1:35	March 30, June 20, September 16, September 18	18:7	February 22
		18:7-8	February 23
		18:13	November 19
1:41-42	April 9	18:41	April 17
5:27-28	June 15	19:10	June 12
6:31	August 17	19:17	July 31
10:27	April 17	22:41	September 12
11:24	March 24, July 23, October 26	22:42	July 7, November 20
		22:44	October 28
		22:61-62	December 3
12:30	September 25	24:21	April 30
14:36	August 18	24:32	September 25
		24:51	September 3

Luke

John

2:19	July 6	1:5	August 25
2:22, 24	August 6	1:12	November 3
5:16	September 17, October 14	4:23	March 14
		4:23-24	November 8

4:24	February 13	8:26	January 28,
5:6	August 16		March 5,
6:5-6	April 1		March 14,
7:7-38	March 21		May 4,
8:47	December 5		July 30,
10:10	January 25		September 29
11:25	April 28	8:26-27	December 8
11:25-26	April 29	8:27	October 15,
14:13	January 12,		December 22
	May 12	8:28	November 15
14:13-14	March 22,	9:21	June 25
	August 9,	10:11-13	March 22
	September 6,	10:17	January 16
	December 15	12:2	February 28,
14:14	September 7		May 24
15:4	September 8,	12:11	February 20
	December 4	12:12	June 26
15:5	November 1	15:4	April 14,
15:7	May 5,		July 15
	September 8,	15:30	December 18
	September 21,		

1 Corinthians

	September 27,	1:25	August 24
	December 24	1:30	January 23
15:9	October 12,	3:6	June 25
	November 1	6:19	August 8
15:13	February 15	10:31	April 23,
16:23	September 21		November 25
16:24	September 10	12:12	July 5
17:1, 4-5	May 19		

2 Corinthians

17:20-21	October 18	1:10-11	November 13
19:5	August 21	3:18	June 19,
20:24-28	May 1		December 27
20:28	May 1	4:7, 16	February 20
20:28-29	May 3	6:17-18	October 13
		9:8	December 2

Acts

1:14	February 24	12:8-9	April 3
14:23	November 2	12:9	September 9,
17:28	July 4		November 1
21:6	June 8		

Romans

Galatians

5:2	October 4	5:22-23	August 19
5:5	October 16,	5:24	October 10
	November 16	6:2	December 26

Ephesians

8:9	November 5	1:15-17	February 18
8:15	December 21	2:4-5	December 23
8:15-16	July 22	3:16	November 5
		3:19	February 27
		6:10-20	December 1
		6:11, 18	December 1

6:18 — March 1,
March 7,
May 30,
June 24,
September 15,
November 7

Philippians
1:4 — July 24
1:4-6 — January 18
1:6 — January 17
1:9 — December 17
2:3 — July 10
2:5 — May 16
3:3 — March 14
3:8-9 — October 20
4:4-5 — August 17
4:6-7 — March 9,
April 5
4:19 — May 27,
Nov. 10

Colossians
1:9 — May 25
1:19 — March 25
2:6-7 — May 2
2:9 — March 29
3:16-17 — December 7
4:2 — January 6,
May 20,
November 6,
December 31

1 Thessalonians
3:12 — January 13
5:17 — January 8,
February 6,
July 21,
September 14,
October 8
5:17-18 — February 8
5:18 — November 4

1 Timothy
2:1 — June 5
2:1-2 — January 12,
December 25
2:8 — January 15,
January 22,
March 22
4:8 — December 14

2 Timothy
1:3 — May 31
1:7 — June 14

1:13 — June 3

Hebrews
2:18 — April 21
4:16 — December 19
6:19 — December 29
7:25 — September 28,
December 30
10:19 — March 22,
October 4
10:19, 22 — August 7
10:25 — October 30
11:6 — October 7
11:13 — January 5
12:1 — October 11,
November 30

James
1:2-3 — April 4
1:5-6 — March 22
1:17 — November 4
2:5 — June 7
4:2 — January 4
4:7-8 — December 10
4:8 — January 19
5:13-15 — February 11
5:15 — March 22,
April 18,
October 23
5:16 — March 16,
March 23

1 Peter
1:13 — May 18
4:7-8 — October 17
5:5 — August 30
5:6-7 — December 11
5:7 — January 1,
January 18,
May 10,
August 4

2 Peter
1:2 — December 2
3:18 — November 22

1 John
1:5 — May 29
2:1-2 — September 11
5:14 — February 29,
May 23,
July 30,
September 27
5:14-15 — November 27

INDEX OF AUTHORS

Anonymous
False Devotion   August 13
Prayer Is Life   July 21

A

Albert the Great
A Pure Heart   May 21

Kay Arthur
Our Provider   November 21

St. Francis of Assisi
The Lord's Prayer   March 8

Saint Augustine
Going Away Again to Pray
                        September 13
Ignorance and Weakness
                        August 31
The Spirit's Help   September 29
Tears and Prayers   June 21
Urged to Pray   September 23

Teresa of Avila
Can Prayer Be Put into Words?
                        July 12
A Daring Prayer   August 7
Devotional Diversity   July 20
Listening for God   June 30
Prayer Beyond Prayer
                        September 1
Really Praying the Lord's Prayer
                        August 28
Stop a Wandering Mind
                        August 21

B

William P. Barker
Discipline in Prayer
                        December 14
Dry Spells   December 8
In God's Grasp   December 11

Lana Bateman
Humility in Prayer   August 30
Why?   February 17

Richard Baxter
Taking God Seriously   July 17

Dietrich Bonhoeffer
Morning Prayer   March 11

The Book of Common Prayer
A Prayer for Our Leaders
                        December 25

E. M. Bounds
Daily Prayer for Daily Needs
                        March 27
Giving All of Ourselves in Prayer
                        November 26
The Greatest Thing We Can Do
                        September 14
Hang On   April 24
Lacking Prayer   April 25
Love and Answered Prayers
                        June 17
Loving Others through Prayer
                        June 16
Passionate Prayers   February 7
The Possibilities of Prayer
                        December 29
Prayer and Consecration
                        December 12
Prayer and Devotion
                        November 30
Prayer and Promise   May 28
Prayer Fuel   September 26
Prayer, Obedience, and Faith
                        October 27
Scene of Love from Paul's Journeys
                        June 8
An Upright Heart   January 15
You Must Ask   April 27

John Bradford
Facing the Day Ahead   August 8

Jerry Bridges
Freedom from Sin
                        November 6

Pursuing Holiness Through Prayer
November 5

Bill Bright
The Basics   November 29

Margueritte Harmon Bro
No Reservations   April 15

Gary M. Burge
The Promises of Jesus
December 15

C

John Calvin
Confident, Humble Prayer
July 23
Keep on Praying   June 26
The Limits of Prayer   July 30
The Necessity of Prayer
February 11
Nurturing Prayer   June 20
Pray Like This   February 10
Why Pray?   June 18

Lee C. Camp
On the Altar   December 10
Praying Together   October 29

John Cassian
Prayer That Makes a Difference
June 22
A Special Prayer   August 2

Oswald Chambers
Confidence Amidst Crisis
March 31
He Is Never Late   April 29
Pray without Ceasing
February 6
Seeing Is Not Believing   May 3
The Wrong Conclusion   April 30

Elizabeth Rundle Charles
The Service of Prayer
February 14
A Willing Heart   June 13

John Chrysostom
A Mighty Weapon   January 30
Pray Diligently   September 24

Patsy Clairmont
The Gift of Prayer   May 10

J. F. Clark
My Grace Is Sufficient   April 3

Claire Cloninger
The Doubter   May 1
The Way Is Open   April 16

L. B. Cowman
Abundant Blessings   July 1
Before We Finish Praying
September 21
God's Sure Promises   January 5
Hold onto Faith   October 23
Pleading God's Promises
July 16
Praying Through   October 21

Harriet Crosby
Resting in Prayer   October 31

Cyprian
Praying in Secret   October 2
Sleepy in Prayer   September 22

D

Marva J. Dawn
Waiting   November 16

Ron DelBene with Mary and

Herb Montgomery
No Prayer Is Wasted   April 18

Henry Drummond
Repentance   December 3
There Is Hope in Prayer
May 23

E

Jonathan Edwards
The Duty of Prayer   January 9
Faith and Prayer   March 22
Prayer Brings Revival   March 19
Prayer for the Spirit   March 20
A Prayer Hearing God   March 15
Praying for Mercy   March 21
Pressing into the Kingdom
of God   March 17
Ready to Help   April 11
The Spirit of Prayer   March 14

Union in Prayer   March 18

F

François De Fénelon
Don't Hold Back   January 1
Early on Their Knees
                         September 18
Filling an Emptiness
                         September 3
, from the Heart   September 7
Keeping Prayer Focused   July 7
A Life of Prayer   February 8
Offering Ourselves   August 6
Quiet Inspiration   July 14
The Territory of the Heart
                         August 25
We All Need Prayer   July 9

Charles G. Finney
Persisting in Prayer   May 6
Personal Responsibility
for the Lost   June 12

P. T. Forsyth
Prayerlessness   February 2
The Spirit Intercedes for Us
                         March 5

Richard J. Foster
Ask What You Wish
                         September 8
Childlike Faith   February 1
Just As We Are   December 23
Not Alone   December 30
Petitionary Prayer   September 20
Prayer as Vocation   April 23
The Prayer That Molds Us
                         December 27
Prayers of Adoration
                         December 13
Waiting   February 22

Thomas Fuller
Forgetting to Pray   March 1

G

Gloria Gaither
More Than We Could Ever Ask
                         December 2

Ken Gire
With Jesus in the Garden
of Gethsemane   August 22

Billy Graham
Before the Day Begins   March 30
Day by Day   October 12
Every Moment   January 7
First Words   November 12
On All Occasions   December 18
Powerful Prayer   March 16
A Prayerful Heart   January 8
Praying for a Broken World
                       November 14
The Privilege of Prayer
                        November 3
Thankful Prayers   November 4
Too Busy to Pray   May 15

Franklin Graham
Boldness in Prayer   October 4
Learning How to Pray   July 28

Jean-Nicolas Grou
Prayer from the Heart   March 9
Teach Us to Pray   May 7
There's Hope in Silence   May 8

Guigo I
Requests for Prayer   August 5

Madame Guyon
Praying the Scripture   May 11

H

Cynthia Heald
Honest Communication
                         August 26

Matthew Henry
Waiting on God   May 22

Walter Hilton
The Nature of Prayer   June 24
On Meditation   June 29
Set Your Sights High   June 27

Charles Hodge
Your Prayer Helper   January 28

George Hodges
In Spirit and in Truth
                        February 13

R. Kent Hughes
Thirsting After Righteousness
July 29

I

H. A. Ironside
Communion with God
January 31

J

David Jeremiah
Know My Heart   January 17
Our Father's Business
December 4
Passionate Prayers   February 20
A Prayer of Surrender
November 20

Nicole Johnson
Surrender   August 23

E. Stanley Jones
More Than a Physical Touch
January 25

Julian of Norwich
The Goodness of God
February 23

K

Thomas Kelly
How to Pray without Ceasing
February 19

Thomas À Kempis
Recovery   August 10

Christa Kinde
An Invitation to Prayer   June 11

Martin Luther King, Jr.
Prayer and the Modern World
March 2

L

Hugh Latimer
Blessed to Be a Blessing   June 25

Greg Laurie
Jesus Gives Hope   April 20
What Do You Want?   April 17

William Law
Give God Your Whole Life
February 4
Healing Love   June 15

Brother Lawrence
God in the Commonplace
September 5
A Habitual Sense of God   May 16
How to Go to God   May 14
Keeping Prayer on Track
September 2
A Little Effort—a Big Reward
August 14
Recognizing God's Presence
May 26

R. Leighton
Cast Your Burdens on the Lord
August 4

Madeleine L'Engle
According to Your Will   May 25
Listening to God
December 28

David Martyn Lloyd-Jones
The God of Our Lord
Jesus Christ   February 18

Anne Graham Lotz
Casting Our Cares   August 12
Eager to Receive   August 16
Meeting with the Lord
October 13
Prayers of Faith   April 14
Praying the Word   July 15
Trust Him at All Times   April 26

Max Lucado
All Who Call   October 25
Barriers to Joy   January 18
Confession Is Good
for the Soul   January 19
Contentment   September 9
Divine Moments   January 21
God Is Listening   January 2
He Hears Our Prayers   March 12
Trusting God   August 24

Martin Luther
Give God Your Troubles
February 16
Our Need for Prayer
October 1
Persistence in Prayer
February 9
Prayer in a Time of Trouble
August 3
Two Obstacles to Prayer
September 10

M

George MacDonald
He Will Answer   February 21
Let Go and Let God
September 30
The Light of Hope   May 29
Praying to a God Who Acts
October 9
Praying to a Good God
October 7
The Prayer That Draws
Others to God   November 13
Unity through Prayer
October 18

John MacDuff
Asking with Hope   May 12

Alexander Maclaren
Continual Prayer   January 6

Brennan Manning
The Prayer of Abba's Child
July 22

H. E. Manning
When God Says No   June 28

Catherine Marshall
Prayerful Dependence
November 1

John L. Mason
No Prayer Goes Wasted
December 16

Alexander McKenzie
Resting in Prayer   February 25

Marilyn Meberg
Praying for the Holy Spirit
September 4
Praying the Psalms   July 25

Thomas Merton
Hoping and Praying   May 18
Prayer Builds Faith
November 22

F. B. Meyer
Linger in the Gallery of Love
June 6
Standing on the Promises of Love
June 7

Joyce Meyer
Fan the Flame   July 27

Calvin Miller
United with Christ   December 7

Beth Moore
Study and Pray   September 25

C. G. Moore
God Has a Plan!   April 1

Leon Morris
Pray Shamelessly   January 29

Andrew Murray
The Chief End of Prayer   May 19
The Danger of Prayerlessness
October 5
Difficult Prayer   October 28
Faith in Prayer   October 22
Glorifying the Father   August 9
The Habit of Prayer
September 12
Hoping and Praying   May 5
Love and Prayer   October 17
Love Conquers Selfishness
June 14
Our Great Teacher
September 17
Persevering Prayer
September 15
Persevering in Prayer   October 8
Persistence in Prayer   March 24
The Place of Prayer   February 24
Pray and Prevail   March 23

Pray As He Prayed   September 6
Prayer and Fasting   October 10
Simplicity in Prayer   July 8
The Spirit of Prayer   October 15
A Strengthening Prayer Life
                      October 26
Time for Prayer   October 19
The True Prayer of Faith
                      August 20
A Two-Way Street   December 5
Waiting on God   February 27
The Word and Prayer   October 6
Your Father Waits for You
                      January 24

Ruth Myers
Experiencing God's Love
                      October 16

N

Watchman Nee
The Answer for Every Need
                      January 23

Reinhold Niebuhr
Toward True Worship
                      November 8

Henri Nouwen
Solitude   March 6
Waiting Together   October 30

O

Lloyd John Ogilvie
Christ: The Greatest Miracle
                      March 25
Constant Surprises   March 29
He Is There for You   April 10

Stormie Omartian
Asking for Help   December 26
A Clean Heart   January 20
Letting Go   April 5
Praying for Each Other
                      February 15
Reaching out in Faith
                      January 16
Setting Time Aside   October 14

P

J. I. Packer
Asking in Jesus' Name
                      February 29
Christ-Based Prayer
                      December 19
Prayer and Meditation
                      November 9
Praying the Psalms   February 5
The Struggle of Prayer   March 3

Eugene H. Peterson
God-Centered Prayer   April 12
In the Wilderness   April 21
Kingdom Prayers   February 12
The Most Vital Human
   Experience   October 20
The Necessity of Silence   May 9
On Our Darkest Days   January 3
The Place of Prayer   April 22
Prayer and the Denial
   of Self   July 10
Right Where We Are   August 15
Single-Minded   March 28
Turn It All into Prayer   May 30

J. B. Phillips
Healing Minds   April 19

Arthur W. Pink
His Mission   April 8

John Piper
Glorifying God in Our Prayers
                      December 24
Let God Be God   May 17
Persevere   March 4
Power to Love   December 17
Praying Big Prayers   November 7

Evagrius Ponticus
Asking for the Right Things
                      August 19
Obstacles to Prayer   June 23
Prayer Beyond Prayer   July 19
Wanting the Right Things
                      August 18

Pseudo-Macarius
Heavenly Harmony   July 5

R

Frederick W. Robertson
Always Be Prayerful
February 28
The Prayer That Transforms
June 19

Richard Rolle
Steadiness in Prayer   August 27

J. C. Ryle
Love and Prayers   June 2
Love and Salvation   June 4

S

Francis De Sales
Christian Meditation   July 6
Cleansing Prayer   July 2
Morning Prayer   July 26
Prayer and Patience   April 4
Preparing to Pray   January 27
Putting Yourself in
    God's Presence   July 4
Shifting Gears   July 11
Silent Prayer   July 3
Solitude and Society   August 17
Tiny Prayers   July 31

Edith Schaeffer
Doing God's Work   December 1
The Work of Prayer   November 2

Lawrence Scupoli
When You Stumble   August 29

A. B. Simpson
A Chance to Bless   April 2
Help in the Hard Times   May 4

Hannah Whitall Smith
The Burden of Self   February 26

Charles H. Spurgeon
Healing Prayer   January 11
Hope in Him   April 7
Needs Supplied   May 27
A Prayer for a Deeper Walk
October 11
Prayer in the Year to Come
December 1
Prayer Makes a Difference
November 10

A Prayer of Thanks
November 11
Turn Your Gaze upon Him
April 13
We Live   April 9

Charles Stanley
Knowing God's Will   May 24
Our Ever-Present Help   April 6
Our Great Intercessor
September 28
Planning with Prayer   August 11
The Power of God's Love
September 11
Praying in Faith   January 10
Praying to Our Father   July 13
The True Goal of Prayer
March 26

Douglas V. Steere
Pay Attention   February 3
Prayer for Others   March 7

Charles Swindoll
Brand-New Prayers   May 2
God Cares for You
November 23
Prayer Changes Me   January 22
Wait upon the Lord   January 4

Luci Swindoll
Celebrate God   July 18
Easing Our Burdens
September 19
Praying with Abandon   March 13

T

Joni Eareckson Tada
Prayer Moves God
November 27

John Michael Talbot
A Prayerful Community
January 13

Hudson Taylor
The Absent Bridegroom   June 1
Answered Prayer   May 31
The Father's Powerful Love
June 10
Pleasing the Father   June 9

Gigi Graham Tchividjian
In the Desert   December 9

Corrie ten Boom
All Things for Good
                            November 15
The Glorious Task of Interceding
                            January 12

Tertullian
He Is Our Example
                            September 16

A. W. Tozer
Courage in Prayer   October 3

Sojourner Truth
Talking to God   June 3

William Tyndale
Praying Naturally   July 24
Secret Prayer   August 21

V

Dave Veerman
The Better Answer   April 28

W

Walter Wangerin
The Lord's Prayer in Gethsemane
                            November 17

Rick Warren
Mayday Prayers   November 25
Prayer As Natural
    As Breathing   November 24

Thomas Watson
Delayed, But Not Refused
                            January 26

John Wesley
The Most Perfect Prayers
                            December 20

George Whitefield
Intercede in Love   June 5

Warren W. Wiersbe
Answered Prayer   September 27

Bruce Wilkinson
Praying for Blessing   October 24
Private Prayers   December 6

Dallas Willard
God in Our Midst   January 14
Pray Your Heart   May 13
Praying with Our
    Whole Selves   May 20

N. T. Wright
Have Mercy on Me
                            November 19
The Prayer of Jesus
                            November 18
Praying the Lord's Prayer
    Today   March 10

Y

Philip Yancey
Disarming Fear   December 21
Our Wordless Prayers
                            December 22

Susan Alexander Yates
Before the Throne
                            November 28